RUSSIA STARTS HERE

Real Lives in the Ruins of Empire

HOWARD AMOS

BLOOMSBURY CONTINUUM
LONDON • OXFORD • NEW YORK • NEW DELHI • SYDNEY

BLOOMSBURY CONTINUUM
Bloomsbury Publishing Plc
50 Bedford Square, London, WC1B 3DP, UK
Bloomsbury Publishing Ireland Limited
29 Earlsfort Terrace, Dublin 2, D02 AY28, Ireland

BLOOMSBURY, BLOOMSBURY CONTINUUM and the Diana logo are trademarks of Bloomsbury Publishing Plc

First published in 2025 in Great Britain as *Russia Starts* Here by Bloomsbury Continuum

A catalogue record for this book is available from the British Library

Library of Congress Cataloguing-in-Publication data has been applied for

ISBN: HB: 978-1-4729-9134-8; TPB: 978-1-4729-9136-2; eBook: 978-1-4729-9135-5; ePDF: 978-1-4729-9137-9

2 4 6 8 10 9 7 5 3 1

Typeset by Deanta Global Publishing Services, Chennai, India
Printed and bound in Great Britain by CPI Group (UK) Ltd, Croydon CR0 4YY

FSC www.fsc.org MIX Paper | Supporting responsible forestry FSC® C171272

To find out more about our authors and books visit www.bloomsbury.com and sign up for our newsletters

For product safety related questions contact productsafety@bloomsbury.com

RUSSIA STARTS HERE

For my parents

And I should raise in the east
A glass of water
Where any-angled light
Would congregate endlessly.
Philip Larkin, 'Water'

Contents

PSKOV REGION

List of Characters (in order of appearance)

Nina
Resident of Baranovo and wife of Nikolai

Nikolai (Kolya)
Resident of Baranovo and husband of Nina

Sergei Kirin
Volksbund employee, ex-Red Army officer

Vladimir Orlov
Head of Vorontsov Volost, former flax-factory director

Artyom
Walking companion, former summer camp volunteer

Lev Shlosberg
Opposition politician in Pskov

Andrei Turchak
Governor of Pskov Region from 2009 to 2017

Semyon Geichenko
Director of Pushkin Hills from 1945 to 1993

Vyacheslav Kozmin
Custodian of Pushkin Hills' Bugrovo, nephew of Boris Kozmin

Pyotr Bystrov
Former artist-in-residence in Pushkin Hills

Boris Kozmin
Custodian of Pushkin Hills' Petrovskoye, uncle of Vyacheslav Kozmin

Father Tikhon (Grigory Shevkunov)
Abbot of Pskov Caves Monastery from 2018 to 2023, rumoured to be Vladimir Putin's *dukhovnik*

Sasha
Boy at Belskoye Ustye Orphanage who drowned aged eleven

Alexander Moskalyov
Doctor at Bogdanovo Psychiatric Hospital

Olga Grudtsyna
Owner of a riding school in Volyshovo

Lyudmila Yakovleva
Chief vet at Volyshovo collective farm

Baroness Hélène de Ludinghausen
Last living descendant of the Stroganoffs

Mikhail Minin
Red Army soldier who raised the red flag over the Reichstag in 1945

Karina Smirnova
Great-granddaughter of Mikhail Minin

Yevgeny Mikhailov
Governor of Pskov Region from 1996 to 2004

Dmitry Markov (Dima)
Photographer, former summer camp volunteer

Svetlana
Widow of Mikhail, a Russian soldier killed in Ukraine

Mikhail
A volunteer Russian soldier killed in Ukraine in 2023

Father Raphael (Boris Ogorodnikov)
Priest with a love of driving, younger brother of Alexander

Alexander Ogorodnikov
Soviet religious dissident, elder brother of Boris

Father Ioann (Ivan Krestiankin)
Dukhovnik of Father Tikhon, Father Raphael and Alexander Ogorodnikov

Lyudmila Maksimovskaya
Writer, historian and former head of Nevel town museum

Tiina Süvaorg
Employee of Estonia's border-guard service, daughter of Helju Tsopatalo

Helju Tsopatalo
Retired librarian, mother of Tiina Süvaorg

Eevi Liname
Resident of Serga, an Estonian village on the Russian border

Fyodor
An Old Believer and retired fisherman living on Piirissaar

Pavel
Local historian, owner of a house on Piirissaar

Preface

From where I stood in the Velikaya River, all I could see on both banks were a few unlit houses and the dark outlines of trees. The red-orange remains of an unseasonably warm September day lingered in the West. I was in the middle of an ancient ford, once part of a busy thoroughfare on Europe's eastern approaches, which had been used for centuries by merchants, diplomats and knights. Under my feet, naturally-occuring, interlocking slabs of potholed white limestone formed a ridge that sat higher than the rest of the riverbed, forcing the water upward and making it briefly shallower. If you didn't know it was there, it would be almost impossible to guess: there were no tourist information boards.

As well as being a place of intermingling, compromise and trade, this area of Western Russia has also been riven by war and divison. Today, less than fifty kilometres from the ford lies Russia's border with the European Union and NATO. Since the full-scale invasion of Ukraine in late February 2022, militaries on either side have monitored each other warily, and civilian crossing points sit eerily empty.

For almost half a millennium, these lands were ruled by the medieval city state of Pskov (pronounced 'Pskoff'). The Velikaya River, comparable in size to the Thames or the Seine, runs through the centre of the city of Pskov. If you were to trace the river's meandering path north-east from the ford, you would pass an ancient church with a black cupola marking the birthplace of St Olga, who went on to become the first Christian ruler of Russia.

Further on, you would find whole villages of *dachas*, the Russian second homes where city dwellers take up residence in the summer months. Then, the grey apartment blocks and industrial ruins of modern Pskov.

Today, Pskov is the capital of Pskov Region, one of 83 territories that make up the Russian Federation. On a map, the region nestles like a kidney below St Petersburg, with its western edge alongside Estonia, Latvia and Belarus.

It's sparsely populated. While Pskov Region is two-thirds the size of Scotland, it has just 620,000 people (compared to Scotland's 5.4 million). Like elsewhere in north-eastern Europe, its relentlessly flat landscape is made up of forests, bogs, rivers and lakes. In summer, temperatures rise to over thirty degrees; in winter they can sink to thirty below. Away from the few tarmac motorways connecting distant cities, packed-earth roads wind through forests and along rivers, linking villages of one-storey houses where firewood is the only source of heating, toilets are in outhouses and water is drawn from wells.

I first went to Pskov Region in 2007 (when I was a university student) to take part in a month-long summer camp run by a Russian charity at a state orphanage for mentally and physically disabled children. It was a life-changing experience, and I returned for several subsequent years before moving to Russia in 2010 to become a journalist. Even while living in Moscow, though, I remained involved with charities working at the orphanage, and travelled regularly to Pskov Region.

As a reporter in the Russian capital, I covered everything from inflation data to oil pipeline corruption, illegal logging, opposition rallies and political assassinations. But I often found myself turning to the people and places I knew in Pskov Region to answer questions from friends and editors about life in Russia. Then, as now, Pskov Region was a prism that reflected unfamiliar and uncomfortable truths.

It was a hot July weekend in 2007 when I visited the city of Pskov for the first time. I remember it as a dusty, down-at-heel place dotted with elegant, whitewashed onion-dome churches.

The roads were cracked and potholed, there were almost no new buildings, and the city's medieval fortifications were crumbling heaps. It was almost impossible to find a restaurant, and box-like *Ladas*, the cars familiar to me from Soviet films, were everywhere. It was like entering a different world. Years later, I came across an article by the British journalist Hector Hugh Munro (pen name Saki), who was a reporter for *The Morning Post* in pre-revolutionary Russia, describing a visit to Pskov in 1905. 'There are few spots in European Russia where one so thoroughly feels that one has passed into a new and unfamiliar atmosphere,' he wrote.

For centuries, the centre of Pskov has been dominated by its *kremlin* (the Russian word for fortress), which sits on a tongue of land between the Velikaya River and its smaller tributary, the Pskova. It is dominated by the large, box-like Trinity Cathedral with its white facade, aquamarine roofs and golden domes. On its 'land' side, the *kremlin* backs onto Pskov's busy main road, a gaggle of souvenir stalls and cafés, and a large square with a statue of Lenin.

But if you cross over the ugly, post-war Olga Bridge to the left bank of the Velikaya, the setting is more impressive. There, you have an uninterrupted view of the *kremlin*'s dressed limestone walls, which rise out of the water like an ocean liner that has run aground.

Fishing vessels and ferries once moored in crowded lines on the embankment below the *kremlin*. Now, it is a paved walkway that is busy on sunny days with families, rollerbladers, cyclists and fishermen. It's a scenic spot, with the Velikaya sweeping away westwards in a gentle curve. The walkway is decorated with a line of faux-gothic, capital letters about twice the height of an average-sized person. They read: 'РОССИЯ НАЧИНАЕТСЯ ЗДЕСЬ' – RUSSIA STARTS HERE. In the dark, they glow with a fluorescent white light.

It's a bold claim. More than one place in Russia can – and does – market itself as the country's 'starting point'. There is the exclave of Kaliningrad, Russia's most westerly territory sandwiched between Lithuania and Poland; there is majority-Muslim Derbent on the Caspian Sea that is the country's oldest continuously inhabited city; there is St Petersburg, Russia's so-called 'window onto Europe' and its capital of culture; there is Moscow where economic and political life has been concentrated for over a century; and there is mainland Russia's easternmost coastline, which faces Alaska across the Bering Strait. The town of Yelizovo in Kamchatka (6,900 kilometres from Pskov) even has a monument of its own proclaiming 'Russia Starts Here'. Unlike Pskov's free-standing letters, the words are inscribed on a stone pedestal supporting two large bears, one with a salmon in its mouth.

This book however takes Pskov at its word. Like any slogan, Pskov's 'Russia Starts Here' contains a kernel of truth. Geographically, Pskov Region has long been a starting point for travellers arriving from the West. And it's where Russians historically began journeys to other European countries, whether as part of diplomatic missions, merchant caravans or fighting in armies. Before the attack on Ukraine in 2022 and subsequent Western sanctions, about 10 per cent of Russia's international trade passed through Pskov Region.

There are numerous accounts of visitors making their first assessments of Russia from Pskov. After arriving in the city in 1578, the Danish diplomat Jacob Ulfeldt was outraged by thieving locals, claiming people 'do not keep their word, and don't consider it shameful to lie, deceive and steal'. But he was impressed by Pskov, his first Russian city. 'The town is located on the flat and surrounded by walls, towers and moats,' he wrote. 'It is decorated with 300 churches and 150 monasteries, according to those who know the exact number of such buildings. Almost all of them are built from stone and sparkle, giving the town a wonderful brilliance.'

Culturally, the wider Pskov Region is home to the family estate of Alexander Pushkin, Russia's most influential poet. It was here that Pushkin penned some of his most famous verses, including 'I remember a wonderful moment' that is widely considered the greatest Russian-language love poem. Historically, too, Pskov Region makes a convincing case. The ancient fortress of Izborsk was one of the first places in Eastern Europe where Viking princes arrived from Scandinavia to rule over the local Slavs, a fusion that created the Russian people; and the Soviet Union was conceived in Pskov when the Russian Empire's last tsar, Nikolai II, abdicated in March 1917 amid spreading revolutionary unrest.

These are the sort of things visitors are supposed to think about when they see 'RUSSIA STARTS HERE' on the banks of the Velikaya. But the slogan can also be understood in different ways. Pskov Region is one of the poorest regions of Russia, with little industry or agriculture. It often tops national ratings of depopulation, death rates, disease and poverty.

After President Vladimir Putin launched the full-scale invasion of Ukraine, my wife and I joined hundreds of thousands of other Russians who left the country at short notice. We spent almost two years living in Yerevan, the capital of Armenia. Even observing from a distance, the horror and shame I felt at Russia's actions was intense. For a while, I stopped working on this book.

Since the start of the fighting, most observers of Russia have, understandably, found it almost impossible to see much further than the terrible, daily violence in Ukraine. The suffering inflicted by Russians on Ukrainians has not only been horrifying, but also difficult to comprehend. How was this war possible? What are the roots of this darkness? Eventually, I came to see this book as a response to such questions. I would even argue there are few better places to look for answers than in the towns, villages and hamlets of Pskov Region.

More soldiers from Pskov Region have been killed in the Ukraine war than any other region in western Russia when the figures are adjusted for population size. And hundreds of these men have been buried in an out-of-the-way cemetery that lies near the ford over the Velikaya River. When I visited the cemetery one cold morning in March 2023, just over a year since the invasion, it was a very different scene to that idyllic autumn evening when I had waded out into the river. Now, the ground was blanketed with snow, the sky grey, and the ice-fringed Velikaya River swirled forlornly. Between the cemetery and the ford lay the remains of a bridge built under the Nazis that was blown to bits by Soviet bombers in World War II.

Pulling into the car park attached to the cemetery, I realized that preparations for a military funeral were in full swing. Men in uniform sat in idling cars waiting for the hearse, while others prepared the burial site. It wasn't a place to linger. As I drove away, green-and-blue paratrooper flags fluttered above the rows of heaped-earth graves covered by wreaths of artificial flowers.

1

The Last Ones

Nina and her husband Nikolai, both well into their eighties, are the future of the village of Baranovo. But they prefer to talk about the past. Nina first moved here in the hot summer of 1941, a few days after the Nazi invasion of the Soviet Union. Just seven years old, Nina remembers helping her three sisters and parents pack their things onto horses for the twenty-five-kilometre journey from their previous family home in the village of Fedkovo. As they trudged along dusty, dirt roads with a cow and heavily laden horses, Nazi planes flew overhead, their vapour trails criss-crossing the clear June sky. With the arrival of Nina and her family, the population of Baranovo swelled to twenty people, including eight children.

Today, the village spreads out along a road, with the land on one side sloping down to the brown meanders of the Shelon River. A small sandy beach used to attract swimmers and picnickers, but it is now badly overgrown. A plastic bottle hangs from a branch to mark the spot where you can wade through the water in summer to the village of Alyonino Zakhonye. In springtime, the lilac bushes lining the track leading to Nina and Nikolai's house fill the air with their thick sweetness. Nearby, a stork's nest sits on an electricity pole. The birds, which mate for life and migrate northwards every year from sub-Saharan Africa, are graceful black-and-white creatures with orange bills. But the pair that made the nest in Baranovo abandoned it, and it now lies empty.

Baranovo was the first place I visited in Pskov Region, and Nina – then in her seventies – was one of the first local people I got to know. She was kind, cheerful, proud of what she and Nikolai had built, and had a wicked sense of humour. Long before the punchlines in her stories, her small eyes would crease up in laughter, her unruly grey hair trembling as she giggled in anticipation. In retirement, Nina and Nikolai spend their days on housework, watching television, looking after the dogs and cats, and tending their vegetable garden and beehives. Summers are filled with activity: chores and guests. There is much less to do in winter when the snow piles up, and the days are short.

My visits to see Nina and Nikolai always began with greetings in their gloomy hallway where, in winter, one of them would hand you a bundle of twigs to brush the snow from your boots. Then you would be offered tea and sweets, or a meal, depending on the time of day. Nina never failed to produce home-made treats for guests: sorrel soup with sour cream, fresh eggs, lightly pickled cucumbers, meat jelly with peppercorns, sea buckthorn jam or thick, yellow honey that she scooped out onto a small dish from five-litre glass jars.

Their home was solid and welcoming: a single ground-floor room with walls of treated tree trunks, a lino floor and a stove of red bricks that reached almost to the ceiling. For centuries, wood-burning stoves have been the centrepiece of Russian rural dwellings. Although now rarely used for cooking, they are still usually the only source of heat through the long winter. Adding logs every few hours during the heating season – September through to April – becomes a routine almost as instinctive as breathing.

The conversation at the table with Nina and Nikolai usually involved village gossip and the retelling of stories from their long lives, which both began under Stalin and followed the arc of late twentieth-century Russian history. Nina was a particularly wonderful raconteur, with an eye for the dramatic and the absurd. Nikolai, more pedantic, was liable to get lost in the detail, and his long and technical explanations often tested the limits of my Russian. When he laughed, Nikolai revealed a mouthful of perfect dentures. If Nina tended toward the comic, Nikolai was touchingly earnest and I have seen him become so swept up in the poignancy of a story that the tears started in his eyes. Married for over sixty years, Nina and Nikolai were deeply caring of each other, their relationship full of bickering and affection.

On a slight rise in the land, Baranovo's four houses cluster around the inside of a curve in the dirt road. This combination of rise and curve can be dangerous for speeding cars, particularly in the winter when the road is covered by packed snow. Nikolai liked to recount how the whine of a car engine suddenly cut short meant a driver had missed the turn and plowed into a snowdrift. Once when I was in Baranovo, a man so drunk he could barely speak knocked at the door seeking a tractor to extricate his car.

At the two ends of the village, the road winds away through a forest: to the south it gradually becomes a rutted track impassable for cars, while to the north it leads past half a dozen other villages to the nearest town, Porkhov, a twenty-five-minute drive. Apart from their house, Nikolai and Nina also own a garage, where they keep a still-functioning Soviet-made car, and a *banya*, or wood-fired washhouse-cum-sauna, where they steam, soak and wash once a week. Sometimes, they slather themselves in home-made honey; a way of keeping the skin soft. Like most Russian rural dwellings, their toilet is outside, a small wooden shack shaped like a guard post. There is no running water, and they rely on what they can draw from two wells. Baranovo water, they would tell me with pride, is the most delicious for many kilometres in all directions.

This is Nina and Nikolai's third house since moving to Baranovo in the early 1990s from St Petersburg: two others burnt down. On neither occasion did they ever find out how the fire started. On neither occasion was there any chance of a fire engine arriving from Porkhov in time to save the house. Twice, therefore, they have rebuilt their lives here from scratch.

When I first came to Baranovo, I was volunteering at an orphanage for disabled children in the next-door village of Belskoye Ustye, living with other volunteers in tents in Baranovo and making the twenty-minute walk to the orphanage several times a day. The walk took us past Nina and Nikolai's yapping dogs, across a bridge over the Belka River and up a small slope to Belskoye Ustye where a giant neo-classical church towered over the nearby houses. The Church of the Holy Ascension was an evocative ruin: its brickwork exposed and its cupolas covered by a patchwork of blanched wooden planks, rusty iron sheets and old copper that had turned a deep green. After sessions at the orphanage, we would clamber up rickety ladders to the church's rafters from where the view stretched over endless forests and fields.

This church is deeply intertwined with Nina's family: one of the last priests to run the parish was her grandfather, Sergei Vasilkov. Like the clerics who preceded him, Vasilkov lived in Baranovo. There is an abandoned priest-cemetery in the forest nearby (when I went to find it one autumn, I discovered just a few fallen headstones and a skull unearthed by grave robbers – or wild animals); and the meadow by the Shelon was known as the 'priest's field'. Appointed to run the Church of the Holy Ascension in 1903, Vasilkov served through the final years of the tsarist empire and the first years of the Soviet Union before being executed in 1937 during Stalin's Great Terror. Nina does not remember her grandfather, but she keeps a black-and-white photograph of him on a shelf, his thinning hair pulled back and his hooded eyes staring straight at the camera. The church operated for much longer than many others in the atheist Soviet Union, but was finally closed down during Khrushchev's anti-religion drive in the 1960s, its crosses cut from the cupolas.

Neither Nina nor Nikolai were religious while the Soviet Union lasted, but they have both adopted Orthodox Christianity in their old age and attend services, which take place in a makeshift wooden church in Belskoye Ustye. The Church of the Holy Ascension has been undergoing restoration for more than fifteen years – but remains unfinished. I always sensed that Nikolai, a more typical product of the Soviet system, was a sceptic, but he indulges Nina, and on religious holidays sends out kitsch, animated videos to friends on WhatsApp. For Nina, religion is not only a question of belief and a connection to village life, but a direct link to her ancestors.

During World War II the whole of Pskov Region was seized by the Nazis and used as a staging ground for the brutal siege of Leningrad unfolding to the north. While Nikolai, two years younger than Nina, was raised in Leningrad and remained in the city as it endured 872 days of shelling and starvation, Nina lived under occupation. She saw her first Germans just a few weeks after the start of the invasion. 'They were from the SS and were on black motorcycles and dressed in black,' she told me one evening, sitting around their table. 'The whole of Baranovo was filled with motorcycles. My mother was down by the well, the one near the *banya*, and was carrying water on a yoke. They stopped, got out their map and, as mother told us later, pointed at the village they needed to get to. My mother was so shaken, her legs were trembling.'

Neither Nina nor her three sisters went to school during the occupation. Soviet partisans, who lived in the forests and bogs of Pskov Region, and who could be as brutal with locals as the Nazis, sometimes visited the village. When a couple of German soldiers were killed in a shoot-out with partisans in her grandfather's church, Nina remembered the all-consuming fear that the Nazis would burn Baranovo to the ground. Excited about their success, the victorious partisans turned up for a little celebration. 'There was a woman among the partisans,' said Nina. 'For some reason I remember her in particular. And how she shouted about them having won a victory! And how they had been shooting! They were all very happy. But we began asking them: "Leave, leave! Otherwise they'll either shoot us all or burn us to death."' When the partisans finally left, Nina was sent out with a brush to sweep away the tracks left by their horses in the snow. The Germans arrived minutes later.

For all the brutality of the Nazi occupation, the hardship did not abate when Baranovo was liberated in 1944. In fact, for Nina's family, things got much worse. Her father, Vladimir, was immediately conscripted into the Red Army and killed at the front the following year. Nina and her three sisters were sent to work on the newly reopened collective farms, which had been dissolved by the Nazis. Tasks for the children included gathering hay and weeding, but the most dreaded chore was helping with the flax harvest. A staple crop for centuries in Pskov Region, flax is known for its pale blue flowers. 'They grew an awful lot of it, there were big fields full of it,' Nina recalled. 'For us teenagers, the hardest job was to carry flax.'

What Nina remembered most from the post-war period was hunger. All across the victorious Soviet Union, the countryside was gripped by near-famine. The tipping point for Nina's family came when their horse and grain stores were requisitioned on the order of the local collective farm. 'That's when our starvation began,' Nina said. 'We had a strip of land: on half of it, my mum planted potatoes, and on the other half was rye. When the rye was ready, they ground it with millstones . . . We boiled up this *muchakha* in the evening and that was our food.' The family also ate dandelions and reeds, but one of their most frequent meals was sorrel: they either cooked it as a fritter, or ate it raw rolled in salt. In early spring, they sought out what Nina called *shindriki*; the soggy remains of potatoes forgotten in the fields that had been frozen solid all winter.

Nina's mother cast around for ways to find food – or get hold of cash. In desperation, she even sold the large cross that her father-priest had worn over his cassock.

To this day, Nina remains prepared for a repeat of such hardship. I remember her laughing about news reports of Europeans rushing to stockpile toilet paper at the beginning of the coronavirus pandemic. In a period of starvation and shortage, she told me, the two most valuable things are matches and salt. She still keeps a store of both in the attic.

The crops grown by the nearby collective farms were strictly off-limits and everyone understood the risks of giving in to temptation. This was the period of high Stalinism, when the ageing dictator ruled the country with an iron fist. 'If you stole an ear of rye you'd get a year in jail,' Nina remembered. 'You'd be walking hungry past these fields of corn, it was very beautiful. Such heads of corn! But we were scared to tear them off. And we didn't. It's difficult to understand that sitting here now. But everyone was scared.'

Nina was sent to Leningrad by her mother when she was sixteen and it was there that she met and fell in love with Nikolai, recently demobilized from his military service with a tank regiment in Dresden. They married four months after their first encounter and studied at night school for more than a decade to make up for the education they had missed in the chaos of war. Eventually, Nikolai graduated from a university in Leningrad with an engineering degree, and Nina finished college. Their two daughters, Olga and Irina, were born in the 1960s.

When Nina took Nikolai to Baranovo for the first time, the countryside was very different from her childhood: the church was shuttered, the collective farms were bigger. But, more than anything else, there were fewer people. Like the grinding of tectonic plates, depopulation has been a powerful force in Pskov Region for the last century – and a backdrop to Nina and Nikolai's lives.

The number of people in Pskov Region peaked in the 1920s at almost 1.8 million and has been falling ever since (it's currently about 600,000). Arguments rage about the reasons, but the start of the decline coincided with the violence of Stalin's brutal war on the countryside in the 1930s, known as collectivization, which destroyed private smallholding and reimposed something resembling tsarist-era serfdom on the peasantry. This was followed by the killings of World War II. In Porkhov, the nearest town to Baranovo, officials following behind the advancing Red Army estimated 1,600 people were left from a pre-war population of 9,562.

When, in the 1960s, Soviet leader Nikita Khrushchev relaxed strict laws that had made it all but impossible for people to leave their villages, a flight to the cities began. Nina and her sisters were a textbook example. Post-war subsidies for agriculture and relatively high rural salaries underwritten by the boom in Soviet oil production slowed the pace of this exodus, but never managed to reverse it.

As Nina and Nikolai spent their adulthoods in Leningrad, Baranovo was gradually hollowed out. Its remaining inhabitants moved to Belskoye Ustye, literally taking their houses apart and transporting them wholesale up the road. By 1981, Nina's childhood home – where her grandfather priest had lived – was the only house left in the village. Empty since the death of her mother, it was stripped of everything valuable by thieves. Passing hunters used it as a place to spend the night and, eventually, the electricity was disconnected.

Nina and Nikolai's decision to settle permanently in Baranovo in 1992 saved the village from the fate of thousands of others: abandonment, ruin and a gradual return to nature. The couple had originally intended to turn Nina's childhood home into a *dacha*, where they could grow vegetables and live during the summer months, but Nina couldn't find any part-time work in St Petersburg and they were worried about thieves. So, they left the city. To help make ends meet, Nikolai took a job as a nightwatchman in the Belskoye Ustye orphanage just up the road.

The full force of rural depopulation was held back by the policies of late Soviet governments, but with the arrival of capitalism, the dam collapsed. In the three decades following the end of the Soviet Union in 1991, the number of people living in rural areas of Pskov Region has halved. Whole villages were left to rot amid rapidly expanding woodland. Public services, from buses to schools and hospitals, were cut, and households of one or two pensioners, like that of Nina and Nikolai, became the norm. Moscow and St Petersburg acted as giant magnets, and Pskov Region increasingly resembled a poverty-stricken backwater. The sight of children in the countryside was a rarity. Data from Russia's 2021 census showed that 2,771 of Pskov Region's 8,355 rural settlements contained no people at all.

Everywhere, collective farm managers, whose success in Soviet times had depended on their political skills, failed to cope with the demands of the free market. Agricultural production in Russia fell 40 per cent in the 1990s, millions of jobs were lost and the average rural wage dropped like a stone. The decline was particularly cataclysmic in more marginal farming areas, like Pskov Region, where winters are harsh and the soil is not nearly as fertile as the 'Black Earth' areas of southern Russia. To this day, the emptiness of the Russian countryside makes a deep impression on city dwellers. On my first visit to Pskov Region for summer camp in 2007, we were regaled with stories about Muscovite volunteers so upset by what they saw on arrival that they burst into tears, or left for the train station in the middle of the night.

One of the by-products of depopulation is rewilding. The fields around Baranovo formerly worked by the collective farm are now all young woods, and species like wolves, elk, wild boar and brown bear are enjoying a renaissance. I moved to live in Baranovo for a year in 2010, and when locals discovered that I walked back from the Belskoye Ustye orphanage alone on dark winter nights, they often expressed surprise – and fear. I should, I was told, be wary of wolves. At the time I paid little heed (besides there was no other way of getting between the villages), but wolves regularly kill farm animals and pets in Pskov Region. Nina believes that, one cold January, her favourite dog, Tima, was dragged away by a wolf pack. Photos of grinning hunters posing with bloodied wolf carcasses often appear online.

The quiet desolation of rural areas was well captured by a Russian writer who published a series of surrealistic sketches about travelling through Pskov Region in 2006. He prepared for his journey as if embarking on a mission to another world:

> I knew for a fact that, before and after Porkhov, for hundreds of *versts* in all directions, until our final destination of Bolshoe Kivalovo, there would be no petrol stations, car garages, shops, hospitals or streetlights in any of the villages apart from one. We faced a bad – in places terrible – road, and after five kilometres there'll be so few bars of signal we'll begin to think our mobile phones have fallen silent forever (the radio will have long since been hissing like a frying pan).

To this day, mobile-phone signal and mobile internet remain extremely patchy in rural Pskov Region as the number of potential users is too small to make the necessary investment worthwhile.

When Nina and Nikolai arrived in Baranovo, food was once again a problem, and rationing was in force. 'We lived very poorly in the 1990s,' Nina said. 'When we went to the shop in Belskoye Ustye where Zoya Konstantinovna worked they wouldn't sell us anything! Only bread. We weren't allowed any sugar, sweets or any type of biscuits because we weren't registered. All our rations were in Leningrad. But Zoya, God grant her health, used to tell me to wait for people to disperse and then she would give me a few things.' Nina and Nikolai sometimes drank tea with pickled cucumbers because biscuits and sweets were so difficult to find.

Hyper-inflation and an alcohol shortage caused by Mikhail Gorbachev's prohibition drive meant vodka was a de facto currency. Nina and Nikolai, neither of them heavy drinkers, delight in remembering how they used bottles of vodka to pay for everything – from hiring men and horses to plough their land to paying for firewood. 'It was a stroke of good fortune that I had coupons for vodka in Leningrad and no one in our family drank,' said Nina. Vodka enjoyed this prized status until the government abolished the state monopoly on alcohol production in late 1992 and the country was flooded with cheap imported spirits. In the years that followed, the iconic *Royal*, 96 per cent alcohol, which was sold in litre-size green glass bottles, was the drink of choice. 'One time I went to fetch water and oop-a! A man was lying there by the well. And he was holding a *Royal*. Most importantly, his head was facing downhill,' Nina laughed. Russia eventually banned *Royal*, but you often come across empty *Royal* bottles in the remains of buildings abandoned in the 1990s.

For several years after Nina and Nikolai returned to Baranovo, their house was the only one in the village. When Nikolai was on his twelve-hour night shift at the orphanage, Nina was alone with her dog, Alissa. However, in the early 1990s, speculators hired migrant workers to put up three other houses, replacing those that had been dismantled in the 1970s. All of them were thrown up quickly and cheaply, with corrugated fibre cement sheets for roofs, and flimsy chipboard walls and floors. Orange bricks were placed in the outer walls of cinder-grey blocks to make crude patterns.

One house was bought by the Moscow charity that organized the summer camp where I volunteered; the second by a woman in St Petersburg for use as a *dacha*; and the last was never finished.

In 1996, Nina and Nikolai acquired their first cow, a traditional signifier of wealth in the countryside. At the time, there were more than a hundred cows in Belskoye Ustye: half owned by individuals, half by the restructured collective farm. Even twelve years later, I remember a sunburnt shepherd bringing a herd of cows down to graze by the Shelon River every morning, the crack of his whip of rope and tyre-rubber audible from several kilometres away. But the inexorable rise of feed costs, veterinary bills and heating gradually meant it became cheaper to buy milk and other dairy goods from the shops. Everywhere, people butchered their cows, or sought a buyer. 'The number of cows shrank and shrank. People had two or three cows, and then some didn't even have any at all. Then it shrank, and shrank again. And, now, in Belskoye Ustye there is only one cow,' said Nina.

After much soul-searching, Nina sold her cow a week before her seventy-fifth birthday. 'We found a woman from Logovino who was interested. We wanted 20,000 roubles for the cow. But she turned up with a small baby and said there were three more children at home and she only had 18,000. So, we said "take it". I didn't want to sell the cow for meat. I wanted her to live a bit longer.'

It was Nina and Nikolai's choice to move to the countryside, and, after thirty years away from the city, it is impossible to imagine them in a high-rise apartment block. They would be lost and unsure of themselves. Relatively speaking, the couple live well. As survivors of the war, their pensions are generous, and their children and grandchildren in St Petersburg help them financially. Thanks to his daughters, Nikolai was one of the first in the area to get a chainsaw. He is also the owner of a laptop and smartphone, and is a regular user of WhatsApp and VKontakte, the Russian equivalent of Facebook. Every day, after Nina goes to bed, he spends several hours online.

But you do not have to go very far from Baranovo to find real deprivation. On one visit, I asked my friend Artyom if he knew any villages with only one resident. He did. In years past, we could have walked to Oogly from Baranovo, but a collapsed bridge meant it was now a thirty-minute car journey. There were five houses in the village, which lay along a low ridge above a stream. Two were empty after the deaths of their owners; the other two had been converted into *dachas*. In the final house was Lyubov, a woman aged somewhere between forty and sixty with a puffy face tinged crimson by years of drinking.

When she opened the door to us, Lyubov shuffled and blinked in the light. She offered us tea, but asked us to first fetch water from the nearby stream. Inside, the house had two small, sparsely furnished rooms. The wooden floors were stained dark with age and sloped alarmingly, the result of rotting wooden supports and the weight of the brick stove, which was itself crumbling. There was no fridge or freezer, and a television in the bedroom played continuously. Lyubov swore repeatedly, and was deeply suspicious. She said she had lived there for seventeen years. In the winter, the road to the next village is not cleared of snow and the only tracks are her own. To get to the nearest shop was a one-hour-forty-minute walk – she did not own a car.

It was not clear exactly how Lyubov survived, but she was likely dependent on some form of social benefit. Her main distraction was alcohol. While half a litre of vodka costs about £2.50 in the shops, a moonshine dealer would deliver the same quantity to her village for half the price. 'You can get used to anything,' she told us.

Nina and Nikolai's two daughters live in St Petersburg – as do their three grandchildren, and one great-grandchild. The grandchildren, each of whom spent the summer months in Baranovo when they were younger, do the five-hour drive to Baranovo with their families for birthdays, anniversaries and to help with potato planting and harvesting. But they are all city folk, and are unlikely ever to want to move to the countryside. Nor has anyone else settled permanently in the other houses in the village. The house owned by the woman from St Petersburg and used as a *dacha* is rarely occupied as she is now elderly, and in poor health. On my last visit, I noticed one of the second-floor windows was smashed. Which leaves just Nikolai and Nina.

If you look at a graph of the number of people in Pskov Region over time, you can see that its 100-year population collapse continues with no end in sight. The line is not bottoming-out. The highest natural population decline of any Russian region means that almost a third of Pskov Region's residents are pensioners. The region's population density is half that of neighbouring Estonia, two-thirds that of Norway, and one forty-ninth of the Netherlands. The two largest cities – Pskov and Velikie Luki – have traditionally seen population inflows, or even slight rises, as they suck up migrants from rural areas. But now even their populations are wobbling. Russian military losses in the Ukraine war, which fall heaviest on deprived regions like Pskov, are only exacerbating the demographic crisis.

For a long time, I wanted to ask Nina and Nikolai what they thought would happen to Baranovo after their deaths. But I could never find a way to put the question. It seemed too cruel – and the answer all too obvious. Perhaps some relatives will want to use their house as a *dacha* once they are no longer around. But villages without permanent residents do not survive long: with no one to keep an eye on buildings, small leaks can cause catastrophic damage, and thieves are free to steal anything of value. A final ruin would likely not happen overnight, but the spectre of Baranovo as yet another ghost village loomed large. We were all much happier discussing the past.

The last time I saw Nina and Nikolai was after Russia's full-scale invasion of Ukraine, and I was nervous to find out what they thought of the war. They are both people for whom I have a great deal of affection, and who have been unfailingly kind to me over many years. I desperately hoped they might harbour some doubts. But I also knew they were Putin admirers, and that one of their few daily links with the outside world was state-owned television. Sure enough, they both turned out to be cheerleaders for the Russian cause.

'We watch it every day. At 8 o'clock,' said Nina, referring to the war coverage as if it was a tennis match. When Nikolai learnt how to use the internet several years ago, it seemed possible he might come across something that would contradict what the television beams into their home. But it never happened.

For both of them, the fighting was a direct continuation of World War II. During his military service Nikolai had trained to be a tank commander and, at a certain point on that grey February afternoon, his tales about tanks in the 1950s seemed to merge with stories about Russian tanks in Ukraine. I suddenly realized he'd spent his whole life regretting that he was too young to join the fight against Nazism, missing out on the glory of his father's generation. Nikolai paced back and forth, arms gesticulating, his eyes wet with tears, his voice breaking and swear words creeping into his speech as he described the sacrifice of heroic Russian soldiers. He told me that the collapse of the Soviet Union, which he saw as an epic tragedy, had led to the current war. He railed against 'fucking Yeltsin', and said Gorbachev had 'pissed everything away'. Back at the table, which was laid with teacups, a tray of sweets and a dish of their delicious honey, he banged his fist. 'You can never conquer Russia,' he said. 'Except through treachery.'

My role in many of the conversations that I had with Nikolai and Nina was that of a careful listener; the respectful young man nodding along to his elders. And, as they spoke about the fighting in Ukraine, I was too cowardly to say anything in protest. I knew that, for them, this was one of those topics where logic would be useless. Instead, I tried to direct us in a less painful direction.

Nevertheless, the war in Ukraine came up again. Explaining to me that both his sisters were now dead, Nikolai admitted he was 'the last one' from that generation of his family and chuckled contentedly as the meaning of the phrase sunk in for Nina and me. Nina reacted with a mock shriek of horror. 'Kolya!' she cried, throwing her hands in the air, as if warning him of the consequences of dying first, and leaving her all alone in Baranovo.

'What?' he replied in pretend confusion.

She paused, her eyes twinkling. 'You'll see! You'll go off in a tank to fight in Ukraine yet!'

Nikolai roared with laughter, clapping his hands in delight.

2

Rising Bones

Porkhov's football stadium lies next to the Shelon downriver of Baranovo. When it was built after World War II, the entrance gate was fashioned of metal cylinders and topped with the word 'stadium' spelt out in yellow letters. Used by local schools, sports clubs and amateurs, it was particularly busy in the summer months. Moments of high drama came during league matches when several hundred spectators would turn out to watch Porkhov's team, recruited from local factories or collective farms. On hot days, dust would rise in clouds from the heavily scuffed pitch.

Occasionally, the footballers tripped over human bones. Visitors may have been shocked, but locals rarely batted an eyelid: everyone in Porkhov knew the stadium had been built on top of a German military cemetery dating from the time of the Nazi occupation. As the ground was churned and pounded by countless matches some of the remains of the dead soldiers rose to the surface – it was just the way things were. If the bones worked themselves loose, they would be trodden back into the earth, or tossed to one side.

When I first visited Porkhov in the late 2000s, the old stadium was no more. In its place was a revamped sports complex with a luminous green Astroturf football pitch, new running track and a high brown fence. It was bizarrely out of place. Like other towns across Pskov Region at that time, Porkhov was dilapidated and depressed, its infrastructure crumbling, its roads potholed and decades of decay painfully evident. The stadium was the only new public building in the district.

It turned out that most of the money had come from Germany. In exchange for permission to exhume the remains of soldiers under the pitch, Germany's *Volksbund*, the equivalent of the UK's War Graves Commission and the American Battle Monuments Commission, paid for the Soviet-era facilities to be revamped. For two months in summer 2008, the stadium was closed to the public while a team dug down into the earth to find thousands of skeletons that were then taken to a modern German military cemetery in the south of Pskov Region, and quietly reburied. The *Volksbund* has been carrying out similar exhumations in Russia for a quarter of a century, their mission to ensure that every German soldier has a marked grave.

One of those who took part in the Porkhov exhumation for the *Volksbund* was Sergei Kirin, a short man in his sixties with tousled grey hair, a dapper moustache and pot belly. A former captain in the Soviet army, Sergei began working for the *Volksbund* in 2000, criss-crossing Russia to track down lost cemeteries, negotiate with landowners and local authorities, organize exhumations and rebury the dead. He estimates he has been personally involved in the location and reburial of more than 100,000 soldiers.

Sergei's job could not be done by a German. The memory of World War II is never far from the surface in Russia, where it is usually expressed through dignity, anger and pain. A German citizen doing Sergei's job would likely encounter obstruction, even hostility. To a certain extent, this reflects the scale of death and destruction suffered by the Soviet Union, which lost some 27 million people, or about 15 per cent of the population, (compared to 11 per cent for Germany and Austria, 1.3 per cent for France and 0.3 per cent for the United States). But these feelings are also stoked by the Kremlin, which has turned pride in the victory of 1945 into an ideology. Every year, Russia's celebrations of Victory Day on 9 May – a national holiday – become more and more like a religious event, with million-strong marches, and tanks, troops and rocket launchers rumbling through the main squares of major cities.

Sergei oversaw the whole of north-western Russia for the *Volksbund*, from the bogs and forests of Pskov Region to the frozen Arctic tundra around Murmansk, and he was well aware that he was not fulfilling some mystical debt to the fallen. His job was for the living: helping create the neat cemeteries that are a place to grieve for friends and relatives, and a warning to future generations. 'Those who were killed do not need all these graves,' he told me. 'I type out all the names [of the soldiers]: when they were born and when they died. How old were they? Eighteen or twenty? They were young men with their whole lives in front of them. Why did they come here? Why do they lie here? Why did life turn out that way? It's not one or two – it's millions.'

Whether you're aware of it or not, anywhere you travel in the parts of Russia occupied by the Nazis you will pass mass graves. In Pskov Region, it was the south that saw most of the fighting, with a series of brutal battles as the Red Army gradually forced the Wehrmacht westward. But all over the region, the Nazis carried out vicious anti-partisan campaigns, and exterminated Jews, gypsies, card-carrying Communists, the disabled and Soviet prisoners of war.

I remember the chill that went up my spine when I first tallied up the official number of war dead in Porkhov: on the other side of the river from the stadium 5,000 civilians were executed by the Nazis; 5,257 Red Army soldiers lie in a grave on the western edge of town; and just to the east are the remains of two Nazi camps for Soviet prisoners where the official death toll is in excess of 85,000. When you add that to the 2,226 corpses in the German cemetery under the stadium, the number of dead in Porkhov at the end of the war was about 100,000. Local historians later told me that this number was inflated, the result of bureaucratic mistakes and Russia's cult of victory that brooks no revisionism. Even so, just a fraction of this death toll casts a long shadow over the 7,000 people who live in the town today.

I arranged to meet Sergei in Sebezh, a town in south-western Pskov Region, near the Latvian border. It is home to the military cemetery where the bodies of dead German soldiers gathered from all over the region are reburied. There is one of these cemeteries in every Russian region once occupied by the Nazis (the biggest is Sologubovka outside St Petersburg with almost 80,000 burials). Sergei and his team meet in Sebezh every year at the end of the summer exhumation season to bury all the remains they have found. When I visited, about 800 skeletons were awaiting internment.

Although he has been out of uniform for over thirty years, Sergei could not hide a military bearing. He moved slowly and deliberately, and, when standing, his arms naturally found their way to his sides as if on the parade ground. He told me to come to a *Volksbund* storage building that was indistinguishable from the other houses on a long, straight road in Sebezh. Even though it was September and the leaves of the trees were already yellowing, it was unseasonably hot. Beyond the unassuming building, the blue water of one of the lakes that surround Sebezh sparkled enticingly in the sun.

Sergei was dressed entirely in black: a black T-shirt tucked into black trousers, and black trainers. Like many older Russian men, he carried a small bag on a shoulder strap for his phone, wallet and other documents. He pressed my hand firmly in welcome and I noticed the black earth ingrained under his fingernails.

Inside, he led me into a room filled with blue, turquoise and black plastic bags containing assorted human bones, piled floor to ceiling on crude wooden shelves. Out of the sun, it was cold, even damp. Exposed bulbs hung from the ceiling, and a simple wooden cross of two planks was nailed to one wall. Sheets of A4 paper in plastic wallets listed where the bones had been dug up, and the remains of how many people had been found: 'Goray 53, Derganovo 21, Pushkin Hills 43, Karatyagino 82, Dno 212 . . .' Sergei pointed out one huge stack of bags that he said contained the bodies of SS soldiers.

'This is the final stage – the finish,' said Sergei as we surveyed the bags, which covered much of the floor. A couple had small tears through which poked mud-encrusted bone fragments. After a last round of checks, the bones would be driven out to the cemetery just outside town, placed in cardboard boxes and laid to rest in a long trench. Each soldier is allotted a plot measuring 50 by 80 centimetres.

The *Volksbund* is responsible for all those killed while serving in the Wehrmacht, so the dead are mostly German. But dozens of other nationalities fought for the Nazis during World War II: Sergei has buried Latvians, Lithuanians, Estonians, Russians, Spanish, Norwegians and Dutch. They all receive identical treatment. Unless they died amid the chaos of a hectic retreat, the Wehrmacht buried its dead in near-identical military cemeteries where each grave was marked by a cross. In the freezing winters, the ground would be blown apart with grenades before grave-digging could commence.

When the Nazis retreated from Pskov Region in 1944, they left behind hundreds of such cemeteries. But these solemn monuments to the Wehrmacht's losses did not long survive the arrival of the Red Army. An order from Stalin to wipe German cemeteries from the face of the earth meant locals pulled up fences and wooden crosses for firewood, and tractors or tanks flattened the graves. The land was given over for agriculture, or to build factories, public spaces and housing. In the case of Porkhov, it became a stadium. As the decades rolled by, the existence of many of these cemeteries was forgotten, or kept alive only in the stories of ageing locals.

It was not until the end of the Cold War and the collapse of the Soviet Union that Germany reached an agreement with Russia to allow the *Volksbund* to begin the mammoth task of locating and exhuming these cemeteries. To find them is complicated, and it cannot be done without men and women like Sergei. They use material from German military archives, talk to surviving witnesses and study Nazi aerial photographs.

Once he has an approximate location, Sergei drives out to a site and begins searching with a long wire probe. It takes a lot of practice to be able to identify a burial through several metres of soil, but Sergei is an expert.

'Bones are a completely different sensation,' he told me. 'You go through the top and the bottom. Even if there's no coffin, you feel a double dip. First you enter the body, then there's dead earth. You can also tell by the state of the soil: it's unimportant how long-ago soil was dug up, it doesn't have the same consistency as undisturbed soil. You'll always know.'

Once the location of a cemetery is confirmed, the most sensitive work begins: obtaining permission for an exhumation. If it's public land, Sergei approaches the local authorities: a time-consuming, bureaucratic process. But if the graves are on private land, each individual owner must be persuaded. These conversations, Sergei said, can only be had in person. Many of the landowners have no idea that their houses or gardens are on top of cemeteries. Others have heard rumours, or have struck bones when digging in the garden. Either way, it's impossible to predict the reaction. Some agree immediately, others ask Sergei to come back at a later date, hold out for money, or flat-out refuse.

I imagined it would be easy to be persuaded by Sergei. He had an easygoing bonhomie and the calm, reassuring manner of a military commander. With reluctant landowners, he told me he tries to explain how well Germany takes care of Soviet war graves; then he argues that German dead should be in cemeteries – not rotting in someone's vegetable garden. As a last resort, he points out that, as a Soviet military officer he, too, was sent to fight, and possibly die, in a foreign country – Sergei took part in the Soviet intervention in Afghanistan in the 1980s. 'When locals get hot under the collar about Germans, I use an example: "OK, take me. Why was I in Afghanistan? Why did I kill? Why did people try to kill me? Who invited me to go there?"'

Despite Sergei's best efforts, some never give permission. Often, this is the product of a deep hatred. Sergei told me there was a generational divide when it came to such refusals; but not in the way you might expect. 'The older generation always surprises me. They're always more willing,' he said. 'Even though they saw terrible things; death, the burning of their homes and so on . . . There are more problems with younger people.' He did not say it explicitly, but the reason is not hard to guess: while younger Russians have no direct experience of war, they have had plenty of exposure to the Soviet Union's cult of victory that has been reinvented and reimagined by Putin.

When they take place, exhumations are carried out as quickly and quietly as possible. If the soil is clay, the *Volksbund* hires a mechanical digger to take off the top layer, otherwise all earth removal is done with shovels. It is hard work. Sergei was obviously physically fit, almost cat-like in his movements, and the muscles in his forearms were well defined.

Often the ground is waterlogged and, in summer, the mosquitoes come in swarms. Aside from bones, Sergei and his team are also looking for the metal dog tags placed on the chests of dead soldiers. These oval discs were worn around the neck and, when the soldier was killed, they were snapped in half: one half left in the grave, the other taken for Wehrmacht records. If the cemetery hasn't been targeted by looters, most dog tags usually survive. For each skeleton, the team also estimate the age of death by looking at the teeth, and guess height by measuring the femur. Sitting with Sergei in his hotel room one evening in Sebezh, he showed me a plastic bag of items recovered from a recent exhumation. As well as dog tags, some badly corroded, there were also personal effects: a rusted pocketknife, rings and a few crosses.

When I asked Sergei if handling the remains of dead men ever made him squeamish, he looked at me in the tired way people do when they have answered the same question many times. 'You can get used to anything,' he replied. Although the vast majority of exhumations nowadays only involve bones, sometimes – even eighty years after the end of the war – the *Volksbund* still has to deal with rotting corpses. With a smile of black humour playing on his lips, watching me for my reaction, Sergei recounted an incident when he was invited to the raising of a Nazi fighter plane from a swamp. 'They set-up hoists, and called in divers,' he said. 'The degree of preservation was incredible. Apart from a few deformed bits and pieces, it was as if it had just come off the factory assembly line.' The fighter was shot down in winter, so the pilot was dressed in warm clothes. 'The arms were inside his flying mittens. It was like they'd only just dropped into the water. Everything was there. His legs were in his fur-lined boots. And the body was dressed in insulated leather,' Sergei said. 'There was a very powerful smell. As soon as they pulled it out, it began decomposing. It was all very real – flesh. All as it should be. I put it in our blue plastic bags – fur-lined boots in one, the hands in the mittens in another. I tied them up and popped them in my car.'

The day after showing me the house used for storing remains, Sergei and I met at a bar in Sebezh overlooking the lake. Sergei had been here many times. It was a Saturday, and those around us were getting drunk as melancholic pop music was blasted from a large speaker. By the time darkness fell, most of the other drinkers were slurring, stumbling or slumped unconscious.

Raised in a military family, Sergei's father was a Soviet officer who served in East Germany and Belarus. His final posting was to Ostrov, a town south of Pskov. As a teenager, Sergei said he was a bit of a rebel: he made his own guitar so he could play in a band, and got expelled from school after he persuaded a crop-duster pilot to take him for a joy ride.

At sixteen, his parents sent him off to a military college in northern Russia to become a reconnaissance officer. When he graduated, he spent three years serving in the dusty steppe of Mongolia, and then five years in bucolic Georgia in the South Caucasus. It was there that he volunteered to fight in Afghanistan. A member of the Communist Party, Sergei said this was his own decision, and that he sincerely believed he should fulfil his 'international duty'. Even an encounter in a Tbilisi hospital with a badly disfigured paratrooper, who warned him not to go, did not change his mind.

The Soviet Union first sent troops into Afghanistan in 1979 to support a local, pro-Soviet government, and, by the time Sergei arrived five years later, it was embroiled in trying to suppress a vicious insurgency led by Mujahideen fighters armed and funded by the West. Part of a reconnaissance unit, Sergei was helicoptered all over the country, often high in the mountains, to watch for the elusive enemy, carry out surprise attacks or protect convoys. There was little food, it was often bitterly cold, and the danger was constant. They hung grenades on the barbed wire strung around their camp at night as a booby-trap for intruders.

It was also far from heroic. 'There were simply stupid deaths,' Sergei recalled:

> Once, we were sitting by the tents eating and a soldier, working as a waiter, was carrying a tray with soup when, suddenly, he was hit by a stray bullet. From where? Why? It hit him straight in the carotid artery. The blood was like a fountain all over our table. Blood everywhere… You could see how the artery was pumping. What a scene. I pressed my fingers to the wound, and the blood went all over the place. We put him on a mattress on the back of a van that was right there, and the doctor came. But he jerked around for a bit, and then died.

In two years of combat duty, Sergei got just a month of leave. He spent it with his wife in Sochi, the palm-filled Russian resort city by the Black Sea. On board the plane back to Afghanistan, the inebriated soldiers around him all fell silent the moment the pilot announced they were entering Afghan airspace.

Eventually, Sergei was wounded. When a mortar exploded in front of him during a firefight he was struck in the head by shrapnel and stones, and deafened by the detonation. 'I was evacuated by helicopter, they couldn't stop the blood from my neck and ears. How my head wasn't blown off, I'll never understand,' he said. Sergei spent more than six months in hospital, after which he and his wife moved to live with her parents in a two-bedroom flat in the industrial city of Cherepovets. By that point, they had two children.

Sergei told me how he pleaded with the military authorities to let him stay in the army, but they told him he was no longer fit. For much of the next decade, he suffered from debilitating pain, and was in and out of hospital. He had memory loss, and was unable to recall events or people from before Afghanistan. As Russia plunged into the chaos of the 1990s, he struggled to adapt to civilian life.

The worst thing was the nightmares. 'I had spoken to veterans who told stories about the war and how they would dream about charging into the attack, and so on. And I thought they were just old men shooting their mouths off,' said Sergei. 'But that's what tortured me more than anything else. When I got back home, every night I was running into the attack. Every night I was shooting. Every night I was killed. I was on the edge of madness. There was a moment when I couldn't take it any longer and I overdosed on prescription sleeping pills.' Luckily, Sergei's wife noticed, and he was rushed to hospital where they pumped his stomach and saved his life. 'After that, I said to myself, "Lad, that was not the right thing to do." And, since then, I have struggled as much as possible.'

The more Sergei spoke about his injury and his PTSD, the clearer their consequences became. I realized how badly his hearing was damaged as he leaned in to catch what I was saying over the thumping pop music. And I began to understand how his professional pedantry was a way of trying to retain control – a form of insurance against an unstable memory. It also became obvious how his job at the *Volksbund* was a lifeline – a way of keeping the darkness at bay. 'You should never have free time,' he told me. 'Because when you have free time, the thoughts start racing from one corner of your mind to the other. And sometimes you get the wrong sort of thoughts.'

Sergei threw himself into locating cemeteries when he started at the *Volksbund*, working through the weekends and refusing holiday. 'I forgot about everything else on earth,' he told me. Once, he said, he expressed surprise when his wife came home carrying a bunch of flowers – only when she burst into tears did he realize it was her birthday. For months on end, he lived out of his car. 'When a person is occupied with something, he has no time to indulge in any nonsense. He's busy. It provides some alleviation, some satisfaction. You cannot allow any weakness – not under any circumstances. I know so many people who simply drank themselves to death.'

Even though hundreds of thousands of Red Army soldiers were buried where they fell during World War II, or still lie in unmarked graves, there is no Russian equivalent of the

Volksbund. Instead, Soviet remains are exhumed piecemeal and reburied by groups of enthusiasts on shoestring budgets. This is partly explained by a long-standing official preference for mass graves, eternal flames and monuments. And there is less point in exhuming Soviet soldiers because the Red Army did not use dog tags, making identification all but impossible. But there is also, as Sergei put it, a 'difference in mentality'. The pageantry of Victory Day is designed to foster unity and collective pride, and it leaves little room for stories of individuals – stories that could raise uncomfortable questions about instances of mass surrender, cowardice, the ruthless tactics of the Stalinist high command or cases of military incompetence.

Sergei is well aware that the nature of his job leaves him vulnerable to a charge of being unpatriotic, particularly from his underfunded Russian counterparts. After all, the *Volksbund* makes no distinction between eighteen-year-old conscripts and SS officers who butchered civilians. Why should he take German money to rebury invaders, killers and murderers in beautifully tended cemeteries when the bones of Soviet soldiers lie rotting and forgotten?

When I put this to him, Sergei ducked the question, saying he was just hired to do a job. Naively, I assumed the nature of his work meant he would be deeply suspicious of tub-thumping patriotism, but, as the evening wore on, it became clear that his nationalism ran very deep. Apropos of nothing, he brought up his aversion to LGBT activism. 'I don't understand it. I don't need it. They say "I owe it". But I don't owe anyone anything,' he said in a lengthy digression on how he believed Russians were patronized by Westerners. Despite working for a foreign organization, and interacting regularly with foreigners, he was fiercely resentful of the West and what he saw as the imposition of Western values and ideas on Russia and Russians.

If necessary, Sergei told me, Russia would be ready to repeat the fire and blood of World War II. Despite his first-hand experience of the horrors of war, when fighting began in Ukraine in 2014, he went to his local recruiting office to remind them he was available for mobilization. 'I haven't lost any of my skills. I can drive anything, from a bicycle to a tank. I can shoot anything from a catapult to a mortar,' he said. 'If someone else wants to invade, have at it! We'll be waiting.'

My meeting with Sergei took place six months before the full-scale invsion of Ukraine, but we stayed in touch. It came as no surprise when he turned out to be an enthusiastic supporter of the Russian cause. In one email, he said it was hard to imagine how the *Volksbund* could continue its work when Russian soldiers were fighting against German-made tanks in Ukraine. He concluded with the line: 'I am a Russian officer and my position is simple. We beat them in the past, we are beating them now and will beat them in the future.'

The final resting place for the Wehrmacht soldiers exhumed in Pskov Region is on the edge of Sebezh. Sergei drove me out to see the cemetery. It was a forlorn place: neat, tidy and full of quiet sadness. When the land was given to the *Volksbund* by the Russian authorities it had been covered in building waste and the concrete remains of a defunct collective farm. Now, it was a well-kept grass field, dotted with stone crosses and paths that, like the spokes on a wheel, led to a central, wrought-iron black cross. There was barely a cloud in the washed-out blue sky, and only an occasional car on the adjacent road disturbed the silence.

Individual graves were not marked. Instead, lining the paths were human-height granite slabs engraved with names, dates of birth and dates of death. It's *Volksbund* policy not to mention nationality or rank.

At least until the war in Ukraine, the cemetery got a steady stream of foreign visitors, mostly relatives of the fallen soldiers. When warned in advance, *Volksbund* staff met those coming to pay their respects. Sometimes, they were handed personal effects in a little ceremony. Recounting one such encounter, the tears shone in Sergei's eyes for the first and only time during our conversation. 'We were visited by the granddaughter of a dead soldier,' he recalled. 'She was a flautist and she sat on the grave of her grandfather and began to play. It made a deep impression.'

Sergei said the passage of time has helped him deal with the trauma of what he saw in Afghanistan. 'You need time for everything,' he said. 'To heal physical wounds, and to heal emotional wounds. Time heals.' His once relentless pace was slackening: he told me he was reducing how much heavy digging he does, and is training up a member of his team as his replacement. Just before the coronavirus pandemic, he was diagnosed with cancer and underwent surgery to remove a tumour. He was in remission when we met. Even so, he has no plans to stop work, and bristled when I asked about the possibility of retirement. His *dacha*, which he built years ago and where he could grow old, plant flowers and raise chickens, looks unlikely to be much used. 'If you sit down, fold your hands and start thinking of yourself as a sick person, you'll perish,' he said. 'I have no intention of sitting still or giving up.'

The last time I heard from Sergei he said he'd been made redundant. He was bitter. More than a million Wehrmacht soldiers may have been reburied in Russia since the early 1990s, but there is much more to do. The soldiers still awaiting exhumation are often those lying in particularly remote locations, or on the property of recalcitrant landlords. Future generations may witness the last Wehrmacht soldier in Russia laid to rest, but Sergei certainly will not. 'There's no end in sight,' he said.

3

Blue Gold

A field of flax in early summer is a bewitching sight. With delicate blue petals and pale-green stems, the plants seem to shimmer and dance. The flowers are extremely fragile, lasting for just a couple of days before dropping to the ground – even less if there's a breeze. In his children's story 'The Flax', Hans Christian Andersen described them as 'even more delicate' than the 'wings of a moth'.

Flax fields were once common all over Pskov Region, and anyone over the age of thirty recalls them with nostalgia. Many people, including Nina, worked in the flax industry. For flax is not just a pretty flower, it's one of the world's oldest cultivated plants. Once processed, it can be made into linen, which is used for clothes and other textiles, or forms the basis for a myriad of other goods, from ropes, banknotes and ship's sails to fire hoses, linoleum and insulation. It's more durable than cotton or wool, and, unlike most fabrics, becomes stronger when wet. It was prized in Ancient Egypt, where embalmers wrapped mummies in linen cloths for their journey to the next world.

In Russia, linen has been worn for at least 900 years, and flax was one of the goods traded by Pskov with the cities of the Hanseatic League – along with beeswax, furs, timber, resin, honey, wheat and rye. But Pskov's flax industry really took off in the seventeenth and eighteenth centuries. North-western Russia's cool, moist climate was perfect for the tricky-to-grow crop, and its location made it an ideal place from which to export to Europe. The Royal Navy was a major client, and Pskov flax was used for rigging, sails and ropes in British ships. For centuries, flax was a cash crop for the Russian Empire, playing the same economic role that crude oil plays for modern Russia, or that fur played for medieval Rus. For some, flax was known as 'northern silk', for others it was 'blue gold'.

Its ubiquitousness meant flax became deeply intertwined with local culture. On the last Sunday before Lent, for example, Pskov peasants would gallop around the fields due to be planted that year shouting: 'Flax, little flax, grow up to be golden and silky!' Some farmers would pay children to do the riding as they believed the further you rode, the taller the flax.

By the middle of the nineteenth century, Russia was the world's biggest flax exporter, and Pskov Region was the source of a third of the country's flax exports. Lenin even devoted a chapter of his book *The Development of Capitalism in Russia* (1899) to Pskov's flax industry, arguing profits were creamed off by landowners and middlemen, leaving the peasants destitute. Well into the second half of the century, there were whole generations of families from Pskov Region who had known nothing but flax. In one of Pskov's libraries, I came across a 1950 book called *Tales of Veteran Flax Growers*. One of the personal stories it recounted was that of Pyotr Figurkin, an agricultural labourer living near the town of Dno who had cultivated flax under both the tsars and the Soviets. 'I was drawn to flax. Fishermen are drawn to lakes, foresters to the forests and me – to flax. What can you do? It's my favourite profession,' he said. 'To be a flax grower with us in Pskov Region is the same as being a miner in the Donbas or an oil worker in Baku.'

Flax's popularity began to wane worldwide in the 1970s as cheap, mass-produced cotton replaced linen. But, in Pskov Region, the centrally planned economy held back the flood of change. Instead, the collapse took place at dizzying speed as Russia embraced capitalism in the 1990s. Like whole swathes of the Russian economy, most of Pskov Region's flax industry was quickly taken out of state hands. Farmers, managers, technicians and mill bosses who had no experience of how to operate in a free market were left to try and navigate the economic chaos. They failed.

Today, there is no flax industry in Pskov Region. No one plants flax, no one harvests flax, no one processes flax into linen. Flax mills lie in ruins, and the fields where flax was once grown have become forest. With hindsight, the industry's end can seem inevitable. But parts of the former Soviet Union, including neighbouring Belarus, successfully preserved some of their flax industry. And it certainly did not seem like total collapse was inevitable to the thousands who struggled through the 1990s to preserve their way of life.

One of those in the centre of this storm was Vladimir Orlov. A cheerful, capable man, Vladimir was put in charge of a Pskov Region flax mill in 1987. It closed down eighteen years later.

Vladimir and I agreed to meet one sunny March morning on the main square of Ostrov, a town famous for its nineteenth-century chain bridge, about an hour's drive south of Pskov. I was waiting when he pulled up in a white Renault Duster. After getting out, he lit a cigarette, explaining that his grandfather, who grew his own tobacco, introduced him to smoking as a child. Now aged sixty-five, Vladimir had a small moustache, receding grey hair and teeth stained yellow from the nicotine. His eyes were a pale, washed-out blue.

It had taken me a lot of searching to find Vladimir. Not only are most of those who worked in Pskov Region's flax industry long past retirement age, but the complete extinction of the sector means there are no organizations to contact: no mills, farms or factories. Instead, I got in touch with local libraries and museums. Two other ex-directors of flax mills whom I found – both women – refused to speak to me. In each case, it seemed they were reluctant to discuss their role in what they saw as a tale of failure and loss. Flax mills all over Pskov Region had fought to survive in the 1990s before furloughing and firing staff and, eventually, selling equipment for scrap. The reluctance to revisit difficult memories was understandable.

In contrast, Vladimir was keen to talk. Indeed, he enjoyed holding forth, telling stories and making jokes. Perhaps his experience at the flax mill had made less of a mark because his career had not suffered. Subsequently elected to head a municipality – Vorontsov Volost – for the ruling United Russia party, Vladimir told me he was currently deciding whether to stand for a fifth term. His position meant he was almost certainly involved in a morass of petty corruption, but he was open, curious and had a disarming sense of humour. Despite myself, I took a liking to him. Married with two sons, Vladimir went hunting in his spare time, and proudly showed me photos of a group of men in snow-camouflage posing with a wolf carcass. He said he didn't want to go to a café, so we sat in his car to talk – him behind the wheel and me in the passenger seat.

Vladimir was only thirty when he was promoted from the post of chief engineer at a collective farm to be the head of Soshikhinsky Flax Mill. At the time, the mill employed about 28 men and women. 'The people knew me, I lived in a village about five or six kilometres from the mill and my aunt and uncle worked there,' he told me. But the job was a step up for a local boy with no university degree whose mother was a nurse, and father a PE teacher. Vladimir was now reporting directly to Communist Party bosses in Ostrov.

At the time, there were 23 flax mills like Soshikhinsky in Pskov Region. In the centrally planned Soviet economy, the amount of land earmarked for flax cultivation was determined in Moscow – and the mills were supposed to process all the flax produced by local collective farms. After harvesting, threshing (to remove the seeds) and retting (to begin breaking down the fibres), the flax was driven by lorries to the mills. Once there, it was 'scutched' and 'heckled' to remove the final bits of flax straw and isolate the prized flax fibres, which resembled grey, iridescent human hair. The highest quality fibres were sent to the nearest textile factory in Velikie Luki to be made into linen.

Soshikhinsky Flax Mill sits by the picturesque Borovenskoye Lake, and is surrounded by pine forest. When the mill was built in 1950, a small village called Priozernaya (literally 'By the lake') sprang up nearby that was mostly inhabited by mill workers and their families. In those days, the mill operated in three eight-hour shifts every day.

When Vladimir was made director, the mill was already struggling. Flax production fell steadily in the last decades of the Soviet Union and mills could not get enough raw material. Immediately after his appointment, Vladimir was thrown into a task of ever-increasing urgency: locating collective farms still producing flax. The more he could find, the more work for the mill. While the Soviet Union was still in existence, this was relatively straightforward as the state covered transport costs and the flax industry was – more or less – still a viable prospect. Even so, Vladimir travelled thousands of kilometres to farms in Belarus, northern Ukraine and the Baltic states. When he found some flax, he would send a column of trucks to collect it.

This period was the heyday of *glasnost* and *perestroika*. Soviet leader Mikhail Gorbachev allowed elements of private enterprise, loosened the Communist Party's monopoly on power, and expanded media freedoms. But, gradually, the reforms escaped the control of Kremlin bureaucrats and, in the late 1980s, they took on a life of their own. The words 'democracy' and 'capitalism' were on everyone's lips. In early 1992, after the dissolution of the Soviet Union, President Boris Yeltsin and his team of pro-Western reformers unleashed a programme of 'shock therapy' designed to embed the free market.

In places like rural Pskov Region, 'shock therapy' and the race to dismantle the Soviet system was accompanied by immense human suffering in the form of hyperinflation, unpaid salaries, job losses and uncertainty. For many, the cumulative experience of those turbulent years was a feeling of abandonment. The ubiquitous Soviet state simply disappeared, like a rug pulled from under their feet. The rules of the game had changed, and people were required to fend for themselves. To add insult to injury, the ideology that had promised a Communist utopia was publicly trashed, suggesting to many their lives had been spent in vain. It's become a truism to say that the arrival of capitalism meant Russians lost not only their past, but also their future.

This sense of catastrophe was on a par with other disasters of the twentieth century. One man who foresaw the enormity of the unfolding tragedy was Mikhail Zvontsov, an artist and World War II veteran who often visited Pskov Region. In early 1992 he wrote to a friend: 'I had thought there could be no ordeal on earth more terrible than the ordeal of the war years, but it looks like I was wrong.'

As Yeltsin's reformers took a sledgehammer to the centrally managed Soviet economy, Pskov Region's already teetering flax industry faced obliteration. At Vladimir's urging, the staff at Soshikhinsky voted unanimously in 1992 for privatization. Vladimir could not remember any euphoria at this pivotal moment; no sense of it being an opportunity. In fact, he had difficulty recalling the details. Either way, the mill was on its own. Shares were divided up according to salary size with Vladimir receiving a 0.84 per cent stake. There was one man who got more because he worked a lot of shifts. 'Nothing' terrible. It was the

Soviet 'Union,' said Vladimir. 'It's now that managers get ten times more than workers. Or a hundred times more. Back then it wasn't like that.'

As the months passed, the situation deteriorated relentlessly. Most worryingly, ever-smaller amounts of flax were being planted: now free from centrally set quotas, farmers simply switched to more lucrative options like meat and dairy. Flax is a capricious crop that requires careful management, and is highly dependent on the weather – suddenly, it did not make economic sense. Vladimir also blamed the relentless rural depopulation, which accelerated in the years following the collapse of the Soviet Union, resulting in a labour shortage. 'If there was not enough people there was nothing you could do,' he said. 'Resist or not the outcome would be the same.' Desperate for raw materials, the mills began accepting increasingly sub-standard flax, which, in turn, put pressure on the textile factories that were struggling to make a profit. 'We were part of a chain,' Vladimir said.

One of the ironies of Russia's transition to capitalism – hailed as a process of modernization – was that it seemed to send the country spinning into the Stone Age. This was epitomized by the rise of barter, which became a common form of exchange. Its prevalence was a consequence of runaway inflation, which reached 2,500 per cent in 1992, and meant goods became a more reliable store of value than money. But barter was also a defensive mechanism: a way for doomed businesses to stay afloat in the short term, masking unprofitability and allowing companies to pay next to no tax. For Vladimir, barter was an everyday reality as he went to ever more fantastic lengths to keep the mill afloat. His descriptions of complex barter schemes sounded exhausting, but he relished the absurdity. When recounting something amusing, his eyes fixed me with a question, as if daring me not to laugh.

In one case, Vladimir sent flax fibre to a sackcloth factory in Narva, a town near the Baltic coast over 300 kilometres to the north. 'They made sacks and sent the sacks to factories that produced flour. And they'd sell the flour in those sacks. I gave the factory flax fibre and they settled with me in flour. Then I took the flour to a bread factory,' he explained. Vladimir would then come to an agreement with the bread factory and the company that distributed loaves to local shops. 'And my people got the bread without paying any money,' he concluded. It was not just bread that the factory workers received in exchange for flax fibre – there were dozens of other items circulating in this goods-swapping economy. Vladimir said he still owned a tracksuit and a pair of boots he got from a 1990s barter deal.

Vladimir oozed an easy affability and I guessed he was a competent manager able to flatter his bosses, inspire loyalty among subordinates, and make difficult requests with lightness and humour. But he was trained in the Soviet system and – even for him – operating in the free market was a steep learning curve. Crestfallen at the memory, he recounted one incident when the mill sold 'two cars' worth of flax fibre to a middleman who promptly dissolved his company and refused to pay.

However, Vladimir admitted his biggest mistake was becoming involved with a group called Northern Flax that gained control of a handful of flax mills in Pskov Region by promising investment and new equipment. From Vladimir's description and a few media articles I found, Northern Flax sounded like an asset-stripping operation: they would take control of struggling businesses and pull out as much value as possible before exiting. Other flax mills certainly suffered at their hands. In a 2002 interview, the former director of the nearby Novousitovskiy Flax Mill broke down in tears when asked about her decision to join Northern Flax, which had yielded none of the promised benefits and only worsened the mill's financial situation.

After closing several mills, Northern Flax eventually disappeared. Nevertheless, Vladimir worried for years about a document he signed that gave Northern Flax the rights to the equipment of the Soshikhinsky mill. Russian business in the 1990s was replete with banditry, sharp practice – even contract killings – and this was the only time Vladimir alluded to the possibility of violence. He was concerned someone from Northern Flax would turn up out of the blue and threaten him with 'other means' – forcing him to hand over the mill's equipment. In a rare moment of seriousness, Vladimir admitted that he was 'afraid for a long time'.

The collapse of the flax industry took place as a series of downward lurches, and within five years of the end of the Soviet Union the situation was already catastrophic. In a 1996 article in *Pskovskaya Pravda* newspaper titled 'Is it Profitable to Grow Flax?' the author summarized the parlous state of the sector. 'The average number of people employed in 1996 compared to 1991 has fallen by more than a half and, in some areas, it's even more. Linen production is one-eleventh of what it was, oakum production one-sixteenth and flax insulation production one-fifteenth,' the article read. 'Because of the lack of raw materials, only one-fifth of the available production capacity of flax mills is being used.' With their customers also struggling, flax mills were starved of funds – meaning the few farmers still growing flax often had no choice but to hand over their harvest for free. In 1996, mills in Pskov Region were, on average, only paying for 20 per cent of the flax they received. By the following year, 80 per cent of flax mills in the region were estimated to be making a loss.

Inexorably, the lack of flax meant mills reached breaking point. Year after year, Vladimir was forced to extend the furlough for staff. Soon it was three or four months, then half a year. Vladimir recounted how he would try and find odd jobs at local farms for his employees in an effort to tide them over financially. In desperation, the Soshikhinsky mill even made a foray into agriculture, renting nearby land and equipment to grow their own flax. Vladimir enrolled local residents and college students to help, but they did not have the resources to cultivate large-enough areas and they lacked the skills. By the early 2000s, most of the mills in Pskov Region had succumbed to the inevitable and closed forever. Soshikhinsky was hanging on by its fingernails.

As Vladimir described the last years of the Soshikhinsky mill, he did so matter-of-factly; it did not appear to be something to which he'd given much thought. Instead, he preferred telling jokey stories. Only on one occasion did he appear to acknowledge the emotional toll of trying to save the mill as everything was in freefall around him. Recounting a moment when the textile mill in Velikie Luki rejected his flax fibre in favour of imports from Egypt, he went uncharacteristically silent. He rested both hands on the steering wheel of his car and stared straight ahead. 'It was not a great way to live,' he said.

Even as the writing was on the wall, most people could not believe the flax industry was headed for extinction. They still hoped for a miracle. In 2003, Antonina Silina, the director of a flax mill in the Pskov Region town of Dno told an interviewer: 'My dream is to have enough flax so the mill can operate steadily.' Silina, who had worked at the mill for thirty years, sat in her office filled with tropical pot plants. 'Sooner or later I will have to retire,' she said. 'I don't want to leave ruins behind me, but a stable and functioning enterprise.' Of course, when she did step down a few years later, ruins would be exactly what she left behind.

Vladimir gave a similar interview a year later when the Soshikhinsky mill had just a few more months left. 'The most important thing is that we have preserved production and that the sale of flax fibre has stabilized,' he told the interviewer, sounding optimistic. 'The town administration has developed a programme for the development of flax cultivation in the district, which means Soshikhinsky Flax Mill should have a future.'

When the end finally arrived for Soshikhinsky, it came with a whimper. Toward the end of 2005 one of Vladimir's old Communist Party bosses, now the head of the district, asked him if he wanted to stand in municipal elections. After some agonizing, he agreed. That year the mill had only been able to source enough flax to operate for two months – October and November – and was about to be mothballed until the following autumn. When I asked Vladimir if there had been a general meeting to announce the closure, he looked nonplussed. 'Why would we have needed a meeting? There were just twenty of us. We saw each other every day. It was just: "That's it. See you later." And then that really was it.'

Even if Vladimir said he realized that the mill's closure was inevitable, that didn't mean he gave up on a revival. And, for several years after the mill shut its doors, former employees living nearby kept an eye on the buildings, which still contained valuable equipment. As Vladimir put it: they were 'hoping for something'. But even that hope faded. One night, there was a break-in, and it became obvious that, without full-time security, thieves would soon strip the place. Vladimir and the other former employees got together and reluctantly decided to sell the equipment for scrap – and split the money. It would be the only financial gain they got from the mill's privatization.

Within a decade of Soshikhinsky's end, there was not a single functioning flax mill left in Pskov Region. A few were converted into other businesses: one mill outside Pskov became a tile- and brick-making factory, and the storage hangers for a mill in Novorzhev were used by a firewood business. Most of the other mill buildings, however, now lie in ruins.

After speaking to Vladimir, I drove to see the Soshikhinsky mill. It was impossible to access the ruins themselves as the territory was fenced off – Vladimir told me there was possible interest from a developer about building *dachas* on the site – so the best view was from the other side of the iced-over Borovenskoye Lake. The mill was a cluster of low-slung buildings around a water tower. Even from a distance it was obvious it was all falling apart, with missing windows and most of the brickwork exposed.

Today, the only functioning remnant of the region's flax industry is a state-run agricultural research centre in the town of Rodina just outside Pskov. When I visited, the entrance hall had a display of dried-out bundles of flax strains with names like 'dawn', 'quartet' and 'chance'. The head of the centre, Alexander Styopin, a muscular, bull-shaped man with almost no visible neck, invited me to chat. In the job since 2003, Styopin had witnessed first-hand the death throes of Pskov's flax industry and said there was no way it could be reborn without massive investment.

'There's no optimism that it's possible, but who knows? Maybe in ten or twenty years' time when everything is again covered by taiga and forest we'll again be burning down trees to create fields for flax,' he said.

At the height of Pskov Region's post-war flax industry, 140,000 hectares of land were sown with flax. Two years before the closure of Soshikhinsky, this had fallen to 7,000 hectares. Now, the 28 hectares attached to Styopin's institute are the only place where flax is still grown. As they have done since before the Russian Revolution, Styopin and his staff use these fields to develop new strains of flax: some are of higher quality; some are more virus-resistant; some are better adapted to the local climate. As much an anachronism as a company fine-tuning typewriters in the age of the computer, they continue their work.

When I went to the centre's fields, which are located on a floodplain of the Velikaya River, it was a scorching hot day in July and white cumulus clouds scudded across the sky. A couple of fields were full of flowering flax, the baby-blue petals shimmering like the surface of a disturbed lake. But there were also fields with half-dried flax, the breeze rattling the golden seed heads. As I walked past sheafs stacked and ready for collection, dozens of wagtails took off ahead of me, chattering and bobbing. A cheerful group of women from the centre, most wearing headscarves, stooped low, working in a field where different strains were marked by white posts. From a distance, it looked like an arable scene from a nineteenth-century painting.

The eldest was Tamara Andreeva, a wizened woman who had worked at the centre since 1967 – likely making her the oldest still-active flax worker in Pskov Region, if not all of Russia. One of the others brought over a wooden stool on which she sat while we spoke. I squatted beside her. With her earth-stained hands, she showed me how flax was harvested before mechanization: grabbing a handful of stems near the ground, she pulled gently upward in a firm movement accompanied with a slight twist. The shallow roots meant the flax came out easily. As she spoke about the different strains, I found it hard to forget that the centre was a relic from a bygone era. Even so, there was also something reassuring in its existence. Tamara's earth-stained hands were a living connection to centuries of tradition. And the seeds from the institute's new flax strains, which are stored in sealed vaults, a guarantee that – at least biologically – there could be a way back.

Periodically during our conversation in his car, the former mill director Vladimir waved at acquaintances who walked past. I guessed he was something of a local power broker, and I believed him when he boasted he had men in the local villages who would do exactly what he asked no matter the time of day. He recounted some of his successes as a municipal head: supplying Ostrov with huge fir trees to be erected on the central square for New Year; arranging support for the families of men mobilized to fight in Ukraine; keeping the roads free of snow. The only issue that seemed to bother him was depopulation, which, he said, showed no sign of ending.

When the Soshikhinsky mill closed its doors for the final time, only a couple of dozen people lost their jobs. Some, like Vladimir, found new employment. Others retired, or turned to traditional village activities: mushroom and berry collecting; chopping wood; keeping cows to provide milk for city dwellers at their *dachas*. When I asked Vladimir if people were angry about the closure, he paused. His memory, he said, was foggy after more than twenty years. But his answer was also full of fatalism, and the futility of struggling against a verdict handed down by powerful economic and political forces. 'There was no anger! What sort of anger could there have been?' he said. 'People bore a grudge, maybe, but not anger.'

So complete was the destruction of the flax industry that, when I first started visiting Pskov Region, I was unaware of its existence. But when I found out about it, I started to see traces everywhere – in other words, I began seeing the landscape through the eyes of people like Vladimir. As well as the ruined mills and reforesting fields, the legacy of flax is to be found in language and symbols: the local newspaper in Palkinsky District is still called Flax Mill; there is a tiny rural railway station just outside Porkhov called Flax Collective Farm; a whole neighbourhood in Nevel is named Flax

Mill; and in Pushkin Hills there is a Flax Mill Street. More than one district in Pskov Region has flax flowers, or sheafs of flax, as part of its heraldry.

Vladimir still drives around the region for work, and he admitted these constant reminders, particularly the physical remains, were a source of sadness. His desperate search for flax supplies to keep the mill running in the 1990s means he knows the location of all the region's former flax mills and collective farms, whether their ruins lie down little-used side roads, or in the centre of towns. Even when not travelling, Vladimir's daily commute takes him past the slowly crumbling Soshikhinsky mill. In his mind's eye he can still picture it in its heyday: machinery humming; workers arriving and departing for their shifts; the nearby fields of blue flowers rippling in the summer sun.

STARAYA RUSSA
VELIKOE SELO
МАГАЗИН
RVY
MIKHAILOV POGOST
NIKANDROVA MONASTERY
E95
ST PETERSBURG
CHERNOBOZHYE
KRYPET'SKY MONASTERY
YELIZAROV CONVENT
ISTANBUL
LAKE PSKOV
TOLBA RIVER
TALAB ISLANDS

4

Back Country

I arrived in Staraya Russa, which translates roughly as 'Old Rus', late one evening at the end of September 2020, on the daily Pskov–Moscow train. After a long history as a major salt-producing centre, the town became a spa destination known as 'Russia's Baden-Baden' in the nineteenth century. I was here because it was the starting point I'd chosen for a walk of some two hundred kilometres that would take me from east to west across the entire width of Pskov Region. All being well, I wanted to finish on the banks of Lake Pskov, part of Europe's fourth-largest lake system, which looks out over the European Union and NATO.

There was not a single hiking path on the way. But I was hoping locals would be welcoming of a walker carrying a heavy backpack, who I wanted to get a better sense for the flat landscapes, hidden holy sites, and hollowed-out villages of Pskov Region.

The spa in Staraya Russa, which had once been patronized by the tsar's family, was made into a sanatorium in the Soviet Union, a sort of cross between a hospital and a resort. Although a bit dilapidated, it was still functioning, and the grounds were full of elderly residents taking leisurely turns along paths. There was a cluster of people around a fountain of mineral water laid out in red marble, and a few were headed into a colonnaded centre for mud-immersion procedures believed to alleviate anything from arthritis to infertility. Women were offered vaginal 'mud tampons'. In a nearby glass building, a line of brass taps dispensed different varieties of the local water. I tried one: it was flat, almost slimy, with a lingering metallic aftertaste.

A friend of mine, Artyom, who I'd met while volunteering at the Belskoye Ustye orphanage, had agreed to come with me on the walk. Although he'd grown up in Moscow, Artyom was living in Pskov Region, where he'd previously worked in a national park. He loved camping, as well as exploring abandoned places, and needed little persuasion to join.

The two of us left Staraya Russa the following day under leaden skies along a road by the Porusya River. One of the houses we passed was purchased by Fyodor Dostoevsky as a countryside escape from St Petersburg in 1876. A small, green, clapboard building, it was where the great writer penned most of his final work, the gargantuan *The Brothers Karamazov*, which grapples with questions of sin, redemption and the existence of God. After a life of moving between rented flats, and with little spare money (in part thanks to his gambling addiction), it was the first property Dostoevsky owned. He only enjoyed it for five years before his death in February, 1881.

Today, it is a museum about Dostoevsky and, inside, it was full of dark wooden furniture and half-drawn curtains. The author's baize-covered writing desk stood in the corner of the study he shared with his wife, below an icon and oil lamp. We were the only visitors, and the museum was cloaked in hushed reverence.

Our walk had been delayed by the coronavirus pandemic, so we were starting well after the end of summer. In all the villages through which we passed later that afternoon, there were apple-laden trees, and piles of chopped firewood ready to be stacked for the winter. Only cabbages were left in the vegetable patches, and the lines of green spheres on squat trunks looked like rows of tiny aliens. Apples turned out to be an unexpected delight on the walk. I had never eaten so many varieties: traditional scarlet apples with dashes of green; late-autumn *Antonovkas*, a bewitching mix of sweet and bitter; small, maroon apples from half-wild trees;

and luminescent green ones, aromatic and delicious. We filled our pockets with windfall, and stewed them over campfires in the evening.

Not long after leaving Staraya Russa, we passed a group of men and women standing around chatting. 'Where have you come from, where are you going, and why?' asked one man, staring in curiosity at our bulging rucksacks. He laughed when we said we were walking across Pskov Region, and told us to help ourselves to apples from a tree down the road on the left. 'It would be quicker to take the bus,' one of his companions deadpanned.

The next day was cloudless, and a light morning mist burnt off as we walked through high grass soaked in dew. At the entrance to the village of Velikoe Selo, we passed a one-legged man, and a sign reading: 'sobriety is an advantage'. During the Soviet Union the bell tower and cupolas were cut from Velikoe Selo's church, leaving a squat, ungainly stump of a building. A man in tracksuit bottoms and a white cap chopping firewood nearby turned out to be the priest.

He wiped the sweat from his face as he came over. 'As you go through the village, you'll see half the houses are empty. Of course, there were lots of people in the past. Even ten years ago there were more,' he told us. 'But there's no work here. There were collective farms, but there's nothing left now. There's a shop, post office, club, boiler station, and that's it. Everyone travels into Staraya Russa. There's nothing to do here, and there are no opportunities for young people. The village is gradually dying.' His tone was matter-of-fact, as if decline had been part of life for so long it was like discussing the weather.

Gradually, the road went from tarmac to beaten earth and muddy track. In one village, a dead sparrowhawk was strung up from a tree, its grey, speckled wings twisting in the breeze. Sitting by the campfire that evening, a man loomed out of the darkness, a rifle slung over his shoulder, making me suddenly aware how far we were from any help. But he turned out to be a hunter, and full of simple curiosity. In his mid-fifties, rotund and jovial, he carried a canvas rucksack held together with string, and chuckled with amusement at finding people in such a remote place.

He said he used a nearby hunting tower – a crude wooden structure shaped like a pulpit – every couple of weeks, sitting alone for five or six hours after nightfall. A field of wheat had been planted below to make attractive grazing. If lucky, he would get a shot at a bear, moose or wild boar.

'How do you see them?' I asked.

'I've got a night-vision sight,' he replied, patting his rifle. 'And you can hear everything. Every beast has their own sound. If a wild boar shows up, you'll hear him a long way off. A moose groans. If it's a bear, he bites into an apple with a crunch.'

In the morning we had another visitor. The dull whine of a tractor built slowly into a roar as it drove right up to our tent, and a rat-like man with a small moustache and deep sunburn jumped out. Lighting a cigarette, he said he earned a living by metal detecting. This was not a hobby, nor was he interested in historical curiosities. Selling scrap metal for him was a source of income. What he was looking for were abandoned villages, defunct collective farmyards, or former Soviet workshops, where used parts were simply tossed aside. Sometimes, he would also find remains from World War II battlefields.

'What else is there to do in the countryside apart from looking for fucking scrap metal?' he asked. He said he was about to fell a tree, tie it to his tractor, flatten the undergrowth – and then go over it with a metal detector. He drove off without shutting the tractor cabin door, which flapped wildly.

We followed animal tracks through the forest, passing piles of brown-bear faeces and being tormented by deer keds: small flies that don't usually bite humans, but which crawled over our exposed skin and burrowed into our hair. Eventually, the trees began to break up and we emerged into a series of grassy clearings. The autumn forest was a breathtaking mosaic of reds, oranges and yellows. In the village of Rvy we spotted a damaged church, a golden spire on its bell tower tilting at a crazy angle and birch trees growing out of the exposed red-brick walls. Inside the roofless building, a man and woman dressed in black were reciting a canticle in praise of St Nicholas, Russia's most-worshipped saint. Occasionally they dropped stiffly to their knees, their eyes flitting to the improvised altar of rubble adorned with guttering candles. We stood motionless as the rough chanting filled the morning air.

Afterwards we spoke to the man, Pavel, who said they prayed to St Nicholas every Thursday. He invited us for tea. Sitting on tree stumps outside his ramshackle wooden house, goldfinches flitted in the bushes. Pavel smelt of alcohol. Despite a thick white beard, his face was childlike, and his kind eyes lit up when he was animated. He told us he was a retired geologist, and described travelling all over the Soviet Union to study the effects of nuclear explosions. 'I ended up here because I came to God. More accurately, God brought me here,' he said. When I asked for details, he was evasive.

'Belief is everything. Do you know what sort of belief there is in Russia?'

The question was directed at me.

'I think so,' I replied.

'You won't find anything like it anywhere else. As Rilke said: "All countries have borders with each other, but only Russia has a border with God." And it's true. That's the essence of it.'

Reluctant to let us leave, Pavel brought out his photo albums, which included shots of buildings warped by nuclear blasts. There were some from Arctic testing grounds, others from what is today Kazakhstan. As we gathered our bags, he filled our water bottles, and insisted we took a dozen apples.

Eventually, we came across a raised grassy track that looked like it could be the Old Russian Military Highway, an ancient road that once started in Pskov. All the villages we passed through on the Highway were typical of rural Russia, consisting of one-storey, wooden houses clustered close together. Sometimes the houses were painted, sometimes they had lean-to porches and, sometimes, carved window frames and eaves. Everywhere, there was an inventiveness born of poverty: old bed frames refashioned as gates, TV antennas made from beer cans, swans carved from old tyres, palm trees built out of green and brown plastic bottles.

Every village was made up of a mixture of lived-in houses, and abandoned 'ghost houses', their ragged curtains flapping behind broken windows. Once the owner dies, empty houses are ransacked and the brick stoves, traditionally a place to hide valuables, smashed open. Later, we would see abandoned shops, and, in one village, an empty cottage hospital with a gynaecological examination chair, like a scene from a horror film.

In Mikhailov Pogost, a shop-on-wheels was parked by a beautiful white, nineteenth-century church with faded aquamarine cupolas. As most villages lack shops and public transport, these vans are a lifeline for elderly residents. Usually, the vans show up once a week, honking and trundling slowly along the road. The shelves inside this van were filled with essentials like pasta, rice, cheese, sweets and bread. At the back was a pile of frozen pig heads.

As dusk gathered, we passed the first of several World War II memorials. Fighting swept over Pskov Region as the Nazis advanced into the Soviet Union, and even eastern areas of the region spent years under occupation. This memorial was in the shape of a small cross, and it honoured two bomber crews killed in a 1942 attack on a German airfield. Artyom said his grandfather, an aircraft mechanic in the war, had told him that the two-seater planes the men had been flying were nicknamed 'cigarette lighters' because petrol tanks in the wings meant they caught fire very easily.

By this point, we had settled into a daily rhythm of waking, making breakfast and then walking until nightfall. Unused to such heavy bags, our shoulders and legs were gathering aches and our daily kilometre count was falling. When we entered Chernobozhye – literally Blackgod – shortly after eleven o'clock one morning, we were surprised to pass a group of men and women drinking moonshine in their coats. They were gathered around the bonnet of an old jeep laid out with a plastic plate of bright-pink sausage and a bottle of clear liquid. The reason for the celebration was unclear until I realized it was Saturday. A little further on, three red-faced men were much further gone in their drinking. Already stumbling, they were taking turns to fire an air rifle at a broken lamp post, and the sound of ricocheting pellets followed us down the road.

Occasionally, we took shortcuts to avoid dusty earth roads. On one such a shortcut after Chernobozhye we found ourselves deep in a forest without a path to follow. It was still and close. We pressed on, briefly following an elk trail, cloven hoof prints visible in the oozing, black mud. Then, we crashed through a sea of nettles well above our heads, protecting our faces with crossed arms. After threading through an alder wood, we crossed a stream flooded by beaver dams. Off to one side was the remains of a long-forgotten road that headed in a direction we did not want to go. It was a relief, finally, to emerge in a clearing, the air instantly fresher. Gnarled apple trees, their lower branches stripped of fruit by bears, were the only sign of a long-absent village. After more nettle thickets, we reached a village that was intact, but mostly abandoned. We didn't see a soul.

In Eastern Christianity, ascetics withdraw to remote places to fast and pray in solitude. This was traditionally the desert, but in Russia, with desert not an option, holy men and women sought out caves, or areas of drier ground in enormous bogs. The Russian word for such holy places, *pustin*, even has the same linguistic root as the word for desert, *pustinya*. Over the centuries, some of these hermit hideouts became monasteries, and it was to one of these, Nikandrova Monastery, that we were now headed. The Indian summer had come to an end, and there was a chill in the air.

The old footpath to Nikandrova Monastery, which had been used by generations of monks was boggy despite the dry weather. In places, rows of tree trunks were laid in the mud as an aide for off-road vehicles – a centuries-old practice known as 'corduroy roads'. The forest floor was littered with mushrooms: delicately creamy ones; grey hooded ones on white stems; vivid scarlet stools with flecks of white; bulbous brown protrusions; orange monsters the size of dinner plates; slimy beige ones.

We realized we were approaching the monastery when, crossing a bridge over peat-black water, we spotted a crude canvas painting of Nikandr, the hermit who spent fifty years living here in the sixteenth century. At the end of a sandy road through tall pines, the golden domes of a church loomed out of the late afternoon murk. A man in a nearby field was using a metal detector, which sent out incongruous beeps. All the monastery's churches and cafés were closed because of coronavirus, but black-clad monks scurried back and forth. A flock of doves emerged out of a dovecote, and flew in tight circles overhead.

After existing for centuries the monastery was destroyed in the 1920s by the Soviets. According to local legend, bricks from the buildings were used in a nearby tank-regiment barracks, later converted by the

Nazis into a prisoner-of-war camp where thousands perished. One pilgrim in the late 1980s recalled how coming here felt like stumbling on the remnants of a lost civilization. Amid the undergrowth, she wrote, 'there were chunks of wall and church lying around that had been blown up'.

Rebuilding commenced in the 2000s, and continues to this day. When we visited, there were three working churches. The whole complex was clearly heated by wood, and there were enormous piles of firewood the size of small houses. For locals, the monastery is most famous for its holy springs. Pilgrims and tourists can plunge into one of several pools of water that remain ice-cold all year round.

The landscape in the centre of Pskov Region felt empty. Sometimes on the walk, we would see just a handful of people each day, and only a few cars. Villages tended to merge into one another, with small differences dictated by their surroundings. In some places the water table was such that there were 'stork wells', which have long wooden 'necks' to pull up a bucket attached to a pole. In boggy areas, we'd encounter home-made 'swamp buggies' with tyres cannibalized from tractors. As we tramped along vehicle tracks in airy woods, I was reminded of Ivan Bunin's 1913 poem 'Pskov Forest':

In the distance is darkness and thickets of trees.
Beneath the red masts, beneath the pines
I stand lingering – on the threshold
Of a world forgotten, but familiar.

As we approached closer to Pskov, we had to get past the E95 motorway, which starts in St Petersburg and travels 2,500 kilometres through Europe before ending up in Istanbul. Emerging onto the tarmac road was like suddenly being back in the city: lorries and expensive cars sped past; our phones picked up 4G; and there was a small café, the first working restaurant we'd seen for more than a week. As we ate *borscht* and reheated pancakes, I counted six car transporters going north, each carrying a full load of brand-new Mercedes.

Reluctant to walk along the motorway, we tried and failed to hitchhike, before giving up and calling a taxi. The driver made a desultory effort at conversation before turning up *Road Radio*, the station that monopolizes the rural airwaves with an endless stream of nostalgic, bitter-sweet ballads and pop hits. Anyone who has spent any time in the Russian countryside is familiar with this type of music, which is played everywhere from public transport to cafés, homes and shops. At the orphanage in Belskoye Ustye it was so ubiquitous it became background noise. As we drove west, the warmth from the car heater made us drowsy, and the 1990s pop star Tatyana Ovsiyenko crooned about childhood innocence. 'I hear my mum's voice across the years,' she sang, 'meaning it's time to return home.'

The final stretch of our walk to the shores of Lake Pskov took us past two of Pskov Region's most famous monasteries. We approached the first, the Krypetsky Monastery, along the 'Yaroslav Bridge': not a bridge in the ordinary sense of the word, but an ancient footpath through a large bog. Legend says it was built by Prince Yaroslav to thank Savva, the monastery's founder, who saved his wife from blindness.

At first, the path was firm and bog rose on either side in mounds of moss and dwarf fir trees. But after a few kilometres, it got wetter, the matted surface of red and green trembling underfoot. We stepped gingerly across rows of birch trunks placed at right angles to the path – more corduroy roads – and the stick I was carrying disappeared half a metre into puddles of brown water. Everywhere there were cranberry bushes, and Labrador tea, a common bog plant whose aromatic flowers can cause nausea and hallucinations. Then, like a summons, we heard the faint sound of monastery bells.

Eventually, the path took us under a russet canopy of birch, alder and aspen. We startled a buzzard, which swooped silently away. When we emerged from the trees, the Krypetsky Monastery was spread out in front of us: an expanse of ground with a cluster of white church buildings that resembled a pyramid. It was as if we'd arrived on an island.

'When Saint Savva came to found the monastery, God showed him the way, the Lord God brought him here.' Father Valentin struck up a conversation with us as we hid from the cold in a tiny gift shop that sold icons, religious books and candles. His face crinkled into innumerable creases when he chuckled, and his nose was deformed from a bad break. His Russian was colloquial and disjointed, and he jumped from tales of monastic history to outrage over avaricious builders. He bemoaned the dangers of cheap alcohol and coronavirus, which he referred to un-ironically as the plague.

The Krypetsky Monastery was shut down after the Russian Revolution and abandoned; the authorities only just dissuaded from blowing it up, like they did to the Nikandrova Monastery. Local poet, architect and campaigner Yelena Morozkina wrote lyrically about the forgotten, crumbling buildings in the 1960s: 'The epic calm of the architecture is inseparable from the surrounding stillness and emptiness; indeed, it's brought forth by them. Strange as it may seem, you don't feel cut off from the world here, you feel its wholeness.'

Only an echo of this beauty survives today, however, as the rebirth of the monastery in the 1990s was overseen by the business-like Abbot Damaskin, who authorized cowboy construction work that obliterated most of the surviving sixteenth-century ensemble. A few days before his death in a car accident in 2007, Damaskin was confronted by a group of heritage campaigners. 'Why do you need cultural heritage if you destroy it, only this time forever, irretrievably, without the slightest chance of restoration?' he was asked.

If the flat wilderness of Pskov Region is an ocean, then its churches are lighthouses that mark the way. And climbing to the top of the monastery's bell tower was an exhilarating experience. We drank in the view, elated by being high up after days of walking on the flat. As we looked, the sheets of grey cloud began to lift from the undulating mosaic of green and autumnal golds. A monk leant on the railings, scrolling through his phone.

Later, as night gathered, we stopped a hunched, elderly woman carrying a bucket of water to ask why her village had outhouses made of limestone, the building materials used in Pskov's medieval churches, but which is now rarely seen. She was confused by the question, and thought for a moment. 'The people who built them all died long ago,' she said.

In many ways, the Yelizarov Convent, which we reached the next day, was the mirror opposite of Krypetsky Monastery: whereas Krypetsky was hidden away, Yelizarov was on the main road going north from Pskov; whereas Krypetsky was charming, Yelizarov seemed functional; and whereas Krypetsky was little known outside of Pskov Region, Yelizarov's political influence stretched into the heart of the Kremlin.

The source of Yelizarov Convent's fame is Philotheus of Pskov, the medieval abbot who developed the ideology of Russia as the heir to the great Christian empire of Byzantium. Born twelve years after Constantinople fell to the Ottomans in 1453, Philotheus' life spanned the relentless rise of Muscovy, which seized huge tracts of land including his native Pskov. In his mind, its success proved that Orthodox Russia was the true heir to Byzantium – and, ultimately, the Christian Roman Empire itself. 'Two Romes have fallen, a third stands, and a fourth there will not be,' Philotheus wrote. The philosophy became a foundation for Russian imperialism, and has enticed tsars, Communist Party leaders and presidents ever since.

Today, the Yelizarov Convent is linked directly to Putin. The first time I heard this was in the early 2010s when a rumour emerged that Putin had banished his wife there amid whispers of an affair with a gymnast thirty years his junior. Journalists would slip into the convent, hoping to spot Russia's First Lady in a black habit. But it was all revealed as false when the Putins announced their separation in an excruciating, live TV interview. Lyudmila went on to marry a triathlon-addicted businessman, and disappear from public life. Even so, the Yelizarov Convent has found it hard to shake its Putin association.

'Everyone asks whether Putin's wife is here. Have you heard that?' Sister Feofaniya brought up the topic after we started chatting.

'Yes, I heard.'

'It's rumours, it's not true.'

We didn't press the issue, but she raised it again when talking about Abbess Yelizaveta, who oversaw the revival of the monastery in the early 2000s. 'She forced her way into an audience with Putin and he allocated money to build the convent. That's why there's a link to his name. And Sister Yelizaveta and Putin's wife were students at the same university. And when Sister Yelizaveta died, Lyudmila came once to visit. That's everything.'

Perhaps it was the allure of the 'Third Rome' idea that swayed Putin when he decided to release the money for the convent's restoration; perhaps the urging of his wife. Either way, it was easy to see why people believed the rumours of an influential patron. Not only was it obviously wealthy, but, in 2010, the Yelizarov Convent successfully lobbied for the transfer of the oldest surviving icon in Pskov Region, the *Spas Yelyeazarovsky*, from a local museum. The small icon painted in 1352 is believed to be miracle-working and, today, forms part of the iconostasis in the convent's main church. Filled with enigmatic dark reds and browns, it showed Christ with serene and compelling eyes, his thumb and ring finger gently touching in the Orthodox sign of blessing. While I gazed at it for a few moments, a young woman wearing golden trainers waited to take my place.

The final kilometres of our walk took us through muddy fields and pine forests to the swirling brown Tolba River flowing into Lake Pskov. We asked around for a lift, and were soon flying down the river in an open-top motor boat that curved through reed beds, and then shot out onto open water. It was drizzling slightly, and the grey sky merged seamlessly into the lake. But the speed was intoxicating, and Artyom and I grinned at each other.

We moored by a wooden pier on Belov, the smaller and more distant of the two Talab Islands. Walking up the only road – nothing more than a sandy track – we saw the hulks of disintegrating boats, and passed a former fish-canning factory, a derelict snowmobile repair centre and a church with faded frescoes on its gateposts. There was a haunted, lost-world feel to the place, and most of the windows of the houses were dark. Fish were carved into some of the fences, and a blue *Lada* was entirely covered by fallen yellow leaves.

Within twenty minutes, we were on the other side of the island. In front of us, a sandy cliff led down to the lakeshore littered with glacial boulders. We dropped our rucksacks and stood among the pines, looking out across the water. This was our endpoint. Night was falling, but the far side of the lake – Russian territory – was just visible, a faint navy-blue smudge. Somewhere to the north-west, where the cloud lay thinner, was Estonia. With a furious beating of wings, a dozen swans on the water below took off, gradually gaining height, their heavy white bodies impossibly airborne against the darkening sky. We watched as they formed up into a V-shape, and wheeled away to the west.

5

Lonely Battles

It was 10 p.m. on Friday in Pskov, and Lev Shlosberg was still at the office. He was tired and hungry. All that week in August 2014, the opposition politician had been dealing with the fallout from a scoop by *Pskovskaya Guberniya*, a small local newspaper, which had presented the most convincing proof to date that Russian soldiers were fighting and dying alongside separatist rebels in Ukraine. The reporting was picked up by media outlets across the world. Although the Kremlin has always maintained no regular Russian troops were sent into Ukraine in 2014, the evidence is overwhelming that Russian military units did, indeed, cross the border that summer. *Guberniya* was the first to prove it.

The scoop followed a tip-off that two paratroopers from Pskov's elite 76th Guards Air Assault Division – Leonid Kichatkin and Alexander Osipov – had been killed in Ukraine. Shlosberg even managed to attend the secret funeral of the 29-year-old Kichatkin, who was laid to rest in the same cemetery by the Velikaya River that I would visit years later. There were dozens of serving soldiers present, and when Shlosberg's identity became known an officer asked him to leave. He didn't argue.

In the days after the *Guberniya* revelations, journalists from independent media outlets in Moscow and St Petersburg descended on Pskov to cover the story. They were met with violence and threats. Several were assaulted; others were followed, or warned to go home.

The atmosphere was febrile. At the centre of it all was Shlosberg: giving interviews, helping reporters and using the national media spotlight to accuse the military top brass of blackmailing bereaved families into silence.

Aware of the danger he was courting by lifting the lid on the Kremlin's covert war in Ukraine, Shlosberg was taking some safety precautions, including not walking home on his own. But that Friday his wife, who usually accompanied him, was on a night shift, and he decided to go alone. The familiar, one-kilometre walk didn't seem like much of a risk: it was a warm August evening and he had agreed to meet a *Guberniya* colleague on the way.

As he crossed a quiet courtyard behind the city's main road, Shlosberg was struck hard on the back of the head. There was no warning, no verbal confrontation, no shouted threat. The blow was strong enough that he immediately fell to the ground and blacked out. As he lay there unconscious, his assailants kicked him all over his head and body. Shlosberg has no memory of the attack or its aftermath and, as there were no witnesses, it was initially unclear how many people took part. Only later did CCTV footage reveal the assailants as two hooded men.

'I don't remember anything. For the space of about an hour and a half, two hours, I don't remember any events, any faces, or movements. Nothing. No memories survive,' Shlosberg told me. But, with a broken nose, severe concussion and bruising on his chest and arms, he managed to pick himself up and continue the way he'd been going. Minutes later he was spotted, stumbling and confused, by Aleksei Semyonov, the colleague he was supposed to meet. Under a lamp post, the horrified Semyonov realized Shlosberg was covered in blood and dirt. He bundled Shlosberg into a taxi, and they were in hospital a few minutes later. 'I woke up when I saw my wife, Zhanna, and asked what happened. "You were beaten up," she told me.'

The attack on Shlosberg was a frightening illustration of the Kremlin's willingness to use violence against political opponents; a willingness that steadily increased in subsequent years. Shlosberg's health dominated the national news for several days before it was eclipsed by the ongoing fighting in Ukraine. Working as a reporter in Moscow at the time, I remember the swirling rumours and rising fear of all-out war. I phoned Shlosberg the following week when he was still in hospital, and was surprised at his dismissiveness when I asked how he was feeling: it was as if nothing unusual had happened. A journalist who visited him the morning after the attack described how Shlosberg was far more interested in discussing a forthcoming *Guberniya* article than the events of the previous night.

It takes courage to be a public critic of the authorities in Russia, and Shlosberg is unquestionably courageous. He is also stubborn: he first stood for election in 1996, but it took him 13 election campaigns over 15 years before he finally won public office. Throughout his political career he has been a steadfast critic of the authorities, resisting all offers of compromise, and holding steady against a political and media juggernaut that outguns him at every level. This gives him a compelling clarity of purpose, but leaves little room for self-doubt – and exaggerates an already formidable single-mindedness. Notoriously difficult to work with, Shlosberg is uninterested in material wealth, well-versed in local culture, and does not suffer fools gladly. He often cuts a lonely figure, soldiering on with no hope of a political breakthrough and the ever-present risk of another beating, or worse.

There was never much doubt the attack was designed to deter Shlosberg and others from exposing Russia's military involvement in Ukraine. In the weeks and months that followed, a police investigation went nowhere. 'The first investigator was taken off the case and replaced by others who demonstratively did nothing,' Shlosberg recalled. 'I think it was clear to everyone what had happened. The attack was carried out with military-style coordination. It wasn't a hit ordered from Pskov, it came from Moscow.'

I spoke to Shlosberg twice while researching this book. Both times he invited me to come to a new brick building in central Pskov, which houses the regional headquarters of the liberal Yabloko Party and the editorial offices of *Guberniya*. Yabloko enjoyed some success in the 1990s before entering the political wilderness during Putin's first presidency. While it lost its last few seats in the Russian parliament in 2007, it still clings on in some regional parliaments and local councils. Shlosberg was head of the local branch of Yabloko for more than a quarter of a century, and remains its most powerful member. The Russian word 'yabloko' means 'apple', and one of the first things I noticed on entering Shlosberg's office was the profusion of apple souvenirs: amid the books, papers and photographs there were glass apples, ceramic apples, stone apples, felt apples, wooden apples, a clock shaped like an apple and apple Christmas tree decorations. Less ridiculously, there were a few photographs of lions: an allusion to Shlosberg's first name, Lev, the Russian word for 'lion'.

Small in stature, Shlosberg's black hair is streaked with grey and it curls in a wave above his right eye. He speaks eagerly and clearly, rolls his Rs vigorously and rarely pauses to gather his thoughts. With age, his face has filled out, but he remains a ball of energy. Each time we met, the moment he finished speaking, he began typing on his computer, or furiously tapping on his phone as I formulated the next question. Shlosberg's intelligence is formidable, and he is a far more effective public speaker than the local functionaries with whom he crosses swords.

Off the public stage, his manner is infused with the polite kindness of a Soviet-educated intellectual. On his YouTube channel, he has the comforting, if outdated, air of a dad-trying-to-be-cool. He married a local cardiologist and fellow Yabloko Party member shortly before his fiftieth birthday. They do not have any children.

Shlosberg was born into a Jewish family of intellectuals and craftsmen from the north of the Pale of Settlement, the giant swathe of Eastern Europe to which the Russian Empire forcibly confined its Jews. By the end of the nineteenth century, this huge area, including parts of what is today southern Pskov Region, was home to half the Jews in the world. The family also has longstanding links with Pskov. One of his grandfathers, a photographer, died in 1943 fighting for the Red Army; the other became an artist. His grandmother on his mother's side worked in a nursery, while his father's mother was a milliner with a hat workshop in central Pskov. Shlosberg's parents, Mark Shlosberg and Bronislava Berkal, both teachers, were part of the generation that rebuilt Pskov after World War II.

Jewishness was not a big part of Shlosberg's upbringing. 'We were not a religious family, we didn't preserve the language, neither Hebrew or Yiddish, and the only Jewish tradition we kept was not declining to be identified as such [a Jew] in our passports. I understood what my nationality was, and felt it from certain interactions. And our Jewishness ended with that,' he said. Shlosberg does not go to synagogue and has never visited Israel. 'I consider myself a cosmopolitan. A person's culture is the one in which he thinks, dreams and in which he writes poetry. I think and write poetry in Russian.'

Much more significant for the young Shlosberg was the history, culture and traditions of his home town. Pskov's moment in the historical sun came in the Middle Ages when, as a mercantile city republic, it stood at the head of a vast trading network, playing off the rising power of Muscovy to the east against the Latin principalities to the west. Its influence peaked in the late fifteenth century before it was absorbed into the rapidly expanding Muscovite empire that would go on to become modern Russia.

The legacy of the Pskov Republic was not only a democratic political culture (princes of Pskov were elected), but the crumbling fortifications, merchant houses and unique churches that filled the city centre. 'I got interested in the history of Pskov when I was fifteen,' said Shlosberg. 'I was keen on photography and wandered around the city taking pictures of the architecture.'

Pskov's churches are its calling card: small and box-like, yet wonderfully subtle, they consist of a simple cube of whitewashed and plastered limestone topped with a cupola on a 'drum' decorated with distinctive patterning. Shlosberg rarely tires of extolling Pskov's virtues. 'Pskov is one of Europe's richest towns when it comes to architectural and cultural traditions. There is a Pskov school of icon painting, there is a Pskov school of monumental art and a Pskov school of architecture,' he told me.

As the Russian Empire expanded westward, however, Pskov lost its status as a frontier city and trading hub, gradually fading into a provincial backwater. And it suffered badly in World War II from Soviet bombing raids and Nazi-ordered destruction. The post-war decades of Shlosberg's childhood saw the emergence of a group of architect-restorers who would not only shape the city's landscape, but also how the young Lev would see the world. Four men in particular – Yuri Spegalsky, Vsevolod Smirnov, Boris Skobelitsyn and Mikhail Semyonov – laboured tirelessly to resurrect Pskov's churches and fortifications and prevent the city's medieval legacy from being lost.

These men exerted a greater influence on Shlosberg's political development than any Western liberal idea. More than anything, they were devoted to Pskov. The awe that the city inspired in them was captured beautifully by architect Olga Arshakuni, the wife of Spegalsky, in a description of her first visit to Pskov after liberation from the Nazis: 'A heavy grey sky hung over the city. It was raining. Over the burned trees swirled flocks of shrieking black birds. Yuri Pavlovich [Spegalsky] led me to the Kremlin. Beyond the twisted, half-destroyed stone walls there opened a spacious square and on it – the Cathedral. Tall, white, striving upwards, it simply soared.

From here, from the high hill, the city spread before us, shrouded in rain, grey from the soot and ash and unforgettably beautiful in its severe and solemn greatness.'

It was by no means easy to persuade atheist Soviet officials to release money for the restoration of Pskov's churches, but Smirnov, Skobelitsyn and Semyonov were decorated war veterans who had fought their way to Berlin, and their moral authority – and Moscow connections – helped loosen the purse strings. In later life they would even flirt with Orthodoxy and nationalism – both ostensibly anathema to the Soviet authorities. 'Culture united everyone,' said Shlosberg by way of an explanation. 'People with liberal views, people with conservative views, people with ultra-patriotic views. Pskov was always a compromise, Pskov was always a territory of compromise.'

Shlosberg's parents made no attempt to stand in the way of the seventeen-year-old's desire to do a history degree, and he enrolled at Pskov's top university. Shlosberg was easily bright enough to have studied in Leningrad or Moscow, but what was the point in studying Pskov's history anywhere but Pskov?

While history shaped his outlook and beliefs, however, it was real life that made Shlosberg a politician. In particular, his experience as a young man following the collapse of the Soviet Union: first hope, then disappointment as democratic dreams were crushed. 'We learnt from real political events. It wasn't textbook learning, but learning from life. The chance was missed. The window of opportunity at the beginning of the 1990s was missed in a ham-fisted and painful way,' he said.

Initially, Shlosberg was a fervent supporter of Yeltsin, the Russian president who kicked in the door of socialism. But no modern Russian politician with electoral ambition can afford to express too much pride in the decisions taken by Yeltsin that pushed millions of Russians into poverty. And Shlosberg is cautious. 'I voted for Yeltsin in 1991. I realized it was the democratic choice. But then I began to understand that those people did not know how to lead,' he said. 'The reformist majority that elected Yeltsin should have been looked after. They were the social basis for change. If you wanted to move forward, you should have taken care of their interests.'

His last vestiges of trust in Yeltsin evaporated during the 1996 presidential election. With single-digit approval ratings, Yeltsin entered a corrupt pact with a group of oligarchs who funded his re-election campaign and helped defeat the resurgent Communist Party in return for access to cut-price state assets. Shlosberg was scathing of those who backed Yeltsin in this Faustian bargain. 'The level of prostitution displayed by the intelligentsia, even the academic intelligentsia, was monstrous. The campaign of 1996 was just a flood of treachery. People sold out their convictions,' he said.

As Shlosberg gravitated toward Yabloko's brand of liberalism, political life in Pskov Region lurched to the right. In 1993 parliamentary elections, 43 per cent of voters in the region cast their ballots for the nationalist, imperialist and authoritarian Liberal Democratic Party of Russia (LDPR). Overnight, this gave Pskov a reputation as the cradle of Russian revanchism – even Russian fascism. Three years later, Pskov Region elected Russia's first LDPR governor, Yevgeny Mikhailov. Many at the time worried that political events in Pskov were the canary in the mine: Russia, they thought, was turning into a tinpot dictatorship.

The groundswell of anger in Pskov Region that fuelled support for the LDPR arose from a seemingly unending economic crisis, as well as the visceral pain and humiliation generated as 'democracy' and 'capitalism' entered the void left by the Soviet collapse of 1991. Ironically, while it was the end of the Soviet Union that propelled Shlosberg into politics, it was the legacy of this collapse that would confine him to the political margins.

For those in Pskov Region, many of the fruits of the freedom that arrived in the early 1990s seemed like a sleight of hand, or a cruel trick. Nowhere was this more evident than when it came to freedom of movement. The end of the Soviet Union meant that, for the first time since the eighteenth century, the western borders of Pskov Region were international borders. Latvia, Belarus and Estonia all emerged as independent states. The paraphernalia of international travel – borders, visas and customs – sprung up and, suddenly, westward travel became immensely complicated. Although the West had condemned the Soviet Union for caging its citizens, what followed was far more restrictive. Widespread poverty meant it was only the super-rich who enjoyed greater freedom of movement. Everyone else was more tightly caged than ever.

This sort of gulf between reality and rhetoric planted the seeds of a deep ambivalence toward what was trumpeted as 'democracy', fuelling disappointment with the West and a longing for the simplicities of the Soviet past. The changes of the 1990s also altered life in a myriad of other bewildering ways: from free markets changing the nature of social ties to a flood of new books, music and films. 'People experienced the fall of the Soviet Union with their hearts and souls,' said Shlosberg.

After joining Yabloko in 1994, Shlosberg embarked on 17 years' worth of unsuccessful election campaigns, standing repeatedly to be both a deputy to Russia's national parliament, the State Duma, and the local parliament in Pskov. His difficulties getting elected were not only testament to a general disdain for liberalism (in elections to the State Duma, Yabloko has never received more than 8 per cent of the vote), but also the genuine popularity enjoyed by Putin after he became president.

Against the backdrop of economic recovery in the 2000s, Putin's patriotic centrism, promise of political stability and re-assertion of state power was a vote-winner. Although Shlosberg would link his eventual electoral victory in 2011 regional parliament elections to the beginning of 'Putin fatigue', naysayers whispered it was nothing of the sort. Actually, they claimed, it was a new Pskov Region governor, Andrei Turchak, who manipulated the results in Shlosberg's favour to help create the illusion of democracy. Either way, Shlosberg became the only Yabloko deputy with a seat in Pskov's 45-member parliament.

When I asked him to describe his political beliefs, Shlosberg replied: 'liberal values of a left-wing orientation'. But beliefs take a backseat in daily political battles. In the regional parliament, his main enemies were deputies from the ruling United Russia party, which was created as a political vehicle for Putin and remains absolutely loyal to him. 'Who are United Russia? They're guardians. They're just the guardians of power. There is no ideology, they just hold on to power,' Shlosberg said.

A powerful speaker, argumentative and pedantic, Shlosberg was well suited to the role of parliamentarian. Even when outnumbered, he remained intellectually head and shoulders above his opponents. One of his most fiery moments came amid the nationalist fervour that accompanied the 2014 annexation of Crimea, just six months before he was attacked in the streets.

When Governor Turchak said in a speech that the Ukraine crisis had led Yabloko to 'tear off its mask' and reveal themselves as a 'fifth column' and 'traitors', Shlosberg responded on the floor of the Pskov parliament. 'The Russian state is again ready to destroy those who do not agree with its actions,' he told the gathered deputies; an uncanny prediction of his beating. Then, he flung the traitor accusation back at Turchak, reading out a long list of the region's political and economic woes and adding, after each point, the phrase: 'this is a betrayal of the people of Pskov Region carried out by enemies of Pskov Region'. As Shlosberg advanced further down the list, he seemed to quiver with rage. His final words were a denunciation of Turchak, who owed his political rise to his father's acquaintance with Putin, and has few ties to Pskov. Shlosberg repeated Turchak's name and patronymic in derision. 'We lived on this land before you, Andrei Anatolevich; it's our burden to live on this land under your rule, Andrei Anatolevich; and we will live on this land after you, Andrei Anatolevich. You're an alien person here, Andrei Anatolevich, it's alien land for you. On this land, you're the chief fifth column.'

Shlosberg's fight is lonely, and unequal. He faces a constant stream of stories spread by state-controlled media outlets and on social networks that seek to discredit him personally, and politically. Some are outright lies; some distorted half-truths; and some tap into anti-Semitic conspiracy theories. Shlosberg knows that, at any moment, the stakes could rise again like they did that August evening. 'They don't have a barrier to the spilling of blood, or a barrier to the taking of life, they have long since passed that,' he said.

Nevertheless, Shlosberg's story is not simply a tale of David versus Goliath. He is known to be a difficult colleague: a micro-manager who works from morning to night and is averse to cooperation and delegation. He prefers acolytes to equals. One of his former colleagues described Shlosberg to me as a 'messianic politician' who has become humourless and less tolerant with age. 'The only thing that will stop him is death,' he said. 'God willing that won't happen.'

At the heart of Shlosberg's politics – his brand of anti-Putin liberalism – is a Europe-centric vision of Pskov and, by default, Russia itself. He talks with pride about the Middle Ages when Pskov was a city-republic tied into European networks: Italian silk, Swedish metal and English wool were all once traded in its marketplaces. This is not entirely fanciful. Unlike most Russian cities, Pskov was never directly ruled by the Mongols, and the fifteenth-century Pskov Judicial Charter drew heavily on Roman Law, rather than Slavic legal norms. Famously, royal secretary Jan Piotrowski who accompanied the Polish king Stephen Bathory during the siege of Pskov in 1581 was astonished by Pskov's wealth, writing in his diary: 'My God, what a large city! Just like Paris!'

In his many speeches and articles on the subject, Shlosberg has compared Pskov to a bridge, a gateway, even a sail that is filled with the prevailing wind, whether it blows from the West or East. These sorts of metaphors may seem naïve in the 2020s amid unrelenting hostility between Russia and the West. But Shlosberg remembers the period after the collapse of the Soviet Union when it was widely believed the accession of the Baltic States to the EU was a big economic, cultural and political opportunity for Pskov. At the beginning of the 2000s even Putin expressed interest in Russia joining NATO. 'Pskov is European land, with European cultural and political traditions,' Shlosberg told me. 'Ties to Europe are natural, we are a part of Europe. It's not "they" who are Europe, we are also Europe.'

Nor are Shlosberg's democratic politics as much an aberration as they might seem in the third decade of Putin's rule. They have a long history in Pskov. Shlosberg likes to tell the story of how Pskov's

9-kilometre defensive walls made it the only medieval Russian city to protect ordinary people, not just the rich and powerful. At the heart of democratic Pskov was the city's medieval parliament, the *veche*, a descendant of East Slavic tribal assemblies. The word 'veche' is even thought to share a common linguistic root with *soviet*, the people's councils that emerged in the Russian Revolution and provided the name for the Soviet Union. The symbol of Pskov's democracy was a large bell that summoned people to *veche* sessions.

There are many legends about the fate of the bell when Tsar Vasily III ended Pskov's independence and annexed its lands to Muscovy. One version holds that it was brought to Moscow for destruction but, on the way, disintegrated into hundreds of tiny 'Valdai bells'; the bells that were used for centuries on horse-drawn coaches (and took the sound of Pskov democracy to all corners of Russia). It was the association between bells and freedom that led the nineteenth-century radical Alexander Herzen to name his famous exile newspaper *The Bell*. And I worked for a few years for an independent Russian media outlet called The Bell, which was set up in 2017. There is even a sculpture of a large bell in one of Pskov's central squares, paid for by local councillors.

It is this democratic heritage on which Shlosberg and his supporters draw, and which they strive to embody. 'Russia has long traditions of paternalism and long traditions of imperialism,' Shlosberg said. 'But in the two hundred years of the Pskov Republic, people didn't dream of a "strong hand". They deposed and chased out princes.'

Whatever the historical roots of democracy in Pskov, the fact remains that democratic politics are profoundly unattractive to most modern Russian voters. In 2021 parliamentary elections, Yabloko got just 2 per cent of the national vote. Even in elections untainted by massive fraud, though, it's impossible to imagine Yabloko being more popular than the Communist Party. Their brand of liberalism is firmly on the margins, tainted by association with the suffering of the 1990s – and there seems little chance of that changing. One acquaintance who grew up in Pskov in the 1990s expressed a typical opinion for her generation. 'The 1990s were an absolute catastrophe for the country,' she told me. 'The more time passes, the clearer this becomes.'

Instead of Shlosberg's vision of a Europe-looking, democratic Pskov, a very different ideology currently holds sway in the city. If Shlosberg would like to see Pskov as a gateway, or a bridge, the Pskov authorities, the governor and the ruling United Russia party would characterize the city as a shield; a watchtower; or a fortress guarding the Western flanks of Orthodoxy from the perfidious West. This is not entirely historically inaccurate, either: Pskov has survived dozens of sieges and invasions. Famously, Pskov repulsed the massed Catholic armies of Stefan Bathory in the sixteenth century and, at least according to Soviet legend, the Red Army won its first victories in 1918 just outside the city. Today, the paratroopers of the 76th Division, whose involvement in the Ukraine conflict Shlosberg helped expose, are at the forefront of almost any military mission ordered by the Kremlin, from Syria to Kazakhstan. Pskov's military prowess is embodied in its heraldry, which features a snow leopard with a raised paw, ready to strike.

Being an ambitious politician in Russia means aspiring to enter federal-level politics. And, despite his deep ties to Pskov, Shlosberg has tried to make the jump to Moscow at least twice, standing to be the national leader of Yabloko in 2015 and 2019. Both times he lost. Just as Shlosberg is unlikely ever to relinquish control over Yabloko in Pskov, so Yabloko co-founder Grigory Yavlinsky, now in his seventies, keeps his hand firmly on the reins of power in the wider party. Perhaps understandably, Yavlinsky sees Shlosberg as a threat, and each time the Pskov politician stood to be leader, Yavlinsky ensured a less talented, more easily manipulated, candidate got the necessary votes.

One of the major political issues dividing Shlosberg and Yavlinsky was their attitude toward Russia's most popular opposition leader, Alexei Navalny, who was far more successful in rallying support, particularly among the young. Navalny, who survived a Kremlin-ordered nerve-agent poisoning in 2020 only to die suddenly in a remote Siberian prison in 2024, began his political career in Yabloko, which he later ditched as too staid, and too liberal. While

Yavlinsky repeatedly launched broadsides at Navalny (some believe as part of a bargain with the Kremlin), Shlosberg's position was more ambiguous. He spoke out against the authorities' treatment of Navalny, and was briefly arrested in 2021 after attending a pro-Navalny demonstration. In other words, Shlosberg is more radical and more wary of alienating young people.

With Russia's ever-growing authoritarianism, there is less and less space for Kremlin critics like Shlosberg, who are forced to walk a tightrope. Despite his ambition, courage and status as one of modern Russia's most successful opposition figures, it seems unlikely Shlosberg will ever lead the national Yabloko party. And his Pskov brand of liberalism, which draws on a Russian democratic tradition and the city's European heritage, looks set to languish. The authorities blocked Shlosberg from standing for the local parliament in 2021, meaning he was left without public office: a personal and financial blow – and a return to the political wilderness.

Jail is a constant risk, and most other opposition politicians in Pskov languish behind bars. The same year Shlosberg left parliament, husband-and-wife political activists Artyom and Liya Milushkin, who have two young children, were each handed sentences of more than a decade in prison on dubious drug charges. The accused in Russian trials are usually held in courtroom cages and, when Artyom's sentence was read out by the judge, he began tearing apart the benches screwed to the cage's floor with his bare hands – a gut-wrenching sight of desperation and powerlessness.

Russia's full-scale invasion of Ukraine made it look as if Shlosberg's balancing act was doomed. One by one, Russia's remaining independent politicians were arrested under wartime censorship laws and, for many months after the invasion, whenever I opened the news, I expected to see photos of Shlosberg in handcuffs. But it never happened. Although an outspoken critic of the war, he has been careful with his language. As long as he operates within certain limits, like other members of Yabloko, he appears to be immune to arrest – a fact that strongly suggests the existence of some sort of informal Yavlinsky deal with the Kremlin. Of course, if Shlosberg were to venture beyond those limits – intentionally by organizing anti-war protests or accidentally by saying something too radical in an interview – he would not remain at liberty for long.

The Kremlin's brutal attempt to seize Ukraine was, for Shlosberg, a catastrophe not just measured in lost human lives and the devastation of a country. The political logic of the situation, he believes, could mean Russia turns away from Europe for generations. In one interview eleven months into the war, he described Putin's confrontation with Ukraine and the West as a 'civilizational choice'. Russia has shown itself to be trapped in the tragedies of the twentieth century. 'We continue to scrabble about in that century with its rivers of blood, awful squalor and terrible number of victims,' he said.

Listening to my pre-war conversations with Shlosberg as fighting raged in Ukraine, he seemed nothing less than prophetic. The last time we met in Pskov, eighteen months before Russian tanks rolled across the border, I asked him about the future. 'Everything will get worse. Much worse. There will be many years of reaction,' he told me, as if stating a fact. However bad it gets, Shlosberg will continue to soldier on, unyielding and alone.

6

Pushkin Hills

When Semyon Geichenko arrived in Pushkin Hills a few weeks before the end of World War II, he found a scene of devastation. All that was left of the ancestral home of Russia's most famous poet, Alexander Pushkin, was the burnt-out foundations of buildings, smashed trees and military detritus. The German army had used the natural rise above the River Sorot, where the Pushkin family estate of Mikhailovskoye once stood, as part of their Panther Line, a massive defensive fortification that was the scene of heavy fighting in early 1944 as the Red Army pushed westward. When the Nazis eventually retreated, they left tens of thousands of mines and dynamited the surviving historic buildings, including the Svyatogorsk Monastery where Pushkin was buried.

'Mikhailovskoye was a picture of sad ruin,' Geichenko wrote years later. 'It was impossible to walk or drive along the roads and commemorative walkways. Everywhere there was rubble, shell craters, and all sorts of enemy rubbish. Instead of villages there were rows of stove chimneys . . . blown-up tanks and artillery. Along the banks of the Sorot were the smashed remains of German bunkers. And everywhere, everywhere, everywhere, rows of barbed wire, and signs reading "Mines", "Danger" and "No access".'

It's sometimes difficult for foreigners to understand the importance of Alexander Pushkin for Russia and Russian culture.

While he is often compared to Shakespeare, Goethe or Homer, that doesn't really do it justice. Despite his death aged just thirty-seven from a duelling wound, Pushkin created *both* the modern Russian language *and* modern Russian literature. His poetry has an elegant simplicity, which belies a treasure trove of meaning, allusion and metaphor. But this is not just about his poetry. Since his death, he has also become a symbol of the Russian national ideal. Nikolai Gogol described Pushkin as a 'unique manifestation of the Russian spirit'. Others were more gushing. 'Pushkin is our all,' the critic and poet Apollon Grigoryev declared in 1854, a phrase that is repeated *ad nauseam* to this day.

Geichenko was not just a visitor to Pushkin Hills, which was one of the Soviet Union's most famous museums. He had been made its director. It would be his job to clear away the debris, and restore what had been lost in the fires of war. It must have seemed an impossible task. There was little in the way of funding, and hardly any exhibits: the Nazis had shipped anything of value back to Germany shortly before they departed. The destruction was such that, like many locals, Geichenko and his wife lived for months in an earth dugout.

The forty-two-year-old Geichenko was an odd choice for such a demanding job. Just over a year previously he had been wounded at the front and left with an amputated arm and bad leg. But the emotional trauma of what he had experienced over the last five years ran far deeper. Once a promising young museum curator, Geichenko's life was comprehensively broken by the 'meatgrinder' of Stalin's Great Terror and World War II. He was extremely lucky to be alive.

Geichenko grew up in pre-revolutionary Peterhof, the town outside St Petersburg where the Russian royal family had one of their most sumptuous summer palaces. His father worked for a cavalry regiment, and the young Geichenko remembered catching occasional glimpses of Nikolai II, the country's last tsar. After attending university following the 1917 Revolution, he returned to Peterhof where he made a name for himself as a tour guide, writer and up-and-coming curator helping to re-package former imperial residences as museums for the masses. He befriended some of the leading cultural figures of the day, including poets Anna Akhmatova, Sergei Yesenin and Nikolai Klyuev. Around this time he married a woman called Irina Velikanova, about whom little is known. They had two children, Fyodor and Natalya.

It wasn't long, however, before the storm clouds began to gather. As Stalin unleashed the Great Terror in the late 1930s, one by one Geichenko's friends and colleagues were arrested or executed: the historian Fyodor Schmidt, an important intellectual influence, was exiled in 1934 and shot in 1937 (the same year as Klyuev); Geichenko's close friend Anatoly Shemanskiy was arrested in 1936 and killed at the front in 1942; and Nikolai Arkhipov, Geichenko's boss at Peterhof, was jailed in 1937. Arkhipov survived the camps, but his wife and only son died while he was in prison.

Eventually, the inevitable happened. Geichenko was arrested in 1941 along with his landlord and probable lover, Natalya Jorgenson. His flatmate Boris Mazing was already behind bars. The accusations facing the three stemmed from a drunken conversation one evening in which they apparently criticized the regime. After a perfunctory trial, Mazing was shot, and Jorgenson and Geichenko jailed. Geichenko received a ten-year sentence for 'anti-Soviet defeatist propaganda'. The fate of Geichenko's family is shrouded in mystery, but he had likely left his wife by the time of his arrest. Some sources claim she fled to Moscow, changing her name and the names of the children; others that the children died. Either way, Geichenko appears never to have had any contact with them again.

In a prison camp in the northern Urals, Geichenko was put to work felling timber. Although released in 1943, he was not at liberty for long: he was conscripted into a Red Army punishment battalion (units for ex-convicts that were used for the most dangerous military tasks). Part of the 372 Rifle Division as it forced the Volkhov River and liberated Novgorod, Geichenko helped push the Wehrmacht back toward the Russian border. After just a few months on the front line, however, he suffered the wound that led to the doctors removing his arm. Contemplating the shards of his shattered life, he must have questioned what sort of a future he could have as an amputee with the stigma of a political conviction. 'I lost everything in the war,' Geichenko later told a journalist.

Nevertheless, he did not die. Remaining friends pulled strings to get him appointed as director of Pushkin Hills – an opportunity to once again immerse himself in creativity and culture. Step by step, against all the odds, Geichenko pushed ahead with the clearing and reconstruction of Mikhailovskoye, the surrounding estates and parks. By his side was his second wife, Lyubov Suleimanova, whom he met while recuperating from his wounds in a hospital in Tbilisi. Looking back years later, Geichenko said that finding her was the beginning of his 'second life'. Nineteen years his junior, Lyubov was a Lak (an ethnic group from the high mountains of the Caucasus).

Even before sappers finished de-mining Pushkin Hills, reconstruction was well underway. The single-storey, wooden manor house of Mikhailovskoye, which was used by Pushkin and his family, opened to the public in 1949. But this was only the beginning. The Pushkin Hills museum covered thousands of hectares – in Russian it is known as a *zapovednik*, roughly equivalent to a 'national park' in the West – and Geichenko set about rebuilding some of the neighbouring estates, which had been burnt to the ground by local peasants during the Revolution. The opening of Trigorskoye, the country house of the Osipov-Wulf family, with whom Pushkin spent many happy evenings, took place in 1962, and fifteen years later this was followed by the unveiling of Petrovskoye, the estate granted by imperial decree to Pushkin's great-grandfather, Aram Gannibal.

Geichenko also oversaw the restoration of the Svyatogorsk Monastery, the construction of a wooden windmill, chapels and a watermill, and pushed for a huge, white-marble 'scientific–cultural centre' to be built in the local town. When his health finally gave out in the late 1980s, he was planning the reconstruction of Voskresenskoye, the estate owned by Pushkin's great-aunt.

All this was done with the approval and support of the Soviet authorities. Despite his background, Geichenko emerged as one of the country's leading museum curators – a public intellectual who was often on the television or radio talking about Pushkin, giving updates about the development of Pushkin Hills, or appealing for volunteers. He was a prolific writer, whose books enjoyed large print runs, and did much to popularize the already-adored Pushkin. In later life, Geichenko was showered with awards and, in 1983, he became the first museum worker to be made a Hero of Soviet Labour (a few days before Boris Piotrovsky, the veteran head of the world-famous Hermitage Museum in Leningrad).

At the heart of everything Geichenko did was Pushkin, whose poetry had been deeply influenced by the landscapes and people of this area of Pskov Region. In perhaps Pushkin's most famous work, novel-in-verse *Yevgeny Onegin*, the protagonist moves to live in a countryside estate obviously inspired by Mikhailovskoye:

The manor house stood in seclusion,
Screened by a hill from wind's intrusion,
Above a stream. Far off, there stretched

Meadows and golden cornfields, patched
With dazzling, multi-coloured flowers;
Small hamlets could be glimpsed around,
Herds wandered through the meadow ground,
And, in its thick, entangled bowers
A vast, neglected garden nursed
Dryads, in pensive mood immersed.

Pushkin is not merely a writer. Such is his influence and popularity that consecutive regimes in Russia have reinvented him as an ideological prop. Pushkin statues are the second most common statues of a person in Russia after those of Lenin, and Pushkin's writing remains a cornerstone of school curricula. Almost anywhere in Russia with more than a few houses there is a Pushkin Street, and there are museums, institutes, theatres, hotels, football tournaments and whole towns bearing his name. Such is the state's involvement in promoting Pushkin that his image, with its trademark sideburns, has become a marker of 'Russian' territory. This makes Pushkin a painful symbol of Russian imperialism in some post-Soviet countries and dozens of Pushkin statues in Ukraine were toppled after Russia invaded in 2022.

The Pushkin Hills created by Geichenko became the epicentre of a Soviet Pushkin cult and, in an atheist state, this ended up looking a lot like a substitute for religion. Geichenko actively encouraged quasi-mystical veneration of the poet, and in later life would compare the atmosphere and purpose of Pushkin Hills to that of a church. In Geichenko's telling, Pushkin's remains were akin to relics, dreaming about Pushkin was widespread, visitors to Pushkin Hills were 'pilgrims', and if you went down, alone, to the edge of the Sorot in the evening and called out for Pushkin, the great poet would answer. Such worship was a caricature of Russia's long tradition of raising its cultural icons to the status of demi-gods. But Geichenko was also brought up as an Orthodox Christian, witnessed the religious pageantry of the imperial court, and likely privately retained some Christian beliefs to which he could never publicly admit. 'For me there's no secret,' he told his biographers in the late 1980s. 'We got rid of religion in 1917, and Pushkin became our religion.'

Inevitably, Geichenko became a lightning rod for this Pushkin-adulation: part confessor, part academic, part guru. Indeed, his own life mirrored Pushkin's in a number of surprising ways. Both Pushkin and Geichenko were notorious womanizers, full of *joie de vivre* and prone to bouts of melancholy. Neither chose to live in Mikhailovskoye: Geichenko was sent there when his life was in tatters, Pushkin was banished there for suspected liberal sympathies. Finally, neither Pushkin nor Geichenko ever travelled abroad, spending their entire lives within the confines of, respectively, the Russian Empire and the Soviet Union.

Tourists in Pushkin Hills loved to seek out Geichenko, who lived just a stone's throw from Mikhailovskoye. Popularly known as the 'house-spirit', Geichenko rose at five or six in the morning, and could be spotted striding around the parks, checking everything was in order and giving instructions to gardeners, cleaners, tour guides and attendants. A tall, lanky man with a large nose, he was difficult to miss. Geichenko rarely pinned back his empty sleeve and it would flap as he walked or when he gesticulated giving lectures. His rapidly changing moods were notorious: Geichenko could erupt in anger as unexpectedly as he could dazzle visitors with his famous story-telling skills. At the end of every working day, he would see off the bus taking museum staff, who he referred to as 'my children', back to town.

Geichenko's job was not that of an ordinary museum curator. How could it have been? Almost nothing survived from Pushkin's time. Instead, it's better to understand Geichenko as a *creator*: a person who used his encyclopaedic knowledge of Pushkin's life and times, Pushkin's writings, whatever expertise was available, and his own imagination to put together something that would enthuse and delight.

Pushkin Hills was a place where reality and fantasy collided. Some compared it to a play (Geichenko was a keen amateur actor), others to a myth, or a fairy tale. It has also been described as a utopia where the Soviet Union came closest to perfection, with all the flaws and happiness of everyday life magnified as if under a microscope. More unkindly, Pushkin Hills has been referred to as a place of unscientific kitsch akin to a Soviet Disneyland. Geichenko himself preferred the analogy of an injection: anyone coming to Pushkin Hills, in his telling, would receive a shot of culture and inspiration.

Perhaps unsurprisingly considering the state of Pushkin Hills after the war, Geichenko was obsessed with material things. The first sentence of his bestselling book *Lukomorye* is: 'When people pass away, they leave behind things', and it is followed by dozens of chapters – sometimes whole detective stories – about how he tracked down objects once owned by Pushkin, his friends and family; or things linked to the poet's life. Magpie-like, Geichenko loved acquiring antiques, and asked local kids to bring him any 'old village stuff', for which he would give them a few kopecks. His collection of *samovars*, displayed to passing tourists in the window of his house, was one of his trademarks.

As well as using objects to help illuminate the life and times of Pushkin, Geichenko also dabbled in oral history, seeking out elderly men and women whose relatives remembered meeting Pushkin. 'Everyone's literate now and they've stopped doubting,' Geichenko quotes one old man as telling him. 'They believe in books like they believe in the Bible, and they don't trust what they hear in conversations.'

What Geichenko created in Pushkin Hills was not an esoteric, dusty museum; it was wildly successful. People flocked there in their millions. Pushkin Hills was one of the most popular museums in the Soviet Union with almost 100,000 visitors a month. Even if many were bussed in on organized tours paid for by trade unions, factories, or other arms of the state, this was an extraordinary number for a museum a day's journey from both Moscow and Leningrad. The busiest time of the year was always the festival on Pushkin's birthday (6 June), when people would descend for readings and speeches by famous writers of the day. Photographs from this annual event show temporary stages and huge crowds milling around the fields and meadows of Mikhailovskoye: a sort of Soviet Woodstock.

In an attempt to understand Geichenko better, I went to Pushkin Hills for a couple of weeks one summer, and rented a one-room flat in a dilapidated apartment block half-an-hour's walk from Mikhailovskoye. The town near Pushkin Hills is called Pushkin Hills (it was known as Svyatagoriye – 'Holy Hills' – under the tsars) and is the capital of Pskov Region's Pushkin Hills district. In most respects it was no different to other small towns in Pskov Region: on the way to my flat I passed the usual array of supermarket chains and a large, silver Lenin head hanging on the walls of a defunct factory. There was just one big difference: Pushkin was everywhere. The long-dead poet was a major part of the local economy, whether that was the stalls selling souvenirs, the services of guides, the demand for rented accommodation, or the many other facilities required by holidaymakers. Browsing the menu in the Pushkin Park restaurant one evening, I found volumes of Pushkin's poetry for sale alongside pizzas, soups, sushi and home-made bread. I soon discovered that Pushkin was the second toast whenever locals drank together. 'To the breadwinner,' people said as they clinked glasses.

Geichenko died in 1993. While there have been some superficial changes since then, the museums themselves are still run more or less as they were while he was in charge. Many of the staff members he appointed are still in post (the current director met his wife as a result of Geichenko's matchmaking). As in Soviet times, a line of elderly local women sell bunches of flowers to those clambering off tour buses on their way to pay homage at Pushkin's grave.

One thing that's difficult to appreciate without seeing first hand is the sheer size of the place: Pushkin Hills is like no other literature museum on earth. In total, the *zapovednik* covers almost a hundred square kilometres. While you can just about see the three main country houses, Mikhailovskoye, Trigorskoye and Petrovskoye, at a breakneck pace in a single day, if you want to absorb the atmosphere you need at least two or three. As Geichenko put it: 'The *zapovednik* is a literature museum, a commemorative museum, a Pushkin museum, a botany museum, an ornithology museum, a geology museum and an archaeology museum. It's got it all. It's got it all. Shakespeare does not have such a museum, nor Goethe, nor Dante! No one else has such a museum! It's only Russia that can allow itself 3,000 hectares!'

The other thing that strikes you very quickly is the beauty. The landscapes have a bucolic Slavic charm that distil something timeless: chapels perched on ancient earthworks, fishermen sitting silently by the river and groves of shimmering birches. Geichenko was a master of drama, and the long, forested approach road to Mikhailovskoye is perfectly calibrated to maximize the impact when you finally reach Pushkin's colonnaded ancestral home with its vista of meadows in all shades of green, the meandering Sorot and distant wooden villages. Tufts of white cloud are reflected in the translucent blue of Lake Kachanye, and the smell of freshly cut grass rises with the summer heat.

You can go inside Mikhailovskoye without joining a tour, but no one does, not least because there are no information boards. Like thousands of other museums in Russia, guided tours are *de rigueur*, and Geichenko actually designed the inside of the house to ensure tour groups could circulate without bumping into each other. I booked myself onto one. Our guide was a slight, mousey woman clutching a straw hat called Tatyana – like the main character in *Yevgeny Onegin*.

Most of all, I enjoyed hearing the details of Pushkin's life: his favourite jam, I learned, was gooseberry jam. Pushkin, Tatyana told us, came to Mikhailovskoye on seven occasions, mostly for just a few weeks at a time, with the exception of two years in the mid-1820s when he was exiled here. He wrote dozens of poems while at Mikhailovskoye and found inspiration for *Yevgeny Onegin*. The most famous love poem in the Russian language, 'I remember a wonderful moment', was also written here as a result of Pushkin's infatuation with a married woman, Anna Kern, who came to visit his neighbours in Trigorskoye.

Tatyana was reverential of Pushkin, and when quoting his poems she adopted a tone like she was reading the Bible. There was no mention of how Pushkin was, at times, deeply unhappy at Mikhailovskoye, how he got a serf-girl pregnant and had her sent to another property owned by his father, or his famously coarse language. When he finally slept with Anna Kern years later, he wrote to a friend that, 'with God's help I fucked [her]'.

That evening I had arranged to meet Vyacheslav Kozmin, the custodian of Bugrovo, a mock-up of a nineteenth-century village that was one of Geichenko's last projects. Kozmin was appointed by Geichenko in the late 1980s and has remained in post ever since. It was a warm July day outside Bugrovo when I arrived: the last tourists were departing and there was a sense of descending peace. With sideburns like Pushkin, Vyacheslav appeared wearing a half-unbuttoned shirt under a faded green waistcoat. His bronzed forearms were scratched, his face tinged red and his bouffant hair streaked grey. One of the first things he told me was that Pushkin

Hills was akin to Communism, because it is 'a fairy tale that will never come true'.

Later, we walked through the forest to meet a friend of his, Pyotr Bystrov, who grew up in an orphanage and was hired by Geichenko in the 1980s as an artist-in-residence. A short, stocky man with a kindly smile and a large moustache, Pyotr lived in an old village school that doubled as his workshop. One room was dominated by an enormous concrete bust of Geichenko that sat on a table surrounded by tools. Pyotr was repairing the bust, which belonged on a giant statue of Geichenko he had created a few years before. Frozen in chiselled concrete, Geichenko was shown with his lips pursed in a smile, a comically large nose and his trademark *skufia* cap, which was traditionally worn by Orthodox priests.

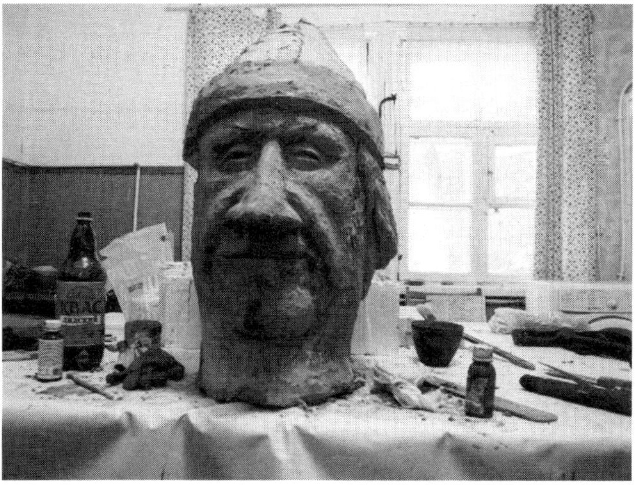

In the kitchen, Pyotr laid out potatoes, pickled cucumbers, sliced pink sausage, sprats, cooked peppers and lettuce. He poured out vodka shots. As the light faded, we talked about Geichenko. Both men had a deep admiration for their former boss, although, whereas Vyacheslav sought to explain away some of Geichenko's excesses, Pyotr was loyal to the point of stubbornness. One of my first questions was about Geichenko's alleged fakery, a subject about which little has been written. Of course, the estate-museums were all imaginative reconstructions, but how far, I wanted to know, did Geichenko actually go? Did he deliberately create counterfeits and fakes?

Pyotr's answer was definitive:

> One day, Geichenko asked me if I could copy Pushkin's handwriting. I told him I would try. He gave me some old paper with watermarks from Pushkin's time. I sat for a long time over it: my eyesight even got worse! I found and copied every tiny little bit, even if it was not visible to the eye. It was some sort of poetry, I don't remember exactly what. I simply copied it. When I'd done it all, I took it to him reverentially, in a folder. 'Here you go Stepan Semyonovich, I've done it.' He looked at it, took the manuscript I'd laboured over and threw it on the floor. [Pyotr mimed stamping his feet.] Not hard enough to tear it. But he wiped his feet on it and picked it up again. Dusted it off and said, 'There you go, now it works.'

The fake was put up in one of the museums, and tour guides told visitors it was an original Pushkin manuscript.

Most famously, accusations of fakery and of the Disneyland-ification of Pushkin Hills were made by the twentieth-century writer Sergei Dovlatov, whose brilliant short stories dissect the absurdity and pathos of Soviet life. Dovlatov spent the summer of 1977 as a tour guide in Pushkin Hills, an experience he fictionalized in a novella that sent up the atmosphere of hushed reverence, the earnestness of the museum staff, and the ignorance of the hordes of visitors – a parable for the whole of the Soviet Union. In the novella, *Zapovednik*, the hard-drinking main character, an alter ego for Dovlatov, is bewildered by repeated questions about whether he loves Pushkin. At one point, he tells his wife that 'these are Comrade Geichenko's dumb ideas. He wants to create an enormous amusement park here.'

As my evening with Vyacheslav and Pyotr progressed, at least one empty vodka bottle already on the floor, I asked about Dovlatov, to this day a hate figure for many at Pushkin Hills. Vyacheslav recounted how he was in the room when Geichenko told staff about the publication of *Zapovednik*. 'I got the sense Geichenko felt only joy at the fact that Dovlatov had found a nerve with which he had been playing for years. The *zapovednik* is not dogma – it's a game,' Vyacheslav said. But Pyotr was far less forgiving. 'He [Dovlatov] was a traitor and a bad person despite his talent,' he said. For Pyotr, not only was Dovlatov underhand, but all Geichenko's tricks were for a greater good; the end emphatically justified the means. 'The most important thing was that he [Geichenko] was telling people about Pushkin. Yes, he made up a lot, but the people loved to listen to him.'

The more time I spent in Pushkin Hills, and the more I read, the more Geichenko's fakery became obvious. It was hidden in plain sight. Across the breadth of the *zapovednik* you find glacial boulders (and a few ancient stone crosses) taken from other parts of Pskov Region and deliberately placed in particularly picturesque spots. Watching one of Geichenko's public appearances that had been uploaded to YouTube, I realized that an anecdote he told completely contradicted versions of the same event given by other participants. Of course, Geichenko's version was far more poetic, and suffused with a seductive symbolism. At first, I took a certain glee in spotting these inaccuracies and inventions, but this 'catch him out' approach quickly became boring. Not only was it too easy, it seemed pointless.

After the appalling hangover from the evening with Pyotr and Vyacheslav had worn off, it was Pyotr's words that stayed with me. Maybe historical accuracy really was less important than the fact that people loved Pushkin Hills: loved coming here, loved reading and re-reading Pushkin, loved believing they were following in the poet's hallowed footsteps. Vyacheslav put it best a few days later. He'd invited me to an event, but was obviously bored, so we stepped outside and stood drinking red wine out of plastic cups. As we spoke more about Geichenko, he quoted a line of Pushkin to me: 'Oh, it's easy to deceive me! / I myself am happy to be deceived!'

The more interesting question is what drove Geichenko to indulge in this make-believe. Part of the answer, no doubt, was the need to make Pushkin Hills popular and educational: Soviet museums were museums for the masses. But the answer was also tied up with Geichenko's personality: his vanity, a desire for success and, most importantly, a deep-seated need to stay on the right side of the authorities. His friend, the writer Yuri Nagibin, encapsulated this in a diary entry he made after visiting Geichenko in the busy summer of 1979: 'Why do you need these hordes of drunks who couldn't care less about Pushkin?' he asked. 'Semyon Stepanovich [Geichenko] is the architect of all this unhealthy clamour, which comes from his own ambition and conceit. He is strong-willed, mercurial and gifted but his artistic background is weak and he needs this chatter, this sparkle, these festivals and this success. The authorities also love it – the imitation of culture – and meet him halfway.'

My next stop was to meet one of Geichenko's longest-serving colleagues, Boris Kozmin. For almost fifty years, Boris has been the custodian of Petrovskoye, the estate of Pushkin's great-grandfather that was rebuilt from scratch in the 1970s. Now in his mid-eighties, frail and partially blind, Boris' job has been taken over by his competent and kindly wife, Lyubov. After an introduction from Vyacheslav – Boris' nephew – I visited Petrovskoye on a warm, overcast afternoon. Petrovskoye is the most distant of the Pushkin Hills estates and the most tangential to Pushkin's life (the poet only actually came here a couple of times). Pushkin's great-grandfather, Aram Gannibal, was an unusual figure for tsarist Russia and of great interest to Pushkin: born in present-day Cameroon, he was captured by Ottoman slave-traders and shipped via Constantinople to the Russian court in St Petersburg. His African origins notwithstanding, he rose high in the tsar's service and, in 1742, was granted Petrovskoye and the surrounding lands. Burnt to the ground in the Russian Revolution, the estate was recreated by Kozmin and Geichenko: a two-storeyed green and white manor house fronted by a large balcony and four white columns. Its elegant gardens and tree-lined walkways lead down to the reed-choked banks of Lake Kachanye.

After meeting me by the entrance gates, Lyubov showed me around Petrovskoye (taking tours, I discovered, is known as 'doing circles' by the guides), and I couldn't help wondering how many hundreds of times she must have recited the same information. Later, over tea in their house nearby, which was filled with Boris' oil paintings, I asked about Geichenko. 'He was a damaged person of course, but not broken,' she said. 'He realized he had won a ticket from death and could devote the rest of his life to Pushkin Hills and love something for real; enriching and creating in the process.' Just like Pyotr and Vyacheslav, Lyubov could tell stories about Geichenko's playfulness – and his fakery. 'He didn't create these myths to exaggerate his own influence but because the times were such,' she said. It was a survival strategy. 'Our generation, the younger generation, do not understand this. They cannot understand what the Soviet period meant – it's over thirty years ago now.'

While Lyubov took a phone call, Boris took me out to his workshop, which was also filled with paintings, covering both the walls and the ceiling. Like his nephew, Boris had Pushkinesque sideburns, now grey and straggly. He walked slowly: one of his pupils was brown; the other an unseeing milky blue.

Boris and Lyubov arrived in Petrovskoye from Siberia with two young sons in 1974. Like all of Geichenko's hires for managerial positions they were Pushkin fanatics and from far away; Geichenko feared denunciations and thought betrayal was more likely to come from locals. 'I was in love with the poems of Pushkin. Nothing better existed for me,' Boris recalled. The couple poured their lives into the rebuilding and running of Petrovskoye, now a oasis of beauty far enough away from Mikhailovskoye to be a world in its own right. At night, when the museum is closed and staff have gone home, they have the place to themselves. As Boris showed me the *banya*, he motioned through the gathering darkness at a picturesque pond in the grounds of Petrovskoye and said he and his guests would hop the fence and jump into the pond after steam sessions. 'I never get tired of repeating that I live in paradise,' he said.

One of the jobs of curators like Boris and Lyubov – and Geichenko – is to entertain a constant stream of visitors: academics, Pushkin experts, writers, musicians and artists. Usually this would be around a crowded table laid with tea and sweets; for more exalted guests, perhaps dinner and heavy drinking, *banya* and a full tour of Pushkin Hills. In Soviet times, intellectuals from Moscow and Leningrad saw Pushkin Hills as an outpost of culture in rural Russia; and Geichenko as one of their own. Although the relentless stream of guests could be a burden, particularly during the busy summer months, it was also a lifeline for Geichenko, who often felt himself to be in exile, and missed the bustle of Leningrad. He and his wife were consummate hosts.

When the composer Benjamin Britten and his partner, the tenor Peter Pears, came to Mikhailovskoye in 1965, they arrived late at night, but Geichenko took them around the estate by torchlight, and fed them. 'After a meal of soup and excellent cold leg of lamb, and a sort of barley with meat balls (so good), marvellous coffee and plum syrup, our host begged to hear the Pushkin songs,' Pears wrote later in his diary. These six songs, which were set to Pushkin poems, had just been composed by Britten and given the title, *The Poet's Echo*. 'The last song of the set is the marvellous poem of insomnia, the ticking clock, persistent night-noises and the poet's cry for a meaning in them. Ben has started this with repeated staccato notes high-low high-low on the piano. Hardly had the little old piano begun its dry tick tock tick tock, then clear and silvery outside the window, a yard from our heads, came ding, ding, ding, not loud but clear, Pushkin's clock joining in his song. It seemed to strike far more than midnight, to go on all through the song, and afterwards we sat spellbound.'

Another of Geichenko's jobs was to convince the authorities that pouring money into Pushkin Hills was justified. Lyubov told me Geichenko's fakes were one of the ways he did this. In other words, Geichenko dissembled, like an actor on stage, to help obtain the resources he needed from Soviet officials. And the plodding bureaucrats who held the purse strings fell for his fake letters, new 'discoveries' and second-hand trinkets – hook, line and sinker. Geichenko knew how to play the system. But, as well as his talent for charming, inspiring and persuading, he was a master shape-shifter. 'I knew one, two, three, four, five Semyon Stepanovichs,' said Lyubov. 'He wore a mask of double-speak that was gifted to him by nature. Or maybe it wasn't given to him by nature, but he developed it to save himself.'

It was in this way that Geichenko could be both a collector of old trinkets and the Soviet Union's first museum worker to be made a Hero of Socialist Labour; a loving husband who had numerous affairs; a member of the Communist Party who restored Orthodox churches; a believer in beauty as the mission of art who loved peppering his conversation with swear words; and a larger-than-life personality who suffered periods of intense loneliness and melancholy.

These apparent contradictions are perhaps one of the reasons his legacy is so closely guarded by those who knew him: they all want to make their Geichenko the canonical version. I've been to Pushkin Hills four times, and it gives up its secrets slowly. Despite repeated attempts, I never managed to get an interview with Geichenko's only child, Tatyana Geichenko, who is locked in a multi-decade conflict with the administration of the *zapovednik*. One researcher told me with bitterness that Tatyana had made it her 'life's work' to block access to information about her father.

Unsurprisingly, Geichenko often spun tall tales about his own past, making any attempt at biography extremely complex. The first account of his life was written in 1990 by Soviet journalists Larisa Ageeva and Vladimir Lavrov, a husband-and-wife team who complained that they couldn't 'figure out where there's truth, fantasy, artifice or when your leg is being pulled'. However, they concluded this wasn't an insurmountable obstacle. 'Something else is important here – it was completely natural for Geichenko to experience the past as living reality.' Even so, thirty years after the biography was published, Ageeva wrote an article admitting to several major errors that had arisen because they did not double-check Geichenko's stories.

Geichenko died aged ninety after a long illness. In the end, the man who had watched the last tsar inspecting troops on the parade ground as a child outlived the Soviet Union. One museum worker told me that a flock of black crows settled over Mikhailovskoye on the day of his death. The economic turmoil of the 1990s, and a crash in ticket sales caused by an end to the Soviet practice of funding holidays for workers, meant the museum was in dire financial straits, and staff had to build Geichenko's coffin themselves. It was Lyubov who found some cloth to cover it, and sewed a sawdust-stuffed pillow for his head. Thousands lined the route as Geichenko was taken on his final journey to a cemetery on the ancient hill fort of Voronich, a stone's throw from Trigorskoye.

My last meeting in Pushkin Hills was with Iosif Budylin, a writer and legendary tour guide in his late seventies. An aged lothario, he died in 2023. Like Geichenko, Iosif's father, a historian and linguist, was chewed up and spat out by the Soviet system, spending sixteen years in the gulag. And, like Geichenko, he went on to become a leader in his field, producing the first Russian-language verse translation of the Quran. Iosif argued that the generation of Geichenko and his father was an extraordinary one, whose achievements could not be understood without their first-hand experiences of deprivation and death. The extremes they had confronted in their life fostered an eagerness for humanity, he said. 'There is a concept of "in spite of",' he told me. 'They humiliate you. They try to wipe you from the face of the earth. But you fight for life and in spite of it all you affirm yourself.'

At the same time, these men and women were never free of fear. Geichenko was eighty-nine when he received an official pardon for the 1941 conviction that sent him to the gulag, and then to a punishment battalion. His illness already well advanced, it was a symbolic righting of a wrong – but it came far too late to make any real difference.

Throughout his 'second life' at Pushkin Hills, Geichenko was haunted by the idea that 'they' could come for him again. In perhaps the most revealing anecdote I was told, Vyacheslav Kozmin recounted coming across a frail Geichenko waiting for a delegation of low-level party officials one bitterly cold winter afternoon in the late 1980s. He wasn't wearing a hat, and Vyacheslav stopped to remonstrate, thinking his uncovered head was the result of carelessness. For Vyacheslav, Geichenko was a great man: a bestselling writer, war veteran and decorated museum director renowned across the Soviet Union. It never occurred to him that Geichenko might have something to fear. But Geichenko refused to listen. 'And I realized,' Vyacheslav said, 'that he had taken his hat off for a good-for-nothing third secretary of some regional committee.'

7

Director of Religion

One grey Saturday in March, 2023, I took the metro to northeastern Moscow to visit a museum called *Russia – My History*. It was in VDNKh, nicknamed the 'Soviet Versailles', an enormous park built to showcase the fruits of Communism and Soviet imperialism. Passing through happy crowds and skirting an outdoor ice rink – the biggest in Europe – I reached Pavilion 57, an enormous, squat glass building that housed *Russia – My History*. It was covered with images of Russian emperors and other notable figures from Russia's past. Particularly prominent was Tsar Alexander III with the accompanying quote: 'Russia has only two allies: its army and fleet.'

The sheer size of *Russia – My History* means most visitors just go to one of its three permanent exhibitions: 'Rurikids' (862–1598), 'Romanovs' (1598–1914) and 'From great shocks to a great victory' (1914–1945). I bought a ticket for the Romanovs. To get there, I climbed the stairs of a concrete amphitheatre past stylized images of Russian soldiers awarded medals for bravery in Ukraine and portraits of Russian rulers. Entering the exhibition was like going underground: there was no natural light, and the gloom focused attention on brightly coloured stands. Video and sound installations alternated with interactive panels, backlit displays and 3D films. One room had a mock-up of a peasant hut; in another you could press a heart-shaped button under reproductions of nineteenth-century paintings to show you 'liked' them. It was a bit like being at the cinema, or playing a video game.

The propaganda was not heavy-handed. Instead, in a style more reminiscent of a school textbook, the words and images burnished Russian history, downplaying military defeats or highlighting cultural achievements. They brimmed with pride in Russia's great destiny, the glory of empire, and the qualities of the Russian people. In each room, there was a little box showing how much land successive Romanov rulers had acquired for the empire. The more it implied, the better. The museum was busy with people of all ages, including young couples apparently on dates.

Russia – My History in Moscow is not unique. At the time, it was one of over 20 such museums across Russia and occupied Ukraine. A few more are added each year. In Pskov, there have been discussions about putting a *Russia – My History* in an, abandoned university building opposite the *kremlin*. They are so easy to recreate because there are no original exhibits. All the displays are identical. Despite this cookie-cutter approach, the museums have been stunningly popular. As of late 2023, over 20 million people were believed to have visited *Russia – My History* exhibitions, one in seven of all Russians.

This blockbuster concept was not dreamt up by a Kremlin official, or an ambitious curator. It was the brainchild of a bishop in the Orthodox Church, Father Tikhon Shevkunov. A conservative thinker known to have the ear of Putin, Tikhon is one of the most powerful prelates in modern Russia, and his interests extend into education, filmmaking and foreign policy. His ambition and charisma mean he stands out among the country's conformist clerics. Some compare him to Rasputin, the mystic who bewitched the imperial family in the years leading up to the Russian Revolution, others to film star Russell Crowe. It's often speculated he could be the next Patriarch.

Tikhon has an eclectic CV. He helped design Russia's school curriculum, wrote one of the most popular books of the last three decades, and has directed television documentaries. He has overseen major construction projects, sat on a Kremlin committee, and founded one of the most influential Orthodox news websites. He has been in charge of anti-alcohol campaigns, organized big literary commemorations, and arranged for the construction of new statues, exhibitions and museums. Ideologically, he is paternalist and a social conservative, contending that homosexuality is a 'cross to bear', women should play a subservient role, and censorship is a force for good. He's also a nationalist and monarchist, suspicious of the West, and susceptible to conspiracy theories. Perhaps most importantly, though, Tikhon is a convinced imperialist, believing empire is Russia's historical destiny. At least in public, he doesn't appear all that interested in religious issues.

There are different ways to wield influence in Russia. On paper, neither Tikhon's relatively run-of-the-mill position as a bishop, nor his committee positions, give him much formal power. He does not own a business, or enjoy an independent fortune. Even his closest admirers do not think the Kremlin consults him about everyday political decisions. Instead, Tikhon's influence lies in the realm of ideas – and his ability to communicate them.

Above all, to one man: Vladimir Putin. Since the early 2000s, a persistent rumour has circulated that Tikhon is Putin's *dukhovnik*, or 'spiritual father'. A role without an equivalent in Western religious traditions, *dukhovnichestvo* involves confession, religious instruction and mentorship. Having a *dukhovnik* became fashionable among Russia's political and business elite after the collapse of the Soviet Union. It is frowned on by more progressive strains of Orthodoxy where it is seen as authoritarian. Obedience is a key part of the relationship, with a blessing from your *dukhovnik* often little more than a direct order. On paper, this bestows an immense amount of power. One priest told me that the relationship was supposed to be about spirituality, but the reality was very different. 'In actual fact,' he said, 'it's all about personal control and manipulation.'

Tikhon has been asked hundreds of times whether or not he is Putin's *dukhovnik*. Each time, he feeds the rumour by refusing to confirm or deny – typically stating it's not his secret to divulge.

In a similar way, there is a cultivated mystery surrounding how and when Putin and Tikhon first met. In one version, they were introduced by then-powerful banker Sergei Pugachyov; in another, Putin turned up at Moscow's Sretensky Monastery when Tikhon was the abbot; in another, they were introduced by a mutual KGB acquaintance; in yet another Tikhon officiated at the funeral of Putin's father. Whatever the truth, the implication is that Tikhon brought Putin, a Soviet-raised KGB agent, into the Orthodox faith.

What we do know is that they met around the time Putin's political career was taking off in the late 1990s, possibly when he was head of the FSB. In a 2001 interview with a Greek journalist, Tikhon revealed an intimate knowledge of Putin's religious beliefs, as well as those of his family. When the conversation was republished in a Russian newspaper, Tikhon was dubbed 'Putin's *dukhovnik*' for the first time. From publicly available information, we also know the two men talk regularly and that they have travelled together. The Kremlin occasionally publishes photos of them in each other's company.

For Tikhon, the relationship has brought extraordinary influence, money and fame. He told an interviewer in 2023 that his first meeting with Putin was 'one of the most important encounters of my life'. For Putin, though, the benefits are less obvious. Perhaps he is drawn to Tikhon's personal charm; perhaps their world views align; perhaps he likes to be publicly associated with the prelate to boost his popularity among Orthodox believers. Pugachyov, the banker who claims he introduced the two men, said Putin took a liking to Tikhon because of his charisma, and because he was deferential. 'If Putin lit a cigarette from a candle or lamp in his church or monastery, he [Tikhon] would simply say: "God's blessing, that's how it should be done." Because it was the president. He's a flexible person. And in that sense he's also a weak person. Putin likes this combination very much.'

I spent almost a year trying to arrange an interview with Tikhon. When I first got in touch on Telegram, he texted back that he was ready to meet with me. But then he went silent, leaving all my follow-up messages unanswered. Perhaps a member of his staff had googled me; perhaps he was too busy. Instead, I found myself watching the many interviews Tikhon has given to television journalists and YouTubers, as well as online recordings of his talks at seminaries, monasteries and universities. Not only does Tikhon obviously enjoy the limelight, I quickly realized he was a consummate performer.

In almost all these appearances, he wears a black cassock and a large silver cross around his neck. He is unfailingly polite, eloquent and confident. Apparently conscious of how he looks, he constantly tweaks his outfit, returning the cross to the centre of his chest, or refolding his cassock. Often when thinking, or holding forth, he takes a fistful of his ample beard in a large, meaty hand, and draws it downward, gradually releasing the hair.

You cannot begin to understand Tikhon without the monastery that helped bring him into the Orthodox faith and where he spent his formative years: the Pskov Caves Monastery. Tucked into a fold in the land around the town of Pechory, it is less than five kilometres from Estonia. For centuries, it was both a spiritual centre, and a military outpost defending Russia's western approaches. Its massive limestone walls and towers mean it's still easily mistaken for a castle.

The monastery gets its name from the network of caves and passageways – some natural, others man-made – that lie under its churches. Cramped and claustrophobic, they are the final resting place for thousands of holy men, the cold air slowing the process of decay. Before he was canonized, this was where the body of the monastery's most famous abbot, Cornelius, was laid to rest after he was decapitated by Tsar Ivan the Terrible in 1570. The reasons for the brutal murder remain unclear, but, according to legend, the tsar immediately repented and carried Cornelius' body, dripping blood, through the monastery. To this day, the path leading from the gates known as the 'Bloody Way'.

I went to the Caves Monastery for the first time in 2010, and I remember being underwhelmed. The pretty cluster of small, golden-domed churches seemed a far cry from some of the spectacular Orthodox buildings in Moscow and St Petersburg. But the Caves

Monastery exudes a quiet power, and, with each subsequent visit, I found myself more and more drawn to its understated, edge-of-world spirituality. Passing its high walls and descending down the Bloody Way felt like entering a place of refuge.

Six years after my first visit, I was invited by the foster mother of a boy from the orphanage in Belskoye Ustye to join them for Easter celebrations and I stayed for two nights in a sparsely furnished dormitory with other pilgrims, attending religious processions and services. I'm not sure what I'd expected, but the experience was a gruelling one. The services, which lasted for three or four hours, began in the early hours of the morning and went on deep into the night. As darkness fell in the churches, they became more and more like the caves above which they sat, illuminated by masses of flickering candles. The congregation does not sit during Orthodox services, which means you cannot doze off and must stand, shifting your weight from one aching foot to another. My mind fogged from lack of sleep and lulled by the billowing incense and the rise and fall of Church Slavonic chanting, I remember slipping into something resembling a trance.

At the time of the Russian Revolution, the Caves Monastery was fairly unremarkable: one of over a thousand monasteries in the Russian Empire, each with their own stories, traditions and history of devotion. But anti-religious campaigns in the Soviet Union led to almost all these monasteries being shut down, their monks and nuns ejected, and their buildings seized. The Caves Monastery, however, escaped closure because a geopolitical quirk put it on Estonian territory for much of the 1920s and 1930s. As a result, today it is the only monastery in Russia that has operated continuously since its foundation, a title that bestows immense spiritual authority.

Tikhon came to the Caves Monastery for the first time in 1980 aged twenty-two, and he credits the place as being the site of his spiritual 'birth'. Two years later, he joined the monastery as a novice. Transferred to Moscow in the late 1980s, he returned in 2018 when appointed abbot.

Born five years after Stalin's death, Tikhon was part of the post-war generation with no direct experience of revolutionary idealism, the gulag or victory over Nazism. Raised to aspire to high moral ideals, many men and women like him ended up becoming disillusioned, unable to see anything in Communism apart from empty ritual. Discovering God went some way toward assuaging these feelings of purposelessness. But Orthodoxy was also exotic, unusual and mysterious – even cool. In their rejection of the status quo, Orthodox believers had much in common with Western hippies. It would be men and women like Tikhon who would drive a late Soviet religious revival.

Finding God, however, was not straightforward. A scarcity of Bibles, and the unwillingness of clerics to proselytize, made it difficult to learn about Orthodoxy. Some churches had been re-opened by Stalin, and, at least on paper, it was possible to attend services. However, the rituals were baffling, congregations were mostly elderly women and the KGB kept a close eye on converts. As a result, the Soviet Union's few functioning monasteries, where religious life could be observed and experienced first-hand, became beacons for curious young people. There were also more prosaic temptations. 'Monasteries were alluring for many of those I knew not only for the "spiritual nourishment" they could provide, but for the daily routine, high morale, solidarity and – what was very important in those years – plentiful food,' one woman who was active in Moscow religious circles at the time told me. 'It was a place where you could survive in all senses of the word.'

Tikhon was told about the Caves Monastery by a university friend, and recalled his first visit as like entering a different world. 'Everything here gave an impression, if not of a fairy tale – because this was obviously real life – then at least of something wondrous,' he wrote. He immediately realized he would never be the same again.

In late 1970s when he discovered religion, Tikhon was studying at Moscow's All-Union State Institute of Cinematography (VGiK), the most famous film school in the Soviet Union. Raised by his mother, a microbiologist, he'd read none of the classics of Russian literature – apart from Dostoevsky – when he enrolled at university. But, according to one student friend, he quickly became a voracious reader, and excelled. Another student remembered Tikhon as 'smiley, soft, and quiet'. VGiK made a deep impression on Tikhon, not only honing his artistic skills and teaching him the power of communication, but pushing him to ask big questions about life, art and belief that would eventually draw him to Orthodoxy. Many years later, Tikhon would conduct the church funerals for several of his VGiK teachers.

In his writings, Tikhon presents his conversion as a series of steps, rather than a sudden revelation. For a while, he dabbled in spirituality, including experiments with a Ouija board that ended when a demon tried to get him to commit suicide. With religious literature hard to find, a pivotal moment was when he was loaned the Bible for the first time. After he graduated from VGiK, Tikhon was baptized in Moscow's Church of St Nicholas just across the river from the Kremlin. Then, against the wishes of his mother, he left Moscow to enrol as a novice in the Caves Monastery.

The abbot at the time was Father Gavriil, a notoriously despotic figure who promoted an authoritarian form of Orthodoxy. Under his stewardship, Christian virtues of obedience and humility were taken to extremes, and discipline was paramount. One monk who lived in the monastery in this period recounted an incident in which Gavriil became so angry about a perceived infraction that he punched an attendant in the face. 'Gavriil was simply a bandit,' said the monk. 'He was rude, and insolent in the extreme.' Tikhon would later write approvingly of other violent incidents involving Gavriil. In one, Gavriil kicked a monk; in another, as a test, he ordered a young man to strike an elderly monk, which he duly did, sending the monk sprawling. In all likelihood, Gavriil was also cooperating closely with the KGB, helping them monitor what was happening in the monastery.

The KGBs interest stemmed not only from the Caves Monastery's role popularizing Orthodoxy, but because it was a destination for foreign tourists – meaning Soviet citizens could meet Westerners, and possibly exchange banned literature. One Belgian–Russian who went on an organized tour in the Soviet Union in 1983 recalled the surveillance. 'The Pskov monastery under Gavriil left the worst possible taste in everyone's mouth,' she said. 'At the front of our group was our guide, and, at the back, came a deacon from the monastery.'

In the 1980s, the monks were mostly a mixture of older men, many of whom had been persecuted for their faith, and relative youngsters like Tikhon, who had embraced Christianity with passionate intensity. Few of them saw Orthodoxy as an intellectual pursuit, and the Caves Monastery was not a centre of religious learning. Little store was put in books, or libraries. However, god and the devil were very real, and the battle against dark forces was one that carried immense, and immediate, consequences. Miracles were real. Exorcisms were real. Demons were real.

Every first-time visitor to the Caves Monastery in the late Soviet Union was struck by the wild cries of possessed men and women who had come for exorcisms carried out by a monk called Father Adrian. In Tikhon's descriptions, this ritual involved people spinning around like tops on the floor, yelling profanities, or oinking like pigs. One visitor in 1982 recalled sleeping in a room with eight other women, including those waiting for exorcisms. 'My roommates were generally quiet,' she recalled. 'But occasionally someone cried-out, or started to snarl and crow like cockerel, or giggle, or swear.'

For people with a conventional Soviet upbringing, such sights made a deep impression. For some, it served as proof of God's existence. For others, it was baffling, or simply terrifying. The crowds thronging the monastery 'seemed like they were from another planet', a woman who was taken there as a child by her parents in the 1980s told me. 'It was frightening to go into the churches because of the wildness, and the madness.'

Novices like Tikhon were clearly intoxicated by the atmosphere, and proud of the spiritual feats performed by the monastery's great elders. Others, however, were not so sure. The monk who witnessed Gavriil punch an attendant was dismissive. 'The brothers in Pechory were totally illiterate,' he said. 'Nobody read anything. The conversation was mostly about devils, the end of the world, and even the Antichrist. Nobody spoke about Christ himself.'

Summoned to Moscow in 1986, Tikhon spent several years working under Father Pitirim, a priest who, like Father Gavriil, is widely believed to have been recruited by the KGB. Finally, a few months before the collapse of the Soviet Union, he became a monk (this was when he chose the name 'Tikhon' after the Patriarch in charge of the Orthodox Church at the time of the Russian Revolution). Accounts differ about why his novitiate lasted as long as nine years – some put it down to spiritual doubts, others to objections from his mother.

When the state began to return church buildings to the religious authorities after the end of the Soviet Union, Tikhon was appointed to Moscow's Sretensky Monastery, a tiny cluster of buildings tucked away in the centre of the city. In 1995, he was made abbot. Famously, the Sretensky Monastery is a five-minute walk from Lubyanka Square, where the FSB have their headquarters – and in one of the versions of Tikhon's first meeting with Putin, the future president (then head of the FSB) dropped in out of curiosity.

Even at this stage, Tikhon was well on his way to becoming a master of spectacle and an adept political operator. One of his skills was an ability to manage large projects, particularly when it came to construction. Many Russian clerics became amateur builders in 1990s as the Church regained control over crumbling sites of worship – but Tikhon, who worked as a builder in his teens, excelled in this role. He was capable of directing hundreds of subordinates and contractors, juggling projects and physically transforming his surroundings. At the Sretensky Monastery, he oversaw the repairs of dilapidated buildings, opened a seminary, organized a large farm outside Moscow, and managed the construction of a huge, gold-domed church with an underground car park. 'He's a very good manager,' a reporter who investigated Tikhon told me. 'He builds everything, restores everything, and, then… he moves on to somewhere else and does the same.'

Tikhon's energy was also on display in his prodigious networking. As he entered Putin's inner circle, he made the acquaintance of influential prelates, film directors, prosecutors, journalists, oil executives, generals and top FSB officers. Perhaps his rush for influence was driven by a sense of inferiority – unlike many senior clergymen, including both post-Soviet patriarchs, he did not come from a clerical family. Brought up by a single mother in Chertanovo, a rough suburb of the Russian capital, he had something to prove.

His dark charisma was a source of fascination for those around him. One academic who sat on a committee with him in the early 2000s told me Tikhon would arrive at meetings in expensive sports cars. 'He looked deliberately crude and unprepossessing. He was unclean, unkempt and there was a sense he had something deeply unpleasant inside,' she said. When Tikhon came closer, she said she was seized by a desire to get as far away as possible. 'There was a whole room of priests, monks and archimandrites, but he concentrated the attention on himself. He only had to move, and everyone looked to see what he was doing. It was impossible to explain rationally.'

The academic had only one association: Rasputin, the Siberian mystic who became close to the Tsar Nikolai II and his wife in the years before the Russian Revolution because of his ability to ease the suffering of their haemophiliac son. While some, including the imperial family, saw Rasputin as a prophet, others denounced him as a charlatan. Dirty and debauched in appearance, Rasputin was known for his sexual exploits: taking part in orgies and seducing high-society ladies.

Comparisons between Tikhon and Rasputin were frequent in the early 2000s (and there remains a undeniable physical similarity), but, as Tikhon became more and more high profile, he seems to have made an effort to clean up his image – now aspiring to be more movie star, less licentious holy man.

Perhaps because of his film-school training, Tikhon has always understood the value of PR. In 1999 he set up a church news website, Pravoslavie.ru, which is today one of Russia's most popular Orthodox media outlets. He produces a steady flow of articles on everything from religious dogma to politics and history. He even did an interview with the French far-right politician Jean-Marie Le Pen. While Tikhon doesn't have a social-media presence, in 2020 his assistant set up an Instagram account for his cat, Vladyka, a giant, ginger Maine Coon. Posts include Vladyka on a plane, Vladyka being cuddled by children, Vladkyka at meetings with black-clad prelates, and Tikhon walking Vladyka on a lead around the Caves Monastery in the snow.

While Tikhon established himself quickly in Moscow, it wasn't until the publication of his bestselling book in 2011 that he became something of a household name. *Everyday Saints and Other Stories* is a whimsical and sentimental memoir that recounts the holiness of the monks of the Pskov Caves Monastery in the late Soviet period. Written in the style of a religious hagiography, or fairy tale, it's easy – almost comforting – to read. And, like *Russia – My History*, it was wildly popular. With more than 3.5 million copies sold, *Everyday Saints* has been a publishing sensation. Its English-language translator, Julian Lowenfeld, was so affected that he converted to Orthodoxy, with Tikhon personally carrying out the baptism. Perhaps the best testament to the book's success, though, is how its stories have entered folk memory and are told and retold by people unaware of their origin. I remember sitting at the table with Nina and Nikolai one evening in Baranovo when Nikolai described a World War II veteran who became an abbot. When his monastery faced closure by the Soviet authorities, the abbot, Nikolai said, pinned on his medals, and threatened to barricade the monastery's gates and order his monks to fight. Only later did I realize that Nikolai's anecdote was lifted from *Everyday Saints*.

Critics of the book claimed it was nostalgic, idealized and had little in common with reality. One religious dissident, Alexander Ogorodnikov, who knew many of the monks featured in *Everyday Saints*, told me that when he saw Tikhon at a book-signing after publication, Tikhon greeted him jovially: 'Well, how did you find it, Alexander? I hope I didn't lie too much?!'

Tikhon's world view has been shaped by conservatives and nationalists. They include Soviet historian Lev Gumilev (Tikhon remembers encountering him as a student), who promoted 'Eurasianist' ideas about Russia's imperial destiny on the steppe, and Ivan Ilyin, a White Russian exile who warned the West was seeking to destroy Russia and espoused monarchism, imperialism and fascism. Much ink has been spilt over the extent to which Gumilev and Ilyin have influenced Russia's elite, including Putin, but both thinkers are undoubtedly widely read in Kremlin circles. Tikhon has described Ilyin as having a 'prophet's gift' and, in 2009, he accompanied Putin to lay flowers at Ilyin's tomb in Moscow.

The essence of much of Tikhon's thinking revolves around what he sees as Russia's immutable imperialism. He believes Russia can only ever be an empire – if it fails as an empire, it fails as a nation. Russia 'should be an empire', he told an interviewer in 2022. 'Not because it wants to be, or doesn't want to be – just because it is.' The boundaries to Tikhon's imperialism, however, are difficult to establish. While it certainly includes the ethnic minorities within modern Russia, as well as much of the territory of the Soviet Union, whether it extends to the entirety of the former Russian Empire – meaning countries like Poland and Finland – is unclear. Perhaps Tikhon would even like to see Russian influence extend deep into Central Europe, or as far as the Bosphorus. Politically necessity, of course, dictates that he cannot be explicit.

In addition to his imperialism, Tikhon believes Russia should be ruled by a monarch. He has criticized modern officials for being too beholden to laissez-faire capitalism, and fetishizing material wealth. And he's argued that education, the media and culture should be far more closely controlled by the state.

Perhaps unsurprisingly, Tikhon's convictions are coloured by conspiracy theories. For several years in the late 1990s he campaigned against barcodes, arguing they contained hidden marks of the Antichrist. 'I was struck by the enormous quantity of 666s in New York,' he wrote after a trip to America in 1998. 'It was like some sort of bad, vulgar game.' And in 2017 he was criticized by Jewish leaders for stating that the killing of Nikolai II was a 'ritual' murder, a false allegation with obvious anti-Semitic undertones. In particular, Tikhon's paranoia comes to the fore when it comes to geopolitics. He's explained to more than one interviewer that the West wants to make Russia its vassal state in order it to precipitate a war between Russia and China that would destroy both world powers in a massive military conflagration. Russia's resistance to the West's plan, according to Tikhon, led directly to the Ukraine war.

At the same time, it would be a mistake to see Tikhon as a dyed-in-the-wool obscurantist. For one, as *Russia – My History* shows, he places a premium on communication, seeking to win people over through entertainment, not just diktat. For another, he flirts with liberalism in a way that puts him out of sync with much of Russia's ruling class. In 2012, he criticized the prison sentences handed to punk group Pussy Riot for being overly harsh, and, during the coronavirus pandemic, he condemned Covid dissidence, which was particularly strong in the Church.

Ever the postmodern éminence grise, Tikhon even makes an effort to maintain contacts among Russia's liberals. At least before the war in Ukraine, he occasionally gave interviews to independent journalists. And when Kirill Serebrennikov, a theatre director whose repertoire includes anti-clerical plays, was put under house arrest in 2017, Tikhon denied speculation he instigated the police investigation. As well as protesting his innocence in interviews, he arranged a face-to-face meeting with Serebrennikov. The theatre director, who now lives in Berlin, told me he was inclined to believe Tikhon had nothing to do with the charges, which were later dropped. When I asked what he made of the powerful cleric at their meeting, Serebrennikov replied only: 'Intelligent'.

The older he gets, the more Tikhon becomes interested in the lessons of history (*Russia – My History* is one of the results). This is far from a nerdish hobby – he appears to sincerely see the past as a way to unite people and justify political action. Above all, he is obsessed with the idea of imperial collapse, writing and presenting long TV documentaries on both the decline of the Byzantine Empire and the 1917 Russian Revolution. They are well-made, polemical parables for modern Russia – and fascinating windows onto his thinking.

In *Death of an Empire: The Lesson of Byzantium*, Tikhon strides around Venice and Istanbul attributing the decay of Byzantium to a weak state, Western hostility, 'liberal' reforms and demographic and spiritual crises. For him, Moscow is the Third Rome, and Russia the successor to Byzantium. 'The vengeful hatred of the West toward Byzantium,' he concludes, ran at a 'genetic level', and 'without an understanding of this striking, but undoubted fact, we risk misunderstanding not only a lot about this distant history, but the history of the twentieth and even the twenty-first century.' His documentary about the Russian Revolution, *Death of an Empire: The Lesson of Russia*, is even more tendentious. Tsarist Russia on the eve of 1917, Tikhon argues, was a flourishing state with a visionary leader, booming economy and unparalleled political freedoms, whose armies were on the verge of occupying Berlin, Vienna and Constantinople. The regime, he says, was destroyed by a liberal 'coup', facilitated by the UK and France, who wished to see a weak Russia. The documentary runs for almost four hours.

For the conservative Tikhon, the Russian Revolution was nothing less than a national tragedy and he reveres Nikolai II, who was executed by the Bolsheviks, as a martyr. However, he is far too canny to condemn the Soviet past, which is the object of such intense nostalgia in Russian society. Indeed, one of his life's missions has been to try and bend the Soviet period into the broader arc of Russian history – bridging the gap between Tsarism, Communism and free market capitalism. The religious continuity at the heart of *Everyday Saints* is one example of such an approach. But Tikhon also refuses to condemn KGB officers, and argues late Soviet leaders were little more than Red tsars ruling over a Red empire. He once admitted to having a soft spot for Soviet songs, which he described as sublimated prayers.

Many observers like to play the speculative game of linking ideas espoused by Putin to specific thinkers, or individuals in his entourage – and Tikhon's name is one that often comes up in such conversations. The dissident priest Andrei Kuraev, who is acquainted with Tikhon, has gone as far as to say that it was Tikhon who acquainted Putin with the crypto-fascist thinker Ilyin, and that the imperialist ideas pushed by Tikhon led directly to the war in Ukraine.

The truth is that Putin's views have always been malleable, and they have evolved over more than a quarter of a century in the Kremlin. Sometime in the early 2020s, though, perhaps as a result of spending long periods in relative isolation during the pandemic, Putin apparently embraced what some have dubbed national imperialism, which moulds together ideas from Tsarist Russia, Stalinism, Slavophile philosophy and the Russian nationalist movements of the second half of the 20th century. There are obvious parallels with the ideology pushed by Tikhon. But was Kuraev right when he claimed Tikhon played a crucial role in Putin's embrace of violent imperialism? Unfortunately, we shall probably never know. It's likely even Tikhon himself does not know exactly how much weight his own words carry with Putin.

The last time I went to the Caves Monastery was a few days before my visit to *Russia – My History* in Moscow. The contrast could not have been greater. I arrived late at the monastery, and, as darkness gathered, it was shrouded in a blizzard. The air was choked with silent snowflakes, imbuing the place with an air of sleepy serenity. There were few people. All the trees were smothered in white, and just a few patches of gold – or gold stars on aquamarine blue – were visible on the monastery's cupolas. I'd been half hoping to catch a glimpse of Tikhon, and perhaps ask him again for an interview. But there was no sign of the prelate. I lingered for a few minutes at a service in St Michael's Cathedral, where those arriving late pushed open the heavy doors, shaking the snow from their coats and hats.

Just a few months later, Tikhon was removed from his position as abbot of the Caves Monastery and made bishop of annexed Crimea. Opinion was split on whether this was a promotion (Putin likes to say that Crimea is as important to Russia as Jerusalem's Temple Mount is for Jews and Muslims), or a demotion by a jealous Patriarch keen to put Tikhon in harm's way. Tikhon himself joked that he was being sent into exile.

One of Tikhon's priorities in his new job has been managing a giant construction project on the Crimean site of Chersonesus, a Greek, (and later Byzantine) colony, where Kyivan prince Vladimir the Great is believed to have converted to Orthodoxy in the tenth century. Under Tikhon's stewardship, builders are erecting at least five museums (including a Museum of Christianity the size of Istanbul's Hagia Sophia), an art school, children's centre, reconstructed ancient town, centre for tourists, archaeological hub, parking for 1,400 cars, amphitheatre and, perhaps, a seminary.

Crimea is regularly struck by missiles and drones as the war rages in Ukraine, and Tikhon finds himself literally serving on the frontlines of Putin's bloody, empire-building project. We will likely never know if this was what he envisaged when he proclaimed imperialism as Russia's destiny, or extolled the virtues of nationalist thinkers in Kremlin corridors. Perhaps being up close to the violence will entrench his national imperialism even deeper. Or, perhaps, it is less inspiring, and more frightening, than he could ever admit. Either way, he is now living what he has long preached. 'Whatever political–social project you introduce in Russia, you'll always get empire,' Tikhon once told a packed auditorium. 'Whether you like it or not.'

8

Orphanage

The road leading to the Belskoye Ustye orphanage is flanked by evenly spaced oak trees, which makes the walk along the cracked, pot-holed tarmac feel like passing through a tunnel. On sunny afternoons, there are usually kids sitting outside, lounging among the trees or playing on one of several colourful climbing frames. If they spot newcomers, there is a flurry of interest. But, more often than not, when you approach, the orphanage is silent, with no evidence it's home to anywhere up to a hundred children. On dark winter mornings, floodlights illuminate the compacted snow around the buildings; the harsh fluorescence keeping the blackness at bay. Staff members at the end of their night shifts huddle deep in their fur coats, their breath rising in steam, as they wait for the bus to take them back to their families in nearby Porkhov.

The orphanage itself is an unremarkable two-storey grey-brick building, about two hundred metres long and ringed by a mesh fence. At one end are most of the dormitories, in the middle a little sports hall and, at the other end, staff offices, a few more dormitories, a computer room and two small halls for plays and events. Gauzy, white lace curtains cover all the windows, making it impossible to see what's happening inside.

When I first visited Belskoye Ustye in 2007, there were nine different types of state orphanage in Russia. They included orphanages for blind children; orphanages for deaf children;

orphanages for children with learning disabilities; orphanages for children with cerebral palsy; and orphanages for children with speech impediments. The one in Belskoye Ustye was for children with serious learning disabilities – so-called 'type 8'– one of two such orphanages in Pskov Region.

For me, the orphanage was where Russia started. In 2007, during my university holidays, I joined a group of thirty Russian and English students recruited by a charity to put on a month-long 'summer camp'. We lived in a house owned by the Russian Orphan Opportunity Fund (or in tents pitched in the garden) in Baranovo, a stone's throw from Nina and Nikolai's house. Every day, we walked up to the orphanage, past the disintegrating eighteenth-century church where Nina's grandfather served, and down the oak-tree tunnel, to put on developmental activities, run sporting events, solve puzzles, play games, stage shows and go on camping trips.

I continued volunteering for almost a decade, including almost a year living nearby in Baranovo, but it was the first visit that made the biggest impression. I had seen nothing like the orphanage. My closest reference point was probably workhouses from a Charles Dickens novel. I vividly remember the smells – cooked food, unwashed bodies, chlorine and urine – and how the children crowded you, grabbing hands and clothes, pinching, pulling hair, jostling and asking questions. Dressed in an odd collection of what seemed to be adult cast-offs, the kids spent most of their waking hours in rooms furnished with just a few scuffed tables and chairs, a bookcase and television. For reasons we couldn't fathom, most of the boys, and some of the girls, had shaved heads with long fringes. At night, and for long periods during the day, cast-iron metal grilles across corridors were locked, confining the older teenagers to their dormitories at one end. Children vulnerable to self-harm were tied up.

Just a few years previously, it had been even more shocking. One volunteer who visited the orphanage in 2000 described it to me in nightmarish terms. 'The children were in rags, dirty and covered in piss,' she said. 'There was one toilet for the whole orphanage. And it was communal, for girls and boys, without any partitions. The smell of urine was all-pervasive. You would leave the orphanage with the smell of urine because the children wet themselves and then weren't changed. The urine just dried into their clothes.'

For me, one of the most disturbing sights was the 'rocking'. Standing or sitting, the kids would rhythmically sway their upper body backward and forward. Lying in bed at night, they would rock side to side, as if in a cradle. At the extreme end was eighteen-year-old Ruslan who was severely bullied. Whenever Ruslan stood still, he would plant one foot slightly in front of the other and rock his whole body forward in a twisting motion until his head was almost level with his knees, letting out an audible hiss. Some rocked so fast that sweat formed on their brows and ran into their eyes. Others only did it when they watched television or listened to the radio. Instinctively, I understood it as a sign of severe emotional deprivation; a comfort mechanism to assuage upset or anger. But it was also a way to pass the time. Worn patches in the linoleum marked the most popular rocking spots and, at discos, groups of kids would cluster around the speakers and rock back and forth in a distressing, zombie dance routine.

One of the children I remember most vividly from my first visit was Mikhail, a tall, thin teenage boy with sticking-out ears. Unlike many of the others, he was quiet and reserved; almost a gentlemanly figure. He was fascinated by history, particularly ancient history, and was able to talk at length about the Punic Wars, Roman emperors and Spartan Greece. While he had difficulty reading and writing, he expressed himself through coloured drawings that he stored in a couple of cardboard boxes: whole armies of legionnaires, gladiators and ancient horsemen.

There is a particular moment that sticks in my mind when thinking of Mikhail. It happened during summer camp when we were gathering for morning assembly outside the orphanage, and he was telling me about Roman emperors. I was only half listening amid a scene of chaos – another boy was hanging off my arm, and dozens of other kids milled around, shouting and running. I didn't hear – or didn't understand – what Mikhail was saying, so he knelt on the ground and, with a twig, drew something in the sandy soil. At the time, I was studying history at university and, when I looked down, a half-forgotten class came flooding back. I recognized what Mikhail had drawn as the Chi Rho symbol that Roman Emperor Constantine had his soldiers paint on their shields. Had they been asked, most of my fellow undergraduates would not have been able to draw a Chi Rho symbol. The next moment Mikhail was happily yelling out our group's slogan: 'Who are we? We're pirates!'

The children at the orphanage ranged from young girls aged five or six to muscled teenage boys who would hang around outside and smoke. As well as learning disabilities, many of them had other medical conditions, which – we were told – ranged from cerebral palsy to autism. Some had difficulty walking, a few did not speak and a couple used wheelchairs. They had an odd, sometimes surprising, collection of skills and knowledge. Mikhail was one example, but there were others who could sing, dance or weave. Their extreme isolation and patchy education meant that it was often difficult to establish the truth. Dima Markov, a volunteer at summer camp who went on to become one of Russia's most famous photographers, put it best. 'At the twilight of their consciousness,' he wrote later, 'there was a mix of reality, fantasy and selective memory of the past.'

Everything about the orphanage was highly regulated, from strict daily timetables to the hierarchies among staff and children. The more time I spent there, the more these power structures – complicated but also very simple – revealed themselves. When it came to keeping order, violence underpinned everything.

Initially, lots of children had disabilities that were not serious enough – according to the official classifications – for them to have been placed in this 'type' of orphanage. Likely shunted down the system as a result of bad behaviour, these teenagers, physically stronger and intellectually more able than most of the others, controlled everything and everyone to the point where it was possible to identify a 'king' and 'queen'. The hierarchy was best – and most frustratingly – illustrated by some of the games we tried to play. When kicking around a football, for example, the weaker children would simply pass to the stronger children no matter which side they were on.

I never saw any of the staff physically harm the children, apart from the occasional cuff or flick on the head. But they were careful in front of volunteers, and there was no mistaking what lurked under the surface. How could it be otherwise when so many children spent so many hours crammed into a relatively small space? I came to understand that, rather than inflicting violence themselves, the staff manipulated the older and stronger children to keep order. For example, when Ksenia, an eleven-year-old girl, bit one of the carers, an older girl punched her so hard in the face that a dentist had to extract the remains of her front teeth. For years afterward, a warning to those who knew, Ksenia went around with a black hole in her smile.

Other forms of violence were less obvious, but no less powerful. Misbehaving children, those who ran away or who were difficult to control, were sent to the regional psychiatric hospital, Bogdanovo. Even more sinister was the concoction of pills taken by most children, who queued up after mealtimes outside the nurse's office.

Each child would get a small plastic cup with their pills and, while we had no idea what they were taking (nor did they), we did see the results. Sedation often turned the children into something resembling vegetables. Some would sleep for long periods, others continued to function, albeit in slow motion. I remember one young boy, Sasha, usually hyperactive, who, when sedated, would take an age to do a basic drawing, the drool slipping out of his mouth and dripping onto the paper.

Among the treatments prescribed in Belskoye Ustye was the antipsychotic drug Aminazin (Chlorpromazine in the West), which was discovered in the 1950s and remains widely used. It was impossible to know whether the children were given appropriate amounts of Aminazin, or whether it was overused as a means of control. Adults who have been prescribed Aminazin in Russian psychiatric institutions describe how it turns the whole world grey, draining your will to live and making you want to cry. In the 1970s it was one of the drugs Soviet doctors used on imprisoned dissidents subjected to punitive psychiatry.

More banal, but just as powerful, was the role played by television. There were televisions in almost every room in the orphanage, and they were on most of the time. Like sponges, some of the children absorbed messages about Putin's might, Russia's greatness and nostalgia for the Soviet past – but what they really enjoyed were soap operas. In the 1990s, Russia was flooded with badly dubbed soap operas that became wildly popular. Favourites included the American series *Santa Barbara*, the Brazilian hit *The Clone* and Mexico's *The Rich Also Cry*. Plot twists were a constant topic of discussion not just in the orphanage but also among locals. When I lived in Baranovo for a year, the soap opera of the moment was a Russian series, *Karmelita: Gypsy Passion*, about the love lives and disputes of a group of travellers. The effect on the orphanage children when the *Karmelita* theme music came on was instantaneous and dramatic: they would rush for their chairs, some beginning to rock violently. The characters and plot twists were completely real for them, a different world unfolding on the other side of the screen, and they consciously and unconsciously mimicked what they saw, particularly the caricatured love affairs.

The children who ended up in Belskoye Ustye came from all corners of Pskov Region. While they were referred to as 'orphans', the disturbing fact was that they were actually 'social orphans' – in other words most had living relatives. Either they had been removed from their homes by social services, abandoned or their parents had been persuaded they would have a better life in a well-provisioned state institution. Often the children would tell you about mothers and fathers intending to come and take them home. But fantasies were the rule when it came to this topic, and visiting relatives were rare.

One evening in June 2010 a member of the orphanage staff called me to say that Sasha, the hyperactive boy, had drowned in a pond a dozen metres from the orphanage's walls. Just eleven years old, Sasha was one of the most likeable in his group. Usually dressed in a tweed jacket and floppy sun hat, he insisted on putting everything in his mouth, and could be wickedly mischievous. Nobody knows how he ended up in the water that afternoon: perhaps he had been particularly heavily sedated. When the carers realized what was happening it was already too late. Several of them jumped into the muddy pond, desperately feeling with their feet for bodies. In total, three children were pulled out. One girl was traumatized, but breathing. Another girl had to be resuscitated. Sasha was dead.

In the Orthodox tradition, burials take place within three days of death. So, three days later, I found myself among a small group of people standing outside the Belskoye Ustye cemetery next to the ruins of the Church of the Holy Ascension. I had been in two minds about whether to attend: unsure about whether I would be intruding. But I needn't have worried. In fact, I had taught regular classes for Sasha's group and realized I probably knew him better than many of the others in attendance.

The sky was cloudless, and the trees shimmered in a gentle breeze as the coffin was unloaded and placed on a wooden trestle. The top was folded back to reveal Sasha's head, deformed by stitches from the autopsy, and guttering candles were put on the four corners. A priest and two female singers conducted a brief service. When they were done, we walked in a line, headed by a man carrying the cross, through the cemetery that sloped down to the Shelon River. Sasha was laid to rest at the far end, next to the graves of other orphanage children who had died in accidents or from illness. When the gravedigger finished his work, he pressed the handle of his spade into the freshly turned earth to make the shape of an Orthodox cross.

It was an unbearably sad occasion, and the bleakest part was how mourners conducted themselves. All told, there were about 30 people there: no family members, just an assorted mix of orphanage staff and charity workers. The older men who held the most senior positions in the orphanage were visibly bored, eager to draw a line under the embarrassing affair. A couple of the carers who had worked with Sasha were upset, their faces stained by tears. But nobody laid a comforting hand on anyone's shoulder; there were no hugs.

Why not? Because everyone was at work. There was no family, no blood ties: Sasha was merely one child among many. There were no toasts and no speeches: no one knew enough about Sasha to be able to talk about his personality or character, let alone the arc of his life. Afterwards there was a criminal investigation, and the carers in charge on the day were fired, but the orphanage routines resumed quickly, closing over Sasha as if he had never existed. A few days later, that year's summer camp began.

Despite all the pain, most volunteers got used to the orphanage very quickly. It helped that everyone was young, and that entertaining the kids required concentration and ingenuity, particularly when Russian was not your first language. Intense friendships between volunteers, and between volunteers and children, formed in a matter of days. The children were fascinated by the volunteers, who must have seemed like aliens with their unfamiliar, outlandish clothes, mobile phones and stories of faraway places. Most kids did not understand the idea of different countries, or different languages, and all the volunteers were referred to as 'Muscovites'.

One of the tragedies of institutional life is that it is almost impossible to form deep attachments – staff are hired and fired, and even other residents can be there one day and gone the next. All the children were accustomed to these fleeting relationships, which, among a host of serious consequences, meant that they were adept at begging sweets and presents from visitors; unconsciously and sometimes consciously leveraging their 'orphan' status.

The more time I spent at Belskoye Ustye the more it gave up its secrets. But much remained shrouded in silence, particularly for outsiders. Sex was one of the taboo subjects and, looking back, I find it hard to believe that sexual abuse was not rife. One year, a volunteer friend and I learned that a teenage girl with whom we had worked was pregnant. Counting backwards, my friend realized with horror she had been teaching the girl to do a human pyramid in the early stages of pregnancy.

The orphanage's contradictions also became starker over time. I learned that the per-month cost of looking after a child was an eye-watering amount for rural Pskov Region – far, far higher than any social benefits you could access as the parent of a child with learning disabilities. And I realized that the orphanage employed almost twice the number of staff – from carers and cleaners to accountants, drivers and cooks – as it had children, yet each child was starved of individual attention. In perhaps one of the saddest examples of this attention deficit, all the children with birthdays in a given month were thrown a joint party on the same day.

One particularly surprising discovery was that many locals, particularly parents, were jealous of how the children in the orphanage were treated: from a steady trickle of presents – charitable donations – to visits from volunteers, and access to facilities like a hairdresser and dental care. There was a widespread belief that the orphanage children should not be 'spoilt' by education but taught 'useful' skills like how to work the land.

Often the reaction of inexperienced volunteers to encountering the orphanage was bafflement: why hadn't this place been shut down and the kids transferred to family-based care? It seemed so obvious. This was also my reaction. I still believe any change needs to be focused on this goal, but I now also understand the power of the forces shoring up the status quo. Not only was the orphanage a keystone of the local economy, it was only a tiny part of an enormous system of state institutions warehousing children from the Baltic Sea to the Pacific Ocean. The chances of it ever being shut down are minuscule.

The village of Belskoye Ustye has long contained a large institution. Before 1917, it was home to an estate owned by a gentry family whose male members enjoyed undistinguished careers in the tsarist military and civil service. As well as a country house, the estate's ensemble included stone storage buildings, a tennis court, ponds, a park extending down the bluffs of the Shelon and the Church of the Holy Ascension. The running and upkeep of the estate provided work for dozens of villagers. A photograph from before it was burnt to the ground in the Russian Revolution shows a two-storey building, not unlike the orphanage in size, with large windows and a balcony.

Today, you can still make out traces of the estate's park, including the lines of oak trees extending toward the Shelon from one side of the orphanage. The sunken tennis court where aristocrats once wiled away summer afternoons now has old tractor tyres buried in the earth for kids to play leap-frog.

It didn't take me long to understand how important the orphanage was to the battered local economy. Nikolai from Baranovo recounted how his nightwatchman shifts in the 1990s had been a financial lifeline for himself and Nina. There were also lots of women living in Belskoye Ustye and the surrounding villages who worked there as cleaners and carers. Monthly salaries were a rare commodity in a place where public facilities – schools, libraries and post offices – had been shut down, farming was in the doldrums, and most people survived on state pensions or benefits. There were also other hidden perks: it was not unknown, for example, to see orphanage children helping staff who lived nearby with weeding, or other household chores.

Nor does the orphanage exist in a vacuum. It is part of a huge system of similar state institutions all over Russia. Most of those who grew up in Belskoye Ustye when I first volunteered there were far too institutionalized – illiterate, unable to cook or take care of themselves – to have any chance of living independently, or even quasi-independently. When they turned eighteen, they were dispatched to places known as 'adult institutions' where they would spend the rest of their lives. Even if they managed to escape the system, the outlook was bleak. There were no statistics, but anecdotal evidence suggested they would end up addicted to alcohol or drugs; in prison; or headed for an early grave.

There was no farewell ceremony for children when they left the orphanage for one of these adult institutions. Everything was designed to minimize disruption and – as leaving was a moment when feelings were liable to run high – it was carefully managed. In the case of Vera, a young woman whose last days at the orphanage I witnessed, she understood she would soon be on her way to a new home – not least because she was unexpectedly taken shopping in the local town, returning with a holdall of new clothes. But the exact day of departure was not settled until the last moment and, like most of the staff and children, I never got to say goodbye. One day when I turned up for a class, she was simply gone. She'd been whisked away early that morning, and driven the two hours to an adult institution. Just like after Sasha's death, the hole created by Vera's departure quickly closed: her favourite clothes redistributed among the other children and her name removed from the dormitory door.

Among volunteers, it was common to make the orphanage administration into bogeymen. But this was usually unfair. Over the years, I got to know some of the men and women who ran the orphanage, and I slowly realized that they looked at things very differently to volunteers like me. For them, the priority was keeping the children alive: fed, clothed and warm in winter. As civil servants, they were skilled in keeping their bosses in Pskov on side, and finding resources to maintain buildings, run buses, service boilers and ensure food on plates. While most of them were not, in my experience, unkind, they had little knowledge about the complex needs of those with severe learning disabilities. The director of the orphanage when I first arrived was a jocular man with a mouthful of gold teeth who had a background in the metals industry. A few years later, he was replaced by a bustling and efficient woman from St Petersburg whose career had been in the hospitality sector.

Most of the orphanage staff were deeply wary of me and other volunteers. At best, volunteers were quietly tolerated; at worst, staff waged a low-intensity campaign of obstruction. Their hostility was easy to understand: most volunteers were inexperienced, condescending, quick to judge and inclined to righteousness. We spent only a few hours a day with the children and saw only a part of the picture. However, this hostility could manifest itself in dangerous ways. The powerful orphanage rumour mill could be set abuzz with the 'news' that one or another volunteer was a paedophile, or planning to steal children to harvest their organs. Snitching was common. The presence of foreigners always aroused particular suspicion and, one year, the local head of the FSB dispatched a state TV crew with a list of pre-approved questions to summer camp. Later the same day, two police officers turned up to find out who exactly was volunteering. We took it as an informal warning.

At the same time, the orphanage staff – whether they knew it or not – had impossible jobs. The system made it so. They had no way to provide the children with what they needed; not even close. Many had no formal training in how to work with young people with learning disabilities, and as the children were almost always in groups, it meant all their time and energy was spent on discipline. Is it better to let a child self-injure, or temporarily tie them up? Is it better to manhandle children than allow them to smash up valuable equipment? These were the sort of daily choices (albeit false choices) faced by staff. Those who invested too much of themselves inevitably ended up hurt, upset or resentful – or a toxic combination of all three.

The staff closest to the children were the carers who supervised groups (mostly containing between five and fifteen children). These women – they were almost all women – were typically overweight and middle-aged, and worked a twenty-four-hour shift one day in three. They were the closest thing the children had to parents and sometimes formed close attachments (there were some cases when they tried to adopt children). But they also circulated through different groups and many – to conserve their emotional resources – maintained a distance. I witnessed once or twice how local carers on their days off would hurry past 'their group' if they encountered them in the village, barely saying hello.

Of course, there were cruel or vindictive carers. But most were kind – albeit indifferent, disengaged and exhausted by a job they couldn't afford to leave. Against all the odds, there were always a few who were young enough, resilient enough or gifted with enough intuition to be empathetic and fun. Inevitably, they were adored by volunteers and children alike.

Over more than a decade of travelling to the orphanage and working for a children's charity in Moscow, my attitude toward the orphanage slowly evolved. Like most of the other volunteers, I was naïve at first, with little understanding of the broader issues, and the risks. When one British social-care expert, a friend of a friend, told me he believed categorically that any cooperation with orphanages was morally wrong, it brought me up short, embarrassed at how I was out of my depth. Family-based care, he argued, was the solution, and any venture – be it a summer camp or a children's village – was only entrenching a system that needed to be destroyed. I told myself that his position was a terrible abandonment of the tens of thousands already trapped within that very system, as well as a misunderstanding of how reform comes about. But it was hard to dispute the logic.

I gradually came to see summer camp as a sort of 'carnival' in which rules could be broken, timetables upended and traditions tested: a breath of fresh air for the children; a glimpse of different ways of thinking for staff; and a potentially life-changing experience for volunteers. But the longer it went on, the more it became a part of the furniture; just another addendum to the system it was supposed to subvert.

In the first few years when I volunteered, little money had trickled down to places like Belskoye Ustye despite Russia's oil-fuelled economic boom of the 2000s. But this gradually changed as the state got wealthier, standards of living rose in major cities, and a culture of charities, donations and volunteering became more mainstream. An enterprising and ambitious director – the one who had come from the hospitality sector – did much to unlock funding. Gradually, the children got new clothes, the orphanage buildings were repaired, the iron grilles on corridors were taken down, the once common smell of urine faded, and welcome additions like wheelchair lifts and a kitchen for the teenagers were installed. Kids were allowed to choose their own haircuts, and given a bit more personal space. The charity that organized the summer camp even won a grant from UEFA to build an Astroturf football pitch on the floodplain below the orphanage.

These days, the dormitories are smaller, and there is none of the once ubiquitous rocking. Violence is less common. Some of the children are still sent to adult institutions when they turn eighteen, but this is the exception rather than the rule. Instead, the director has overseen the construction of two houses in a nearby village where older children are transferred. Here, they can attend workshops to learn skills like carpentry, or are given manual jobs in the orphanage kitchens, or as cleaners. They spend the rest of their time looking after enormous vegetable gardens, cooking, cleaning and, of course, watching television.

At the same time, the money has done nothing to change the essence of the orphanage, which remains implacably true to itself in the face of big grants, small improvements by staff and edicts from Moscow. The orphanage is still a part of a largely unreformed system. And the children are still deprived of the individual attention that they all need. If one of them were to die, his or her funeral would be better funded, perhaps better attended, but just as heart-breaking as Sasha's on that sunny afternoon.

9

Ward No. 6

At the Belskoye Ustye orphanage, one of the most terrifying words you could hear was 'Bogdanovo'. Carers would scare children with being sent to Bogdanovo as punishment, and kids would repeat the threat to one another. Conversations about Bogdanovo tended to be whispered: it was a destination that inspired dread, and a frisson of ghoulish excitement. During staff meetings, I witnessed carers trying to persuade managers to dispatch unruly children to Bogdanovo to get them off their hands. And when teenagers returned from Bogdanovo, they often seemed more adult.

Bogdanovo is the nearest psychiatric hospital to the orphanage, one of two in Pskov Region, and the kids at Belskoye Ustye fell under the remit of its medical staff. Of course, being sent there was supposed to be for treatment. But it was seen among the orphanage children and staff as a punishment; perhaps one of the most feared punishments because so much about the place was unknown.

For me, too, Bogdanovo was somewhat mythical. If I had been asked to point to it on a map, I would have been at a loss. But in early 2023, I asked the photographer Dima Markov whether he could introduce me to Alexander Moskalyov, a psychiatrist at Bogdanovo who had been treating orphanage children for decades.

Dima had worked extensively with the orphanage after the 2007 summer camp, and when we spoke about Moskalyov, it was clear Dima saw him as one of the 'good guys' – an enlightened figure who understood the effect of institutional living on children, and recognized the advantages of children's villages or sheltered accommodation. Dima recounted how Moskalyov told him that, when he was appointed, Bogdanovo was full of patients running around naked, or tied up. 'He said straightaway that there should be no more violence. And he has struggled against it [ever since],' said Dima. At the same time, of course, Moskalyov was obviously also a man of the system.

When I found out that Moskalyov was in charge of Ward No. 6 at Bogdanovo, it immediately rang a bell. 'Ward No. 6' is also the title of a Chekhov short story. I remembered it had been one of the books I had read one summer while volunteering at the orphanage.

In fact, 'Ward No. 6' is one of Chekhov's best-known short stories. In it, he takes the reader inside the psychiatric ward of a squalid provincial hospital in the Russian Empire at the turn of the century. Disturbing and damning, 'Ward No. 6' is a dissection of everyday violence explored through a philosophical clash between the educated Dr Ragin, who believes in the transcendental power of suffering, and his patient, Ivan Gromov, a long-term Ward No. 6 resident, who is only too familiar with the lived reality of pain. In the end, Ragin, who spends more and more time in conversation with Gromov as the story unfolds, is committed to his own psychiatric ward. As he is beaten up by an orderly, he recognizes the bankruptcy of his world view.

When it was published in 1892, 'Ward No. 6' caused a sensation. Perhaps inevitably, it was taken as a metaphor for Russia as a whole. Not only was Chekhov's Ward No. 6 a place of violence; it was a place to which anyone could find themselves committed through little fault of their own. Those in charge, like those ruling Russia, had little understanding or empathy for the privations and humiliation suffered by inmates. The writer Nikolai Leskov, a contemporary of Chekhov's, wrote that: '*Ward No. 6* depicts our general character and customs in miniature. *Ward No. 6* is everywhere. It's Russia . . .'

Just like the orphanage, Bogdanovo was eerily quiet from the outside when I arrived to meet Moskalyov on a Monday morning.

It was a beautiful winter's day with an azure sky and the sun reflected dazzlingly off a part-thawed blanket of white snow. The limits of the hospital and its grounds were marked by concrete blocks topped with coiled barbed wire, and there were half a dozen cars outside. It was surrounded on three sides by pine forest.

The buildings were not dilapidated, but there were advertisements for next-day loans pinned up on the bus stop by the gates and, even in the sunlight, a quiet melancholy hung in the air. I was reminded of Chekhov's description of Ward No. 6, which was located deep in the countryside: 'The rear looks out on to open country, from which it is cut off by the grey hospital fence topped by nails. These nails, with their points sticking upwards, the fence and the building itself have that mournful, god-forsaken look that you find only in our hospitals and prisons.'

I was early for the interview, and stood outside for a while, observing the vehicles driving through the red, corrugated-iron gates. I tried to imagine what it would be like to arrive here – as the orphanage children did – after a two-hour journey in the back of the orphanage's *bukhanka*, a type of dumpy green van with benches instead of seats. Some kids stayed at Bogdanovo for a few weeks; others for months on end. As midday approached, I went inside, and a security guard behind a glass pane entered my details into a ledger. He handed me a handwritten pass on yellowing paper. I would find Ward No. 6, he said, by skirting the main building, and cutting diagonally across the courtyard.

There has been a psychiatric hospital in Bogdanovo for decades. But in 1985 the old cottage hospital with its stove-heating and intermittent water supply was demolished, and a new facility built in its place. The changes were part of a broader restructuring of psychiatric care in which the region's six psychiatric hospitals were replaced by two giant institutions. Like the orphanage and many other public buildings, the new hospital was constructed out of cheap, ash-grey bricks. It can hold up to 500 patients at a time.

Walking toward the main building, I passed a wooden church with two elegant, tapering cupolas. Put up in the 1990s, it was named after Saint Panteleimon, a fourth-century healer martyred by the Romans. Later, I discovered that the church had been the initiative of a local priest, Father Adelgeim, whose reputation as a dissident reached far beyond Pskov Region. Adelgeim lost a leg in a Soviet prison camp and, decades later, as a parish priest in Pskov with a flowing white beard and beatific eyes, became a critic of the Orthodox Church's overly familiar relationship with the Kremlin. In 2013, he was stabbed to death by a man reportedly suffering from paranoid schizophrenia.

After some searching, I found Ward No. 6 on the second floor, up a flight of stairs with metal grates stretched between the bannisters. I rang a bell to gain entrance, and the door was opened by a bustling female orderly in a white coat, who ushered me inside. Sitting behind a desk strewn with case files and a brown phial of liquid, Moskalyov had thinning, mousy hair and seemed long ago to have stopped caring about his appearance. His face was kindly and he chuckled warmly, but his demeanour suggested he could also be uncompromising.

Just as Dima had said, Moskalyov was categorical about the harm that large institutions inflict on young people. 'An institution is a measure of last resort,' he said with a shrug, as if stating the obvious. He argued that orphanages should be as small as possible, and structured around family-type units. 'Good institutions are always small institutions. And that means you need to train staff. The most important thing is always the employees.'

At Bogdanovo, Moskalyov was in charge of all the adult males – defined as anyone older than fifteen – and he has seen hundreds of young men from Belskoye Ustye over the years. There are 57 beds in his ward, of which he said two or three were usually occupied by Belskoye Ustye patients. They get sent to Bogdanovo because of acute psychiatric problems or aggressive behaviour, self-harm, escape attempts, alcohol consumption and drug use. 'They come here to be cured of their condition and then returned to their place of residence in Belskoye Ustye,' he said.

As we spoke, two phones – a landline and a mobile – lay on the desk, and Moskalyov answered calls about every fifteen minutes.

One call was from someone enquiring about documents, another concerned a sectioned soldier. Moskalyov's gentle efficiency and practicality put him a long way from Chekhov's Dr Ragin, who was negligent and callous to the point of cruelty. Nor did Moskalyov ever seem to be left alone for long: a heavily coiffured nurse came in several times, leaving papers on his desk or filing them away in a large cupboard. After answering one call, Moskalyov made his apologies and left to deal with an emergency admission. As he stood up, I saw his large beer belly, which gave his body the shape of an inside-out hourglass.

Waiting in the hall for him to return, the sunlight streaming through the dusty windows, I couldn't help notice how similar the decor of the hospital was to the orphanage. There were the same sturdy brown plastic doors; the same gauzy white lace curtains; the same cheap benches with red plastic coverings; the same colour scheme in the stairwell (dark green to hide scuff marks, white above head height); the same smells and the same atmosphere. I felt like I didn't need to go into one of the wards to see what they looked like – or visit the canteen to see what the patients were fed. Years spent volunteering at the orphanage meant I already knew.

One aspect of institutional living often difficult for visitors to comprehend is the boredom. Perhaps understandably, it rarely occurs to those who come and go how dreary life can get in places that are designed to contain, not to stimulate or excite. Chekhov, however, described it vividly in 'Ward No. 6':

> Probably nowhere else in the world is life so boring as in this building. Every morning the patients – with the exception of the paralytic and the fat peasant – go into the lobby, where they wash themselves from a large tub and dry themselves on the skirts of their smocks. Then they drink tea from tin mugs which Nikita brings from the main block. Each patient gets one mugful. At noon they have sour cabbage soup and porridge; in the evening they have the porridge left over from lunch. Between meals they lie down, sleep, look out of the window and pace from corner to corner. And so it goes on day after day.

Of course, Bogdanovo's psychiatric hospital and the Belskoye Ustye orphanage are extreme examples of Russian institutions. But there is a common thread running through all such places, which include the country's sprawling armed forces, prisons and care homes. Millions of Russians have passed through at least one such place. Inside all these institutions, the boundaries between sleep, play and work are broken down. Everywhere, there are the same rhythms and the same hierarchies; the same meals of buckwheat, sweet tea and baked cottage-cheese pies; the same lurking violence; the same premium on evasion and survival; the same helplessness in the face of arbitrarily exercised power.

When he returned, Moskalyov told me how he ended up in Pskov Region. It was not a decision he'd made through choice: he was sent here as a result of the Soviet system that dispatched medical graduates to work in far-flung towns and villages. On completing his medical degree in Leningrad in 1986, he was ordered to take up a job in Bogdanovo. Initially, he said he felt trapped in this provincial backwater, and wanted to return to friends and family. But after a few years he got used to it, and ended up settling in Pskov. He has been in charge of the adult male ward for over twenty years.

Having spent his entire professional life in Bogdanovo, it is hard to imagine someone more invested in Russia's sprawling institutions than Moskalyov. And, while he was clear-eyed about the terrible effects of institutional living on children with learning disabilities, like those in Belskoye Ustye, he certainly did not think that Russia should disband its institutions. He was no revolutionary. He believed institutions had an important role to play in the care of the country's most vulnerable people.

Many, if not most, of Moskalyov's patients come from the 'adult institutions' where children raised in Belskoye Ustye were once routinely sent when they turned eighteen. These facilities serve a function somewhere between a prison, care home and a secure unit, and are used to house people, usually with mental illnesses or learning disabilities, who are unable to live independently. Some have grown up in orphanages like Belskoye Ustye, but residents include a whole spectrum of adults from the chronically ill to frail elderly people with no money and no family support. The vast majority of those consigned to such places will never leave.

The makers of a 2009 film adaptation of Chekhov's 'Ward No. 6' chose to set the action in a real adult institution housed in an old monastery outside Moscow, and many of the scenes featured patients alongside actors. Across Russia, there are estimated to be almost 180,000 people living in 523 adult institutions. In Pskov Region, there are nine such places. Activists seeking to reform the system describe it as a 'modern gulag' where 'death comes before life ends'.

Moskalyov was far more measured. He argued that some of the children leaving Belskoye Ustye are better off in adult institutions, particularly if the alternative is living in one of Pskov Region's dying villages where there are few opportunities for work, and the temptations of alcohol impossible to resist. 'If there is drunkenness all around them, they lose their humanity,' he said. 'If they get drunk all the time, their intellectual capabilities deteriorate and their characters are spoiled. It's a pity when they lose their humanity. In such cases, an institution is better.'

As we spoke, I realized we had very different views of the Belskoye Ustye orphanage. Whereas I saw an institution that should be broken up in favour of family-based care, Moskalyov did not think anything of the sort. For him, the orphanage was part of a Soviet system of care for disabled children that had been designed to bring jobs, employment and well-trained staff to remote parts of the country, creating local hubs. Those with mental illnesses or learning disabilities may have been isolated by this system, but they were looked after by trained professionals. At least that was the aspiration. While he didn't say it out loud, Moskalyov's implication was that this Soviet model of care was the one that Russia should be trying to resurrect. For him, the problems with the current system were a consequence of neglect and under-funding – not fundamental flaws.

Moskalyov pointed out that there was a facility for children with speech impediments in Porkhov, the nearest town to Belskoye Ustye, and a similar set-up for deaf children in Pytalovo. 'Today the population is smaller and there are fewer specialists. But back then Porkhov was a developed town when it came to the study of disabilities,' he said, pointing out that patients also came from nearby Estonia and Latvia. 'I wouldn't say it was in the middle of nowhere. Although it has turned out like that now.'

The early part of Moskalyov's career coincided with the final years of the Soviet Union and the turmoil of the 1990s, which saw a massive collapse in healthcare funding. Perhaps as a result, he appeared to combine a Soviet outlook with a visceral appreciation of the relative prosperity of the Putin era. He made snide jibes about Western practices when it came to mental health, and was keen to stress the 'civilizational' differences between how Russia treats its mentally ill, and how they are looked after in Europe and America.

Even before the Russian Revolution, Russia's approach to the mentally ill was very different, Moskalyov told me. 'Russia has always had humanized psychiatric hospitals,' he said. 'Unlike Western Europe, we didn't have bedlams . . . the attitude toward patients was always as victims, not as people guilty of something.' It's true that the Russian word for a lunatic, or an insane person, is *dushevnobolniy* – literally, the 'sick of soul'.

As he spoke, I recalled a conversation I'd had in 2009 with the psychologist in the Belskoye Ustye orphanage, who had lamented the loss of pre-revolutionary practices. Back then, she said, the disabled were often seen as 'holy fools', whose behaviour was shocking or unconventional, and who were prized in Eastern Orthodox ascetic traditions. 'In Russian, there is a very interesting word "ubogiy" – "person of God" – meaning he is of God, from God,' she told me. 'We're given these people because they show us the value of our own lives.'

In particular, Moskalyov lamented the mass closure of asylums in the West in the 1960s and 1970s that was the result of a shift in thinking about the effectiveness of institutions, as well as the appearance of powerful anti-psychotic drugs that allowed, at least in theory, care to take place in the community. He pointed out that these closures, which had no parallel on the other side of the Iron Curtain, left thousands of vulnerable people on the streets.

For Moskalyov, the end of the Soviet Union was a tragedy, and nostalgia seemed to inform much of what he said. This was particularly striking when I asked whether he had seen a rise in drug-related admissions during his time at Bogdanovo. In his answer, he linked the appearance of what he ironically referred to as 'Western democracy' in Russia with an explosion of drug use. Of course, the heroin that flooded into Russia after the fall of the Soviet Union came from Afghanistan, not the West. But he blamed the Western values that triumphed over Communism. 'When Western democracy arrived it arrived along with drugs,' he said, pausing for a moment to chuckle at what he knew was, at the very least, a reductive comparison. 'And this problem hasn't left us.' It wasn't obvious whether he meant democracy, or drugs.

Moskalyov was a firm supporter of Russia's war in Ukraine. Without any prompting, he brought up a rumour rife in Pskov at the time: Bogdanovo was apparently full of Russian soldiers who had gone mad after torture or castration at the hands of the Ukrainian army. The rumour had seemed ridiculous to me when I heard it in Pskov a few days earlier – the sole evidence of wartime castration at that point was videos of Russian soldiers inflicting it on Ukrainian prisoners, and it seemed a fairly transparent retrospective justification. Moskalyov denied the rumour outright. But his denial was less a healthy disregard for propaganda, more an echo of Kremlin narratives designed to maintain a facade of normalcy. 'It's completely untrue,' he said. 'I only have one patient from the war zone. And he's as fit as a fiddle.'

The more Moskalyov and I spoke, the more ridiculous it seemed to draw any parallels between the doctor in front of me and Chekhov's Dr Ragin. At one point Ragin tells Gromov: 'So long as prisons and madhouses exist someone must be shut up in them. If not you, I. If not I, some third person.' There was no chance of Moskalyov indulging in such relativism.

In the final scene of Chekhov's masterpiece, Ragin, now incarcerated in the ward he once ran, demands his release, for which the orderly, a large-handed ex-soldier called Nikita, gives him a vicious beating. Of course, Ragin knew Nikita was violent with patients, but being on the receiving end is a revelation; turning his whole philosophy about the moral equivalence of patient and doctor on its head. 'Through the chaos in his brain there flashed the terrible unbearable thought that these people, who seemed now like black shadows in the moonlight, had to endure such pain day by day for years,' Chekhov wrote.

Throughout our conversation, Moskalyov was guarded. But he seemed to relax a bit toward the end as I asked about the social problems behind admissions. Did the hospital hold a mirror up to Pskov Region as a whole? A 'typical' Bogdanovo patient, Moskalyov replied, does not differ much from a typical psychiatric patient the world over – adult men suffering from schizophrenia, delirium and hallucinations. Although, he conceded that the Pskov Region patient profile did reflect local levels of poverty, alcoholism and depopulation.

Having one of the oldest populations in Russia means Pskov Region generates a lot of elderly patients. 'Diseases accumulate with age,' said Moskalyov. 'On top of that you get the appearance of diseases particular to old age – often linked with dementia or psychoses of the elderly, like schizophrenia. And some have lost their close relatives by this point. Some have lost their children. Some have lost their wives. And they are left all alone.'

Moskalyov also painted a grim picture of the scourge of alcoholism. The most common diagnosis on admission to Bogdanovo, according to Moskalyov, is acute alcohol-withdrawal syndrome, or delirium tremens (the Russian term is *belaya goryachka* – literally 'white fever'). This usually arises after an alcoholic emerges from a drinking bout: in its milder form, it leads to aggression, vomiting and seizures; in more serious forms, it results in hallucinations and death. 'They start experiencing hallucinations, problems with perception, scary visions or noises from which they need to save themselves,' said Moskalyov. 'In a state of terror caused by delirium tremens, one of my patients even climbed to the top of a crane on a building-site.'

Tales of hair-raising brutality fuelled by binge-drinking and delirium tremens are easy to find if you trawl through local news. One site published an article in 2020 about 13-year prison sentences handed to two men from Porkhov who committed a murder reminiscent of *Crime and Punishment*. According to the report, the men got drunk, broke into the flat of a ninety-one-year-old woman and beat her to death to steal goods worth £36. A year earlier in Pskov, media reports detailed how a sambo expert, Ivan Mikhailov, broke the back of a female drinking partner after they consumed a bottle of vodka together. He then stabbed her 22 times, and buried her body in woods near the city. In court, Mikhailov stated that the victim, Lidiya Yegorova, started the violence by attacking him with a knife – he claimed she was suffering from delirium tremens.

For alcoholics who drink so much that they end up with delirium tremens, the outlook is not good. More often than not, their addiction has gone too far. 'Most of those with delirium tremens are discharged, but, unfortunately this doesn't frighten them. They start drinking again,' said Moskalyov.

Through most of our conversation, Moskalyov peppered his answers with technical medical terms. But when talking about what ultimately happens to sufferers of delirium tremens he allowed himself to use more colloquial language. Perhaps he was trying to shock; perhaps he wanted to be truthful; perhaps it was just callousness born of experience. It was the only time he allowed himself to allude to some of the horrors of his job.

'It all ends one wonderful day when alcoholic psychosis either kills them or they are confined to their bed, paralyzed with alcoholic neuropathy and brain damage – half the brain has died. They are a chunk of living meat that pisses and shits and sometimes doesn't recognize anyone,' he said.

'Where do they go?' he asked rhetorically, looking me matter-of-factly in the eye. 'To an institution.'

10

Stroganoff Estate

It would have been easy for Olga Grudtsyna to find a job on a local farm after finishing her horse-breeding studies in Kazakhstan. Instead, she yearned to return to Russia's heartlands. She had grown up in Saratov on the lower reaches of the Volga River, and the hot expanses of Central Asia never felt like home. 'I really didn't like it,' she said. 'The steppe is okay, but there are no bushes or trees. It's empty, windy, dusty, and sandy. You clean everything, but then the wind gets up and everything's dusty again. It's a disaster for your hair! I was totally against it. I said I wouldn't live there.'

Horses have always been at the centre of Olga's life. 'I've got horses in my blood,' she told me. 'My grandad looked after the horses at a collective farm and my grandmother was obsessed with horses: she even said she'd marry the man who turned up on the best horse.'

And it was horses that determined where Olga went after Kazakhstan. Specifically, a breed called the Russian Trotter, which is used for harness racing; a breakneck sport in which jockeys sit in low-slung, two-wheeled carts known as sulkies. The most famous stud farm for Russian Trotters in the Soviet Union was Volyshovo, and this name cropped up again and again as Olga toiled over her dissertation, compiling equine bloodlines and trawling through race records. A former tsarist estate, Volyshovo sits at the very heart of Pskov Region, and Olga found herself marvelling at photos of elegant horses amid an ensemble of classical, baroque and art-nouveau buildings. It was a world away from the Kazakh steppe, and she decided it was where she wanted to spend her life.

In its nineteenth-century heyday, the Volyshovo estate was made up of a manor house, stables, ornate dog kennels, a church, cricket pitch, large English gardens, greenhouses and a swimming pool. Hundreds of peasants in the nearby village were employed as craftsmen, servants, gardeners and stable workers: a whole mini-economy. It was made into a luxurious rural retreat by the Stroganoff family, who had made their money as salt producers, and were second only to the ruling Romanov dynasty when it came to wealth.

The magnificent Stroganoff palace in St Petersburg was chosen by the KGB as a headquarters during the Soviet Union, and is now one of Russia's most famous art museums. In the West, the Stroganoffs are best known for the eponymous dish of sautéed beef cooked in sour cream, which was invented by French chefs in their service.

Proximity to the imperial capital of St Petersburg meant Pskov Region was dotted with aristocratic estates. But Volyshovo was by far the most magnificent. The manor house alone boasted more than 40 rooms, and the sumptuous decor included fireplaces of white marble, doors of half-fossilized oak wood extracted from bogs and imported European paintings. An alabaster bust in the entrance hall was decorated with a helmet made from the skull of a lion. Upstairs, the bedrooms looked out over the carefully tended park.

But Volyshovo's real draw was its hunting. Guests had use of several large stables and dog kennels, and would ride out into the surrounding meadows and forests in search of wolf, fox, wild boar and hare. In the 1889 autumn season alone, 279 hares and nine foxes were killed. Schoolteacher and local historian Galina Proskuryakova was a young girl in the early twentieth century and remembered how hunts were an event for the whole village. 'Those who were not taking part themselves attended like an audience at a play,' she wrote in her memoirs. 'After the hunt they used the game to make a hotpot that made its way to villagers. On top of this, everyone was offered gingerbread.'

When Olga landed a job at the local stud farm in 1984, most of these old-world traditions were relics of a distant past, long ago swept away by Communism. Only horse breeding and the estate buildings themselves remained as reminders of the illustrious Stroganoff period. Olga and her husband moved to Volyshovo in the middle of a cold winter, and she recalled it looking like a Russian fairy tale when they arrived. 'Everything was covered in snow, and the snow was sparkling, amazingly white. You can imagine my feelings after Kazakhstan. These houses, the estate – everything was in white,' she said.

For the stud farm where Olga soon began working, these were years of plenty. Decades of careful breeding meant Volyshovo's horses were highly prized. 'It was the best stud farm in Russia for the Russian Trotter,' said Olga with pride. 'Every year, horses were sent abroad to the Berlin hippodrome, the Venetian hippodrome . . . There was a phenomenal mare-breeding stock.' Admittedly, the ravages of age and neglect were showing on the estate itself, but almost every building was in daily use. The manor house was a school, the stud farm had the stables, and the church served as a social club with a stage for plays and concerts. The Stroganoff menagerie, where curiosities like bears were once kept for the amusement of visiting aristocrats, had been transformed into a small factory to treat Arctic fox furs produced by the local collective farm. On her arrival, Olga was put up in another Stroganoff stable that had been converted into flats.

When I went to Volyshovo to meet Olga it was a cold, damp morning in mid-March 2020, with low, leaden skies. She had instructed me to come and find her at the stables where she keeps horses for her riding school. The tsarist-era building was half-derelict, but you could make out the large gates once used by Stroganoff carriages. Inside, the floor was cobbled and the horses stood quietly behind the iron bars of their stall doors. Olga turned out to be a short woman in her early sixties wearing a faded white jacket and mud-encrusted boots. Her face was deeply lined, but she gave off an air of cheerful candour, and was disarmingly matter-of-fact. Brushing aside my introductions, she launched into tales of the estate, its people and her beloved horses. We set off to walk around the village. It wasn't so much a conversation as a monologue: a steady stream of anecdotes and stories, with a hand thrown out occasionally to warn me to watch my step or direct my attention to a specific building, a particular view.

The first place we ventured into was a beautiful square marked out by a sandy earth road. At one end was the manor house, a two-storey, U-shaped building modelled on a French château. Most of the plasterwork was missing, leaving exposed red brick. The main door, with Corinthian columns either side, was topped by three circular windows and a space for the family crest. Facing it at the other end of the square were the English Stables with striped red and white brick columns and two cast-iron horse heads on the walls. In the centre of the square was an ornate dovecote, and the two sides included a church, offices, kitchens and a Gothic house for the estate manager.

All but one of these magnificent buildings was empty. In the forty years since Olga arrived in Volyshovo, the estate has become a picturesque ruin, gradually abandoned and looted. Most people in Volyshovo now live in a cluster of wooden houses and low, grey-brick apartment blocks that stretch in the direction of the main road. As we stood there, I was struck by the quiet. Apart from Olga's voice, the only sound was the occasional rumble of distant farm machinery.

The more or less intact facades meant it was easy to picture how the estate might once have looked: the graceful architecture a stage for chattering peasants, carriages and whickering horses. In winter, there would have been sleigh tracks on the packed snow and smoke rising from the manor house's wood-burning stoves. On hunt mornings, pandemonium with baying packs of borzoi hounds, and guests saddling up on Arab chargers. But now it was a ghost town. Suddenly, a chunk of plaster fell off a building in front of us and shattered on the ground. We both started. The extent of the damage became starker the closer you looked: the former kitchens were nothing more than a mound of rubble, while all that remained of the estate manager's house were cracked exterior walls. Amid the stillness of that March morning, the sense of melancholy was overwhelming.

Most poignant of all was the manor house. The first time I visited Volyshovo, in 2007, the majestic old residence had been locked and boarded up: dilapidated, but intact. In the intervening years, it was gutted by a fire that destroyed walls, ceilings and original parquet floors, apparently started by a fifteen-year-old boy who snuck in late one night and tossed away a cigarette butt. Now, the manor house was open to all comers, its roof largely burnt away and its exposed chimneys poking upward like teeth. As Olga guided me into the ruins of the cavernous entrance hall, we were greeted by the sight of the grand marble staircase, imported from Italy in the 1890s, chipped, blackened and covered in fallen masonry. Shattered pieces of stucco littered the uneven floors of the rooms. I bent down to pick up the remains of one artfully twisted flower, once part of the ceiling's ornate crown moulding, and its leaves disintegrated in my hands. The sound of dripping water came from all directions and there was a distinct sense the whole structure could collapse at any moment. We didn't linger.

Volyshovo's sorry state is not an exception. Across Pskov Region, you find tsarist-era ruins in secluded woods, fields, or, incongruously, the middle of villages. Within twenty kilometres of Volyshovo, there are at least a dozen such places: Krasnie Gorki with its manor house and collapsing church; Vyaze's crumbling stately home and park; Aleksandrov's abandoned nineteenth-century hospital; the derelict church overlooking a lake in Goromulino; lost foundations in Krasniy Bor; estate outhouses in Polonoe and Dirini Gorki; and the fractured remains of ornamental parks in Belskoye Ustye and Zaozerye. These teetering church towers and gutted manor houses are fragments of a lost world, eating away at the communities still clustered around them.

They are also a direct link to the culture that provides the backdrop to nineteenth-century Russian novels, from Turgenev to Tolstoy. The estates that survived the violence of the Russian Revolution and the dispossession of the aristocracy were repackaged by the Soviets as hospitals, schools, sanatoria and warehouses, or abandoned entirely. After the end of the Soviet Union, a few were converted into hotels or private residences, but most were left to rot. Travelling through Pskov Region, I became adept at spotting traces of this former grandeur: a line of specially planted oak trees here, a section of crumbling wall there.

By the time the Soviet authorities took control of Volyshovo after the Revolution, there were few movable items left. Some had been stolen, some trashed, while others found their way to museums or into private hands. The manor house was turned into a college, then a school. Despite being requisitioned by the Nazis as a military headquarters it was miraculously unscathed by World War II.

When the travel writer and Arctic explorer Vladimir Sanin passed through in the 1960s, the manor house was serving as summer accommodation for children from Soviet youth organizations. He was struck by the neglect, noticing how cupboards had been nailed to parquet floors. 'Even covered in a layer of cheap whitewash it's difficult to tear your eyes away from the wonderful sculptures on the walls and ceilings,' he wrote. Sanin's guide, a local chemistry teacher, bristled when challenged about the state of the place. 'Do you think our own hearts don't bleed?' he responded to a mild rebuke. 'But where is a simple village school supposed to get the money for restoration?'

When Olga arrived in Volyshovo, the estate buildings were still intact and used as flats, offices and farm buildings. She remembers those early years as a uniquely happy time: she was young, had her dream job and Volyshovo's horses were at the height of their fame. But it wasn't to last. The estate would soon be almost totally deserted, locked into a vicious spiral of disintegration and decay.

Even as Olga settled into life in Volyshovo, events in Moscow were moving at a breakneck pace. Olga is far from being a Communist – then or now – but she defines the course of her life by the tumultuous events of 1991 when the Soviet Union entered its death throes. 'Everything was fantastic until 1991 when everything fell apart,'

she said. As the centrally managed system was broken up, supply chains went haywire, and subsidies were withdrawn. Millions were impoverished and left to fend for themselves, an abandonment that has not been forgotten or forgiven. 'Live how you want – that was the spirit of the times,' said Olga. In Volyshovo, the stud farm spun toward bankruptcy.

Amid the upheaval there was no time to worry about the estate buildings, which began to disintegrate. In an essay written many years later a Pskov intellectual, Yuli Seliverstov, declared it a horrible irony that Volyshovo survived the violence and looting of 1917 only to be destroyed in the country's second revolution of the century. 'Volyshovo was terribly unlucky,' he lamented.

In the late 1980s, locals moved out of the estate buildings and into new housing with running water. Watchmen were laid off, and money for upkeep dried up. Slowly at first, then with increasing speed, people helped themselves to anything of value from the empty buildings: window frames, doors, tiles, stoves, even bricks. Cast-iron railings were torn out and sold for scrap and the ornamental heads of a wild boar and a wolf, symbols of Volyshovo's hunting traditions, were prised off the English Stables. One night a small crane even tried to rip two iconic griffon statues from their pedestals flanking the entrance to the manor house. A timely call to the police stopped the would-be thieves – but officers later returned to collect the statues themselves. To this day, the griffons stand guard outside Porkhov's police station.

The arrival of capitalism brought Volyshovo's stud farm to the brink of ruin. Across the country, state-owned racetracks went under, and the demand for horses fell off a cliff. With no revenue, the stud farm cut livestock numbers and began a desperate search for other sources of income. A new director elected in 1990 under rules introduced by Gorbachev turned out to be a heavy drinker.

Olga described the atmosphere as a 'war of the worlds' in which managers had few good choices and employees grabbed what they could. One day she and her husband accosted the director. 'What are you doing? This is gold,' they told him, gesturing at the horses. 'Don't you see you'll destroy it all? It's taken people decades to put it together, and you'll run it into the ground in two or three years.' Their pleas fell on deaf ears. In truth, there was probably little the director could have done. Olga and her husband quit the stud farm and set up on their own. As they forged a new life, they watched with horror how the remaining horses were treated – barely fed and confined to the stables. 'It was a catastrophe,' said Olga. 'Like some sort of Buchenwald. When I went to have a look, my heart stopped. How could you do that to horses? It was impossible . . .' She trailed off, shaking her head.

Against all the odds, though, the stud farm is still going. Olga arranged for me to see Lyudmila Yakovleva, its chief vet, who has been employed there for over 40 years and also bore witness to the estate's long decay. We met early the next morning in a building once used by the Stroganoff estate managers. The stairwell was unlit, and I was directed to Lyudmila's shared office through a cramped room occupied by a friendly dog. Severe-looking, with glasses and permed, rust-red hair, Lyudmila was sitting behind her desk when I entered, and she stayed there until the end of our conversation. She watched me closely as she spoke. Horse-breeding is a loss-making business and they only have 100 horses (down from more than 600 in Soviet times), she told me, so the stud farm makes money selling milk and meat from their 800 head of cattle. Gone is the thrill of racetracks and derby winners: all the foals are sold on the cheap to amateur riders. Indeed, the only reason to keep horses at all is out of deference to tradition.

Lyudmila's manner was clipped and formal, but she became more animated the longer we spoke. It was clear she was deeply hurt by Volyshovo's abandonment. Just like Olga, her working life has spanned the decline of the once beautiful Stroganoff buildings, and she told me how she spent years writing to officials, even submitting questions to Putin's annual televised Q&A sessions – the modern equivalent of petitioning the tsar. She was ignored every time. 'No one needs this estate,' she said, a phrase she repeated over and over. There have been countless promises of help, always followed by silence. I knew that, to her, I was just one in a long line of people to take an interest.

Living in Volyshovo has turned both Lyudmila and Olga into amateur experts on architectural preservation. A few years ago, Olga raised money for repairs to the indoor riding arena, risking criminal prosecution by violating building regulations. After all, Lyudmila explained, the best way to save a building is to ensure it is occupied: if people are around they spot leaks and patch up holes. Experience has taught them that when people move out, buildings do not survive. 'A kilometre from here is a place called Dorogini where we had a stable,' Lyudmila told me. 'We left in 2005 and in the fifteen years since then almost everything has disintegrated. There were good warehouses and good hay stores, but we left and everything fell apart.'

The English Stables looked set to meet the same fate: the stud farm moved out the year before my visit and its roof was now leaking badly. The building where I sat with Lyudmila didn't appear to have long left either: the floors sloped at alarming angles and the exterior wall was visibly crumbling. 'The door frames are sinking,' said Lyudmila, her eyes sweeping the room. 'The director has tried to do some cosmetic repairs, but it's scary just to be here sometimes.'

The stud farm's expansion into cattle means Volyshovo is today a moderately prosperous village, offering employment to a handful of labourers, milkmaids and tractor drivers. There is a post office, a nursery and 86 children attend the village school. But the faded glory of the Stroganoff estate is a permanent backdrop to everyone's lives. The ruins themselves are full of litter, which accumulates at the back of the manor house and lies thick on the banks of a nearby stream. It is a particular sort of grief to live your life among the vestiges of a more prosperous history.

Those invested in trying to save the estate tend to be older people, like Olga and Lyudmila, who remember its place at the heart of the community and still harbour hopes of reclaiming what has been lost. Lyudmila, in particular, has attended countless roundtables and discussions about Volyshovo's future, made presentations, given talks and tours and heard hundreds of unfulfilled promises. Her love for the place is plain to see and has led to repeated, aching disappointment. During our conversation, bitterness occasionally crept into her voice. 'When I was taking tours, people would come up to me, beating their chests and boasting that they will get their foot in the door of Putin's office . . . and that the day after tomorrow everything in Volyshovo will be in scaffolding,' she said. She even joined A Just Russia, one of the Kremlin-approved political parties that provide token opposition while remaining loyal to the authorities. 'I am angry, I'm disappointed, and I'm offended,' she said. 'It's very painful and very sad. When you see what was here, and what has survived, it is, of course, an insult.'

The only tsarist-era building in Volyshovo where people still live is the colonnaded kennels that once housed the hunting hounds. It was converted into flats in the 1960s and Lyudmila lived there in the 1980s. After we parted, I walked up to see the building, which is perched on a rise above a stream. The walls were exposed red brick, and the entrance through four whitewashed pillars. Although there was nobody around, there were signs of habitation: a red T-shirt hung on a washing line strung between the columns. One wing of the building was empty, its floor littered with masonry. The other had been turned into a wood store. This time of the year, when the bare forests are free of snow, people fell trees for the following winter's firewood, and there were huge piles of alder, oak and aspen logs towering well above head height. It wasn't much, but some life still clung to the Stroganoff estate.

To be saved from total collapse, Volyshovo would need a wealthy benefactor with political connections. There have been plenty of redevelopment ideas – retirement home, hotel, horse-riding centre – but the most recent cost estimate for a full restoration was £67 million and the chances of turning a profit are nil. Restoration would have to be a vanity project: perhaps for an oil executive fascinated by the Stroganoff dynasty, or a government minister mad about horse riding. Such a patron – a modern-day Stroganoff – would mean a return of culture, status and purpose for locals like Lyudmila and Olga. Instead of a rural backwater, Volyshovo would once again become a destination for high society, and reforge glittering connections to the Russian capital.

The model in most people's minds when they think about the rebirth of Volyshovo is, of course, the splendour of the late nineteenth century. The owner at the time was Count Sergei Stroganoff, a naval officer, horse fanatic and keen hunter who inherited the colossal family fortune aged just twenty-nine. A surviving photograph shows him on an elegant black horse, surrounded by hounds, outside the entrance to Volyshovo's manor house. Thickly bearded, he wears a bowler hat and sits stiffly upright, one hand clenched on his left thigh, the other on the reins. Sergei revelled in his time in Volyshovo, but in 1884 he was struck by tragedy when his young wife died after a botched gynaecological procedure. A friend described Sergei's agony in his memoirs: 'Sereyozha built a glass-house over the grave and used it as a chapel where he would spend days on end, praying for her and reading the Holy Scriptures.' He left Volyshovo soon after and spent decades wandering the globe. He visited India, Singapore, England and the Americas, and undertook several journeys across deserts of the Middle East in search of pure-blood Arab horses. According to local legend, the rooms in the manor house were cleaned daily in anticipation of his return, but he never set foot in Volyshovo again. He died, childless, in southern France in 1923.

In his last years, Sergei would not have been able to return to Russia even if he had wanted. The Russian Revolution saw the empire's great noble families persecuted, jailed and executed, and many fled abroad, their property expropriated. As the Soviet Union entrenched, fewer and fewer émigré aristocrats believed they would ever see their homeland again. But the Stroganoff family was fated to intersect one final time with Volyshovo.

Baroness Hélène de Ludinghausen, Sergei's great-great-niece, grew up in 1950s Paris. Head-hunted by French fashion icon Yves Saint Laurent when working as a shop assistant, she went on to become one of his most trusted executives. In TV interviews, she has a distinctive gravelly voice; a striking combination of aristocratic poise and French haute couture. A Russian-speaking

Orthodox Christian, she married, then divorced, a fox-hunting obsessed member of the English gentry.

Although raised speaking Russian, it wasn't until age forty-two that Baroness de Ludinghausen visited Russia for the first time, flying to Volyshovo by helicopter shortly before the dissolution of the Soviet Union. One friend who accompanied her recalled how de Ludinghausen shed tears when greeted by villagers who implored her to 'take them back'. She offered to fund a restoration, but when the authorities told her she could only have a forty-nine-year lease on the estate that she considered her own, she took umbrage. Refusing the terms, she ditched her plans.

As Russia opened its doors to the West in the 1990s, de Ludinghausen made it her mission to do well by the family name: she set up the Stroganoff Foundation and poured money into the restoration of ex-Stroganoff properties across Russia, including the Kazan Cathedral and Stroganoff Palace in St Petersburg. Eventually, she was persuaded to come back again to Volyshovo, now scarred by years of looting and neglect. It was autumn 2006 and de Ludinghausen was in Russia for the lavish reburial of the repatriated remains of the last tsar's mother, Maria Feodorovna. After the ceremony, she set out for Volyshovo.

Many of those waiting for her understood only too well that this was the last chance for the estate. No other patron had emerged in the fifteen years since the end of the Soviet Union, and Volyshovo's destruction was gathering pace with every passing year. What better person to be their saviour than a direct descendant of the Stroganoffs?

The visit was a disaster. 'They brought a load of people with them including the press and TV, and the event was full to the gunnels,' recalled Lyudmila, who was in the welcoming party. 'The director and I met the cortege when it arrived. We came out onto the steps as Hélène got out of the car, and she immediately pointed at the estate kitchens: "What's that?" she said, "we had lunch there in 1991, but now it's in a terrible state! What have you done?"' Things went from bad to worse as they led de Ludinghausen around the grounds in the rain. 'She wasn't interested at all. She didn't even want to see everything. Instead, we went straight to the barbecue lunch,' said Lyudmila. It became clear the baroness blamed locals for the damage. 'When I came in 1991 with three rich friends and was ready to restore everything to its original state, I asked for just two hundred hectares of land . . . What did the authorities say? That they could offer a lease of forty-nine years,' de Ludinghausen told Lyudmila. 'But why should I rent what belongs to me by right? Today, I no longer have the resources to help you.'

It now seems that both dynasty and estate will soon disappear. In a 2018 documentary, de Ludinghausen said she had wanted children, but married late and suffered two miscarriages. As she has no siblings, and both her mother's two sisters were also childless, de Ludinghausen is the last living Stroganoff – the final representative of a dynasty stretching back more than 600 years. The Stroganoffs and Volyshovo await the same doom: just as the next few decades will see de Ludinghausen's death and the end of the Stroganoff bloodline, so they seem certain to bring Volyshovo's final ruin.

The grounds of Volyshovo are large, and it takes several hours to see everything. On the day I met Olga, she led me from the estate buildings on a long loop through the park, stopping to point out a rare fir tree imported from northern Italy. We didn't make it to a large, grassy clearing where the Stroganoffs once had their cricket pitch, which I remember bathed in golden afternoon light on a previous visit. In thirty-five years, Olga told me as we walked side by side, she had only once thought about moving away. That was in 2006 after her husband died. 'I was ready to leave,' she said. 'I was angry at my lot and wanted to give away or sell everything . . . but then a friend said to me: "Where will you go? Who will you go to? You have everything here. You have land, and you have wonderful horses."' She stayed. Her riding club today is part commercial venture, part outreach project. By the old riding arena, an elderly man asked if his visiting niece could go riding. 'Of course,' said Olga. It was unspoken, but it looked unlikely that money would change hands.

Eventually, we made our way back to the stables where we had started. The March damp had crept into my bones during more than three hours of walking, and I was hunched deep into my coat. Olga seemed unaffected. A couple of teenage girls were waiting outside, and Olga reminded them to brush down the horses. They chattered away while their charges whinnied and shuffled in the stalls.

As we stood in the gloom of the stables, we returned to the improbable prospect of the estate's restoration. Olga gestured around her as she spoke, taking in the estate, the horses, this place that had been lost by degrees, then let her arms drop to her sides with a shrug. We were silent for a moment. 'What is it about Russia?' she asked finally, turning back to me. 'It's a country of slaves and masters. That's the honest truth.'

11

Flag over the Reichstag

Mikhail Minin was one of hundreds of Soviet soldiers waiting in the cellars of bombed-out government buildings in central Berlin as darkness fell on 30 April 1945. Checking their equipment, discussing attack routes, and trying to catch a few hours of rest, the men were preparing to embark on one of the most symbolic battles of World War II: the storming of the nearby Reichstag. The war was in its final days. Neither the Soviet soldiers massing for attack, nor the German defenders of the bullet-ridden Reichstag, knew that Adolf Hitler had committed suicide that afternoon in a bunker less than a kilometre away.

Ever since the tide of the Nazi invasion was turned at Stalingrad in 1943, the capture of Berlin had been the Red Army's ultimate goal. Keen to seize the German capital before the Americans, British and French, Stalin encouraged competition among his generals. And when Soviet soldiers eventually entered the city, the Reichstag was the focus of their efforts. Even if it was mostly unused by the Nazis, who despised it as an icon of German democracy, taking the hulking, neo-Renaissance building came to represent the ultimate prize for the troops who had decimated the Wehrmacht and brought the Nazi Empire to its knees.

The Battle for Berlin took longer than anticipated and, as Stalin got impatient, commanders on the ground sought to be the first to get their men to the Reichstag. The desire to be the one to deliver the coup de grâce was also evident among those in the cellars with the twenty-two-year-old Minin that evening. Many had home-made red flags stashed in their pockets, hoping to unfurl them over the ruins of Berlin. Their officers had promised that the person to achieve this feat would be made a Hero of the Soviet Union, the country's highest military honour. Even though several assaults on the Reichstag earlier in the day had been repulsed, spirits were high.

Minin was one of a group of reconnaissance soldiers from the 136th artillery brigade who had volunteered for a special squad led by Captain Vladimir Makov to try and be the first to raise the red flag over the Reichstag. A tall man with thick brown hair who suffered from rheumatism, Minin had enlisted in 1941 and fought all the way to Berlin. Aware of the extreme danger, each of the men in the squad put a final letter to their families in the right pocket of their tunics, along with a single bullet. They promised one another that those who survived would make sure the letters of the dead were delivered.

Collapsed buildings debris, and the difficulties of crossing the nearby Spree River meant that no tanks and only a few heavy weapons had been brought up to support the attack. Just that morning, the road under a Soviet T-34 in the vicinity of the Reichstag had collapsed, sending the tank and its crew plunging to their deaths in a flooded U-Bahn system. The assault on the Reichstag would be an old-fashioned infantry one.

The softening-up artillery bombardment began at 9:30 p.m. As shells rained down on the building, the German soldiers inside scuttled down to the relative safety of the cellars. Makov's group of five including Minin, were sandwiched between units from the 150th Rifle Division that had been issued with special red flags emblazoned with the hammer and sickle. A few minutes before the shelling was due to end, Makov ordered his men to scramble out of a window and begin sprinting through the darkness.

It was not an easy approach. First, they had to get across Königsplatz, the large square in front of the Reichstag that was cluttered with shell craters and the remains of abandoned German defences: dug-in tanks, rows of trenches and machine-gun placements. Most dauntingly, they had to get to the other side of a a flooded U-Bahn cutting. But they had memorized the route after studying the area through binoculars that afternoon, and one of their number, Gazetdin Zagitov, had identified a large pipe that they used, one by one, to get across the deep water. When the green rockets went up on the Soviet side as a signal the attack should commence, Minin and his comrades were already on the other side of the canal, hurrying towards the Reichstag's grand, colonnaded entrance.

Built at the end of the nineteenth century to house the German parliament, the Reichstag was a squat, six-floor building covered with ornate statuary. Even before the beginning of the Battle of Berlin, it had been badly damaged by bombing and its huge, central glass dome was shattered. All the windows were bricked up, except for machine-gun slits.

The German soldiers inside were mostly from elite units, including those charged with protecting Hitler and Himmler, and probably numbered less than a thousand men. They were armed with light firearms and anti-tank weapons, including *Panzerfäuste*. The Soviet soldiers were lucky the towers on the four corners of the Reichstag, formidable defensive positions, were mostly unmanned while they crossed Königsplatz.

Bounding up the granite steps toward the colonnaded entrance, Minin and his comrades raked it with a burst of gunfire. The massive doors were locked shut, and there was no other obvious way to get inside. Within minutes, soldiers from the 150th Division began to appear, and a small crowd started to form. Some of the men tried hammering on the doors, others put their shoulders to them, but they would not budge. With each passing second the danger of the Germans emerging from the cellars and realizing they were under attack increased. Eventually, two members of Makov's group – Zagitov and Alexander Lisimenko – ran back down the steps and returned with a wooden beam. With the help of about a dozen other soldiers, they used the beam as a battering ram, as if they were breaking down the gates of an ancient castle. After a couple of blows, the doors burst open and the soldiers flooded inside. Zagitov was first across the threshold.

Time was of the essence. It was pitch black and no one knew from which direction the Germans might emerge – or when. As nervous soldiers sprayed bullets along corridors and tossed grenades down staircases, Makov decided he would remain on the ground floor. But he ordered his group to head for the roof. Zagitov had the only torch, so he led the three others as they ran upstairs, bounding several steps at a time. Whenever they reached a landing, they opened fire into the dark corridors, or threw grenades. Down below, Red Army soldiers were still rushing into the building. Some fanned out at ground level, taking up defensive positions in a bid to stop the Germans from getting to the main stairwell; others followed in the footsteps of Minin, Zagitov, Lisimenko and the group's fourth member, Aleksei Bobrov.

On emerging into the cavernous attics of the Reichstag, Zagitov spotted a large chain, apparently part of a cargo winch, that went through the ceiling in the direction of the roof. One by one, the four men shimmied up the chain and through a window. They found themselves in the night air. Although they had reached their objective, they realized they didn't know where on the roof they should actually tie the red flag.

Suddenly, everything was lit up by an exploding shell and they spotted the enormous *Germania* sculpture that stood directly above the main entrance. About four times the height of a man, the central figure of the sculpture was a queen on horseback. They decided that was where the flag should be raised, and Minin hastily scribbled their four names on the red material, barely able to see in the dark. Zagitov tore his handkerchief into strips that they used to tie the flag to a piece of piping Minin had grabbed on their race up the stairs.

With the help of the others, Minin clambered onto the statue, cutting his hands where the bronze had been damaged by shrapnel. Balancing precariously, the blood dripping from his hands, he found a hole in the crown of the queenly rider and thrust the makeshift flagpole into it, using more strips of Zagitov's handkerchief to tie it firmly in place. It was 10:40 p.m., just over an hour since the attack had begun.

In Minin's memoirs, he recalled the exhilarating moment:

> Only when the military objective had been fully achieved did I realize the danger of my position. I was still standing on the bronze horse, holding on to the crown of the giantess. Shells and mortars were exploding on the roof of the Reichstag and the bronze statue was shaking in the blast waves. It seemed as if the rampaging horse was hanging over the roof gable and the whole bronze ensemble was on the verge of crashing to the ground below – and taking me with it.

When he clambered back down, Minin and the others embraced. The adrenalin must have been pumping. Medals and fame beckoned. Perhaps they imagined television interviews, full-page portraits on newspaper front pages, or even an audience with Stalin.

A few minutes later, they were joined on the roof by an elated Makov, who hugged and kissed them all. When he informed his superiors by radio that the red flag was now flying over the Reichstag, military discipline slipped. Different accounts give different versions of his words, but when asked where exactly the red flag was flying, it seems likely he yelled: 'On the crown of some German whore!'

Meanwhile, fighting was intensifying on the lower floors as the Germans launched repeated counter-attacks. The building echoed to the explosions of grenades, and bursts of small-arms fire. Despite having no chance of success, the last German defenders would only surrender some thirty-six hours later. In one of the firefights in the small hours of that morning, Zagitov was seriously injured when a bullet struck him in the chest, narrowly missing his heart. However, he continued fighting until he was ordered by Makov to evacuate.

It was not until dawn that Makov, Minin, Lisimenko and Bobrov received orders to withdraw. Just after 5 a.m. they made their way to the other side of the Spree River, picking up a surprisingly lively Zagitov from the first-aid post on the way. It was a sunny, oddly quiet morning and the sky over the German capital was filled with the smoke of burning buildings.

The men immediately reported the events of the night to senior Red Army officers and were put forward to be Heroes of the Soviet Union. Official photographs were taken, and they sat down for an interview with a correspondent from *Pravda*. The previous night's events would never again be as clear as they were that euphoric morning in Berlin.

Of course, the Kremlin had been focused on the end of the war long before the first Red Army units entered the outskirts of Berlin. Even aside from the foreign-policy implications, it was clear that – whatever the human cost – the defeat of Hitler was an epic military triumph that could be used to cement Stalin's grip on power. As the war's crowning act of symbolism, the raising of the red flag over the Reichstag would need a canonical narrative that could be broadcast to the Soviet people.

Minin and his comrades were not chosen for this role. None of them were made Heroes of the Soviet Union, instead receiving the lesser Order of the Red Banner. And nothing about their exploits appeared in *Pravda*. We don't know exactly when Minin realized he was not going to be credited, but as the days turned to weeks he must have guessed something was wrong. Amid the chaos of the fighting in and around the Reichstag, alternative contenders for the title of first to raise the red flag had emerged: Mikhail Yegorov and Meliton Kantariya. Sometime after Minin's exploit, when the fiercest fighting was over, these two scouts from the 150th, accompanied by Lieutenant Aleksei Berest, made their way to the top of the Reichstag and planted a flag they had been given before the assault. Unlike Minin's scrap of red fabric, this was a proper red flag with a hammer and sickle in the top left corner. Later, the 150th's name and battle honours would be daubed on it in white paint.

It's not entirely clear why Yegorov and Kantariya were selected to be written into history as the first flag-raisers. Some believe it was simply because of the confusion of that night. Others because Yegorov was Russian and Kantariya was Georgian – like Stalin – and that the ethnic mix of the pair would make better propaganda. The two men were also from the 150th, whose commanders led the assault on the Reichstag, and their flag, unlike that of Minin's group, survived the fighting. Likely Marshal Zhukov, who commanded the attack on Berlin, was faced with dozens of competing accounts – and he made a judgement based on limited information.

Fear also played a role. In an earlier attack on the Reichstag, when a group of Soviet soldiers briefly reached the walls of the building, an eager officer reported the building had fallen – information that was passed to Moscow and broadcast to the nation. Terrified of angering Stalin, it appears senior officers from the 150th agreed a false account of events among themselves that included Yegorov and Kantariya and aligned with this earlier mistake. In the version they decided on, the storming of the Reichstag took place ten hours earlier than reality. After a successful attack, Yegorov and Kantariya were said to have raised the red flag on the roof of the Reichstag at 2:25 p.m. on 30 April.

Following approval from generals and the Kremlin, this was the version relayed to the world. The commanding officers from the 150th involved in the assault were made Heroes of the Soviet Union that month, while the more junior participants, including Yegorov and Kantariya, received the honour the following year. The awards guaranteed their silence.

The visual images of the Reichstag after its capture only added extra layers of confusion. When you think about the Battle of Berlin, you probably picture the iconic photograph taken by Red Army photographer Yevgeny Khaldei showing a soldier balancing precariously on the Reichstag roof and holding a hammer-and-sickle flag billowing in the wind. In the background lie the shattered remains of Berlin. It's one of the most iconic images of World War II, and has been endlessly republished. However, it was staged: the flag used for the photo was sewn together in

Moscow from a couple of red tablecloths; the three soldiers pictured were picked at random; and it was taken thirty-six hours after Minin and his team reached the roof of the Reichstag. Khaldei even admitted later to having doctored the photo to add more smoke and remove evidence of Red Army looting (one of the soldiers was wearing a watch on each wrist).

In the same way, video shot by documentary filmmaker Roman Karmen showing a group of Red Army soldiers running toward the Reichstag with a huge red flag – footage that has been used in almost every documentary about World War II ever since – was filmed well after the fighting was over.

Demobilized in 1946, Minin returned home to Pskov Region. The war hero was the son of agricultural labourers from the tiny village of Vanino, perched on the banks of the Velikaya River as it curves toward Pskov. Curious about Minin's roots, I visited Vanino one morning in March 2023. It was uninhabited during the winter months, and getting there required wading through a kilometre of untouched snow with a brittle crust that collapsed under my weight. Some of Vanino's seven houses were abandoned, others used as *dachas*, the snow piled in drifts against their walls. The only signs of life were dog tracks and bullfinches flitting between the birches.

Minin did not settle in Vanino after the war, instead taking a job in the nearby town of Palkino as a newspaper editor. In 1952, aged thirty, he returned to the army, where he would spend the rest of an unremarkable career. By the time he retired in the late 1970s, he had reached the rank of major.

Under Brezhnev, World War II replaced the 1917 Revolution as the founding myth of the Soviet state. Not only did the authorities realize that the scale of the slaughter meant it could bind people together in mourning, but who could refuse to take pride in the destruction of Nazi Germany, liberating Europe and saving the motherland? The day the Nazi surrender was announced to the Soviet people, 9 May, was made a public holiday: a celebration, as the overused saying goes, marked with 'tears in the eyes'. For Victory Day in 1965, Brezhnev ordered a massive military parade through Red Square that included Yegorov and Kantariya and the flag they had raised over the Reichstag. Wildly popular, the parade became an annual tradition that continues to this day.

There was never any question about Minin's loyalty to the Soviet authorities. Even in later life, he was unrelentingly patriotic in interviews, proper to the point of insipidity. He never criticized, or showed anger. His family remember him as an outspoken atheist: strict, inflexible and intimidating – albeit with a kind heart and a sweet tooth. In short, a good Communist and loyal soldier. It seems impossible he would ever have come to prominence without the war. But history thrust Minin into the spotlight and the injustice meted out to him and his comrades would gnaw away at him all his life.

It was one thing not to receive any credit, it was another to see Yegorov and Kantariya feted as heroes on television and radio, in newspapers and books, and in speeches and tributes. As the war became more and more central to public life, it was harder and harder for Minin to find any respite from constant reminders of how he and his friends were written out of history.

Cautious by nature, Minin was careful to whom he told the true story of the storming of the Reichstag. He likely worried he would be met with bafflement, dismissal or, most painfully, laughter. Perhaps, he even feared official repurcussions. Instead, he became an expert on the events of 30 April 1945, collecting documents, watching films, and reading books and articles. Most of all, though, he took to writing letters. Over the decades, Minin wrote to newspapers, magazines, historians, government agencies, deputies in the Soviet parliament, Communist Party functionaries and military officials. He wrote to Brezhnev and, later, he would write to Yeltsin. He wrote to anyone he thought might listen.

I first found out about Minin's letter-writing from watching a news report aired after his death. Following a shot of paratroopers firing a salute over Minin's grave, it cut to an interview with Pskov archivist Marina Safronova, leafing through a pile of Minin's letters that looked at least 30 centimetres high. 'This is his correspondence,' she said to the camera. 'Who didn't he write to?'

Hoping that Minin's letters would provide insight into his character and his campaign for justice, one autumn morning I went to the archive in Pskov where Safronova worked. I was allowed into a reading room, and provided with what the archivist said were all the documents they held on Minin. Everything was in folded white sheets of A4 paper, and carefully labelled. There were none of his letters, but there was a photo, some medals and, most interestingly, a manuscript titled 'Facts and legends about the storm of the Reichstag'. Minin had compiled these notes at the end of his life, and they included an account of his futile attempts to correct the historical record.

Amid the political thaw under Khrushchev, there was a push to de-Stalinize history, and one of the events Minin described was a 1961 meeting in Moscow attended by surviving members of the attack on the Reichstag. Despite the lies of some, Minin said it became obvious to 'everyone present at the meeting that, in order to please I. V. Stalin, the commanders and political leadership of the 150th Division, 79th Rifle Corps and the Third Shock Army manipulated the facts about Yegorov and Kantariya being the first to raise the Red Banner'. However, attendees were told there was no appetite for a complete rewriting of the record of that day, and that Yegorov and Kantariya would not be 'chucked out of history'.

More revealingly, Minin detailed a 1968 meeting he had with Timofei Kuprikov, the deputy head of the Communist Party's Propaganda Department, who told him that officials were well aware of his version of events. While they wanted some clarifications, Kuprikov said that, even if Minin provided the necessary details, they would never allow his account to be published.

Kuprikov was true to his word. With characteristic meticulousness, Minin recounted in the manuscript how journals and newspapers repeatedly turned him down. Just a year before the fall of the Berlin Wall, the Soviet Union's Military–History Journal rejected an article of Minin's for the fifth time. Even the dissident journal *Noviy Mir*, which had published Solzhenitsyn's novel *One Day in the Life of Ivan Denisovich*, his revelatory account of life in the gulag, demurred. Minin finished his memoirs in 1982, but no one would print them. 'I simply wasn't allowed to speak out,' Minin wrote.

As I pored over the document, I realized this was the only time I had seen Minin express bitterness. In one section, he mentioned the 'made-up heroics' of Yegorov and Kantariya; in another he ridiculed a book called *We Stormed the Reichstag* by Ivan Klochkov, a war veteran and Hero of the Soviet Union. Klochkov, he said, was 'a liar' who 'sells his honour and conscience for money'.

From both Minin's account and other books on the subject, it's clear that the inaccuracy of the Yegorov and Kantariya version was an open secret for anyone in the Soviet Union with more than a passing interest in the storming of the Reichstag. But the still-living participants – decorated military veterans and Red Army commanders with immense authority – were all trapped in a lie that had ballooned into something too big to be allowed to fail. Renouncing their words could even have been dangerous. Just as Minin felt the strain of living a lie, so it must have been difficult for these other men to continue repeating what they knew to be false. But it was in none of their interests to pursue the truth. Perhaps, with time, they even began to believe what they were saying.

For the thirtieth anniversary of the end of the war, the director Roman Rozenblit invited Kantariya (Yegorov was dead by this point) and the surviving commanders of the operation to be filmed for a documentary. But no documentary was ever released: this group of war heroes were too scared to say something that would undermine the official version of events. Rozenblit remembered how 'there was such internal tension in the group that it was difficult to be around them'. Even in official footage broadcast on Soviet television that year, their excessive bonhomie rings painfully false.

Only with the media freedoms that came with the collapse of the Soviet Union did the story finally begin to unravel. It had been held together by Soviet ideology, fear and the Kremlin's political decision to elevate the victory over Nazi Germany into something resembling a religious cult. So, when the fear dissipated, Soviet ideology was ridiculed and the cult of victory faded from political life for a few years, Minin's articles began to be accepted by newspapers and journals. A thousand copies of his memoirs, *Difficult Roads to Victory*, were published in 2001 with the financial support of the regional government. He could not be made a Hero of the Soviet Union – the Soviet Union no longer existed – but a political group that denied the legality of the break-up of the Soviet Union and continued to hand out Soviet awards conferred the honour on him in 1997.

At the same time, other truths about the raising of the red flag over the Reichstag began to receive publicity for the first time. The role of Lieutenant Berest, who accompanied Yegorov and Kantariya, was widely discussed – apparently he was denied a Hero of the Soviet Union by Marshal Zhukov because he was a political officer, and Zhukov hated political officers. According to his wife, Berest nurtured a grievance about the snub all his life.

It also turned out that two other soldiers – Rakhymzhan Koshkarbayev and Georgiy Bulatov – had reached the Reichstag in the teeth of Nazi machine-gun fire several hours before Minin's group and planted a red flag on the building (the façade not the roof) – before retreating. While there was some reporting of this in the Soviet period, it was not well known. Bulatov's friends said he told them about a personal audience with Stalin in which the Soviet leader acknowledged he had been the first to raise the red flag on the Reichstag. Like those in Makov's group, Koshkarbayev and Bulatov were put forward to be made Heroes of the Soviet Union. Neither received the award.

Despite all the new public evidence, the Yegorov and Kantariya version was never officially repudiated, and remains common currency. When Minin took part in the Victory Day parade on Red Square in 2000 – the first of Putin's presidency – the ceremony, as is traditional, began with a copy of the Banner of Victory being marched across the cobbles to the strains of a large brass band. Minin's feelings as he waited with thousands of other veterans, wearing his military uniform and a full chest of medals, can only be imagined. Perhaps it was a blessing that he could not hear the TV commentators who told the millions of viewers that the Banner of Victory was first raised over the Reichstag at 2:25 p.m. by Yegorov and Kantariya.

As Russia heads toward the hundred-year anniversary of the end of World War II, the storming of the Reichstag and the raising of the Banner of Victory is not an issue for dusty history books. Putin has revived and adapted the Soviet cult of victory to serve as the ideological cornerstone of his regime, with the rhetoric of sacrifice saturating public life. A large model of the Reichstag built in 2017 in Moscow's Patriot Park is regularly used for historical re-enactments, including by children. And the 150th Division in which Yegorov and Kantariya served was re-formed in 2016 and heavily involved in the invasion of Ukraine. Indeed, the war in Ukraine has been framed by the Kremlin from the very start as a rerun of World War II, with Russian soldiers allegedly battling 'Nazis' and 'liberating' occupied territory. Russian units operating in Ukraine regularly fly Yegorov and Kantariya's Banner of Victory on tanks, and it has been raised over shattered Ukrainian towns by Russian soldiers in a deliberate cosplaying of 1945.

After his retirement, Minin lived in a small apartment in the suburbs of Pskov. At his *dacha* in a village near Vanino, he kept bees. When Klavdiya, his wife of thirty-eight years, died, he married another woman with the same name.

In 1999, Minin was invited by the BBC to go to Berlin for a documentary about the Reichstag – a trip he had dreamed of making for years, but could not afford. The film crew took him out for a meal in the German capital, and he admitted in his memoirs this was the first time he'd been in a restaurant since the fall of the Soviet Union. The seventy-six-year-old Minin only appears in the final cut of the documentary for a few minutes, and the on-screen labels identify him as a 'beekeeper' despite his army uniform and medals. His ample jowls meant his face was almost square, and his eyebrows were straggling, but he held himself upright and spoke stiffly, as if on a parade ground.

A few weeks after I visited Vanino, I met Minin's great-granddaughter, Karina, who lives in a flat in the centre of Pskov. Drinking tea in her kitchen, which contained an aquarium of giant snails, she said her soldier boyfriend was recuperating from a wound received in Ukraine in the next-door room.

Brought up just outside Pskov, Karina's only memories of Minin were of a kindly old man. But she described how all the family members had experienced disbelief, ridicule and insults when recounting the exploits of their ancestor. Her mother, Minin's granddaughter, was teased by friends, she said. And she suffered the same fate. 'Even my classmates in school didn't believe me. They said "it's in the textbooks that it wasn't him! It was Yegorov and Kantariya!",' Karina told me. 'It's written like that everywhere. They'll never correct the inaccuracy in the textbooks. Yegorov and Kantariya will always be there.'

Of all the Red Army soldiers who claimed to have been the first to raise the red flag over the Reichstag, Minin lived the longest – by a long way. Yegorov was killed in a car accident in 1975; Kantariya died in 1993 as a refugee after his house was destroyed in post-Soviet violence in the South Caucasus; Berest was run over by a train in 1970 as he saved a little girl on the tracks; Koshkarbayev worked as a hotel manager and passed away in 1988; Bulatov was imprisoned twice, took to drink, and hung himself in a factory toilet in 1973.

Minin also survived all the other members of Makov's group: both Makov and Bobrov took to alcohol and died in the 1970s; Zagitov was killed in a car accident in 1953; and Lisimenko died from cancer in 1979.

Karina told me that, in the final months of Minin's life, he cut off all contact with his family and went to live in a hostel. In the advanced stages of cancer, he didn't want his loved ones to remember him as weak, or incapable. He died aged eighty-five in 2008.

I never did find Minin's letters. When they turned out not to be with the other documents in the archive, I kept searching. I discovered that the archivist, Marina Safronova, who had shown them to the cameras after Minin's death, had herself passed away. I was put in touch with the archivist now responsible for the twentieth-century collection, who told me the letters had likely not been accepted for the permanent collection. She said they'd probably been binned. While she promised to look for them, she never got back to me.

This final injustice reminded me of how Minin had chosen to end the manuscript of his that was preserved in the archives. He'd written: 'History does not forgive lies. Sooner or later, the truth will out!' Then, he crossed it out.

12

Man of all Parties

It's odd to think that Yevgeny Mikhailov once inspired fear. But his 1996 victory in Pskov Region's governor elections on a platform of extreme nationalism made headlines across the country, sent a shiver of panic through the Moscow elite and triggered an international sell-off in Russian stocks. Photographs from that time show Mikhailov as a thin, pale man with a pencil moustache, bouffant black hair and an arrogant glance. He appears a bit lost in baggy suits and large glasses: more likely to be blown over in a high wind than mastermind a right-wing electoral triumph.

Nevertheless, with more than a quarter of a million votes, Mikhailov became the first governor in Russia from the rabble-rousing and misleadingly named Liberal Democrat Party of Russia (LDPR); his victory an illustration of the desperation of the 1990s. During his campaign, he promised revanchist imperialism and attacked Yeltsin's government for its market reforms, corruption and a chummy relationship with the West. 'Some five per cent of the population is lording it over the ninety-five per cent. How is that possible?' he asked in his 1995 autobiography-cum-political manifesto *Burden of an Imperial Nation*. 'It's possible because we Russians are divided and disorganized, and cannot unite to stand up for our national interests. One by one, we are being beaten, robbed and sold like livestock. Today's government is funded by Western money: nothing more than a well-organized, thieving corporation bent on the stealthy destruction of the Russian people.'

This sort of rhetoric found a ready audience in Pskov Region in the aftermath of the Soviet collapse as people suffered from a brutal and apparently endless economic crisis. Some in Moscow believed Mikhailov's win indicated support for the LDPR was spreading across the whole country, propelling Russia toward authoritarianism, and risking armed conflicts with the newly independent states along the country's borders. Most liberals saw the LDPR as nothing more than a bunch of proto-fascists: Russia's own goose-stepping brownshirts.

Ahead of the vote, Mikhailov and his supporters toured the small towns of Pskov Region in cars and coaches decked out in LDPR blue and yellow. The star attraction was the flamboyant and fiery party leader Vladimir Zhirinovsky, a veteran of two presidential elections. 'The cortege went around all the districts and people gathered inside buildings and out on the streets. Thousands turned up,' according to Mikhailov. Zhirinovsky joked with supporters and opponents alike, and delivered speeches laced with conspiracy theories to packed halls. In one piece of footage from the campaign, Mikhailov and Zhirinovsky are shown wearing long black coats with upturned collars: Mikhailov in aviators, Zhirinovsky with a cigar clenched between his lips. 'There was a town we hadn't been planning to visit because it was out of our way. But several hundred people from the town blocked the road we were travelling on and asked us to come and see them. We were obliged to visit,' Mikhailov recalled. 'People were hoping something would change.'

Yet, for all the glory of his electoral win in 1996, Mikhailov never became a lifelong LDPR man. Far from it. Instead, his career is a story of opportunism. It's a story that illustrates the fiction of Russia's post-Soviet democracy, and the triumph of informality over institutions. In less than three decades, Mikhailov has switched between Russia's three major political parties: the Communist Party, the LDPR and United Russia, the political vehicle created for Putin. For several years he served in the powerful Presidential Administration (the 'chancellery' of Putin's court), and was briefly a minister in the Donetsk People's Republic, a Russia-backed rebel statelet in eastern Ukraine. Latterly, Mikhailov would become a regular guest on YouTube shows advocating for the genocidal dismemberment of Ukraine. Throughout it all, his belief in Russian nationalism has burned bright, sometimes helping his star to rise, sometimes pushing him to the political fringe.

Mikhailov is no firebrand. He is a pragmatist who dislikes public speaking; what you would call a backroom politician – always planning, plotting and managing. He tacks to the prevailing political wind, and has an innate understanding that, in Russia, personal loyalty will always trump position and ideology.

I met Mikhailov in 2020 on a dull November afternoon in Moscow. His grey suit gave him the air of a middle manager, and he was jarringly out of place in a café full of students and freelancers. He was pleased to reminisce, and chuckled dryly at past ironies. Sitting across the table, I recognized the hard, rodent-like eyes from the photographs of the 1990s, but there was little left of the insubstantial, pale man who was elected governor. His dishevelled hair was mostly grey; his ample face tinged red around the nose.

Like Lev Shlosberg, Mikhailov was born in 1963, came of age in the final years of the Soviet Union, and studied history at university. Like Shlosberg, one of his grandfathers was killed in World War II. But whereas Shlosberg is from Pskov's intelligentsia, Mikhailov was born into a working-class family in Pskov Region's industrial capital, Velikie Luki. His father, a sailor, never knew of his existence, and he was raised by his mother who worked long shifts at the local radio factory. His stepfather was an alcoholic. In his autobiography, Mikhailov described spending many hours playing outside because of the cramped conditions in their communal flat, which was also home to his sick grandmother. 'From my earliest childhood, I remember there were endless, relentless arguments between neighbours in our communal flat. Swear words and foul language were the norm.'

Unlike Shlosberg, Mikhailov would have probably ended up as a politician even if the Soviet Union had endured. He was active in the Komsomol (the Communist youth organization) and became a candidate member of the Communist Party aged just twenty-one. After leaving school he trained as a builder and spent his military service in a construction battalion in southern Russia. Once back in Velikie Luki, he decided to do a history degree. 'I loved reading,' he told me by way of explanation. In particular, he consumed the works of the Western authors published widely in the Soviet Union (Jules Verne, Alexandre Dumas and Arthur Conan Doyle), as well as history books like the official history of World War II, which he read over and over. Finally, on his third attempt, he was accepted onto a history degree at the prestigious Moscow State University. High marks earned him a Lenin stipend, but he still worked extra jobs: as a street cleaner; security guard; and, briefly, at an ice-cream factory. Throughout his studies, Mikhailov's mother made his clothes by hand.

Like most young people at the time, Mikhailov was a supporter of Gorbachev and applauded the gradual opening up of the Soviet Union. 'I welcomed perestroika with all my heart,' he wrote several years later. After becoming a member of the Communist Party in 1988, he was appointed the last ever ideology secretary at his university's history department. Two years later, he won election to the Moscow Soviet, the political body that ran the Russian capital, and joined a new intake of reformers challenging the older Communists. As a deputy, he received a flat on the outskirts of Moscow. He decided to put his studies on the back burner. 'After that it was mostly politics,' he told me.

The last months of the Soviet Union remain imprinted on the memories of all who were alive at the time. Like many, Mikhailov had mixed feelings. While he was losing his faith in Communism, he was horrified by anything that diminished the power of the state, or threatened the Soviet empire. He was worried by Moscow's failure to crush national movements in the Baltics and the South Caucasus, and sympathized with the preservationist aims of hardliners who attempted a coup in August 1991. Around this time, he began reading Russian nationalist writers: the Pan-Slavist ideologue Nikolai Danilevsky; the monarchist Konstantin Leontiev; Ivan Ilyin (the religious philosopher who influenced Father Tikhon and Putin); and the writer and gulag survivor Alexander Solzhenitsyn. He attended a seminar led by rocket scientist-turned-theatre director Sergei Kurginyan, who preached a mystical brand of Russian nationalism. 'My views changed pretty radically,' Mikhailov recalled. 'I was a Soviet patriot, but a lot of new information appeared and I had to re-think my position. I remained a patriot – just not a Soviet patriot.' With the Communist Party increasingly a home for political dinosaurs, Mikhailov returned his membership card.

Instead, he was drawn into the orbit of the LDPR. Founded by a cabal of KGB officers and Kremlin managers in the last years of the Soviet Union, the party was an attempt to ride the dragon of

Russian nationalism – and it went on to enjoy a success few had anticipated. Even more than ideology, Mikhailov was drawn to the larger-than-life figure of Zhirinovsky, who exerted a hypnotic effect over his supporters: a father and mentor as well as leader. The party faithful referred to Zhirinovsky as their *vozhd*, a Russian word for leader that was used as an epithet for Stalin. When I asked Mikhailov about Zhirinovsky it was clear some of the boyish hero-worship remained even thirty years later. 'Volfovich was head and shoulders above any other politician,' he said, using Zhirinovsky's patronymic, a sign of comradeship. 'Back then he said what people wanted to hear. Things that no one was saying apart from him. And he said them clearly, firmly and vividly. His charisma was on show.'

Mikhailov joined the LDPR in 1993. Looking for ways to make himself helpful, he began travelling to his native Pskov Region to set up a local LDPR branch. Ahead of his first visit, there were just ten LDPR members in the entire region. But voting patterns suggested support was much higher, and he redoubled his efforts ahead of parliamentary elections in November. When the results came in, they were staggering: across Russia, the LDPR won 23 per cent of the total vote, their highest ever result in national elections. And their best result was in Pskov Region where they got an all-time LDPR record of 43 per cent, rising to well over 50 per cent in many rural districts. One of the new LDPR deputies to the State Duma from Pskov Region was Mikhailov.

It was an exciting time to be a politician in Moscow, and Mikhailov relished being at the centre of national debate. Politics in those years was dominated by the military disaster unfolding in the southern republic of Chechnya. In the summer of 1996, as the First Chechen War drew to a close, Mikhailov took advantage of a perk available to elected officials and went on a subsidized holiday to the Black Sea resort city of Sochi. Staying in the same neo-classical sanitorium was fellow LDPR deputy Aleksei Mitrofanov, an obese nationalist politician and occasional TV producer who hung out with celebrities, and would later flee to Croatia to evade fraud charges. It was Mitrofanov's idea that

Mikhailov should run to be Pskov Region governor. 'Everyone was in a good mood,' Mitrofanov recalled when I spoke to him by phone. 'He [Mikhailov] was intending to go to America for a seminar for deputies organized by an American university. I said to him: "Now, listen, wait a moment, there's a huge detonator in Pskov Region and enormous opportunities as the LDPR vote is already significant. Maybe you'll give it a go?"'

Mikhailov agreed. Back in Moscow, he sat down to consider ideas for his election campaign. 'The big aim of the programme was that we needed to buy the voters,' he said with a chuckle. 'What else does the electorate go for? Money, of course.' But his selling point was, in fact, an offer of lobbying power. Mikhailov promised voters that every LDPR deputy could negotiate, cajole and arm-twist for federal money for Pskov. The better your contacts in Moscow the more state money you get, and the importance of influential connections is something any Russian living outside the capital understands only too well.

More important, though, was the economic and social catastrophe that had unfolded in Pskov Region over the last five years. Figures only hint at the scale of lost jobs, slashed incomes and broken lives. But between 1991 and 1995 annual inflation in Russia averaged 871 per cent (peaking at 2,608 per cent in 1992); life expectancy fell by five years; unemployment doubled; and the number of annual suicides increased by 50 per cent. In the same period, Pskov Region's economy shrank to half its size. Mikhailov told me the collapse in industrial output in Pskov Region was twice as bad as in Russia overall.

On top of this, there was the psychological effect of losing an empire. Nowhere was this more potent than in military units stationed in Pskov Region that had been pulled back to the Russian frontier from Germany and the Baltics as Communist governments were swept from power. A sense of betrayal, a belief that the Soviet Union had been stabbed in the back, was everywhere.

After the polls closed, Mikhailov and his small team gathered in a three-room rented flat in Pskov that doubled as their campaign headquarters. By the early hours of the morning, it was clear he had won by a big margin and congratulations poured in from LDPR bigwigs. Mitrofanov recalled phoning Mikhailov from South Africa, where he was travelling with a parliamentary delegation. 'It was a symbol of a new upturn, a new wave,' Mitrofanov told me. For Mikhailov, it was the pinnacle of his political career. He described it to me as his proudest moment.

Mikhailov's victory became a symbol for nationalists. The old Slavic lands around Pskov had always attracted Russian nationalists, and this interest intensified as the collapse of Communism fuelled a demand for spiritual and political renewal. One of those fascinated by Pskov was Mikhailov's acquaintance Alexander Prokhanov, nicknamed the 'nightingale of the General Staff' for his links to the military top brass, a giant man with a mass of silver hair who preached a heady mix of pagan esotericism, Russian chauvinism and Soviet nostalgia. Those like Prokhanov were drawn to the Caves Monastery, Pushkin's estate and Pskov's traditions of martial prowess.

Several years later, Prokhanov created something called Sacred Hill: a huge cross on a mound near the ancient fortress of Izborsk several kilometres outside Pskov. Soil was added to the mound from places important to Russian and world history, including the battlefields of Stalingrad, the city of Jerusalem and the surface of the moon. 'Come to Izborsk,' Prokhanov urged in one television apearance. 'Go up to the hill and pour upon it the earth of your heart. Press your head to the huge boulders and you will hear the mysterious roar of Russian history.'

In the aftermath of his win, Mikhailov, however, had other priorities. Russian governors are like mini-presidents, arbiters of local power who often rule over areas bigger than entire European countries. And Pskov Region was in deep crisis. Mikhailov's immediate concern was to gather a team and establish control over money flows, including smoothing the way for the LDPR's financial backers to take a slice of the local economy. He got involved in a turf war with the local chief of police that got so bad the Kremlin stepped in to mediate. Summoned to Moscow, Mikhailov put his case to Putin, who was then an unknown bureaucrat working in a junior role in the Kremlin.

At the same time, Mikhailov tried desperately to negotiate bigger subsidies: Russia's federal system means tax money is redistributed via Moscow, and Pskov Region was always a net recipient. 'I knew the Finance Ministry because I'd been on the budget committee in the Moscow Soviet. I understood the nuances, and could speak to them in their language,' Mikhailov said. 'But really there was little they could do. If I'm honest, the situation was a total mess. Every year they reduced the subsidies. And then there was inflation. And on top of that they didn't give us everything they promised.'

In 2000, Putin swept to victory in presidential elections. As always, Mikhailov read the room. It was clear Putin was intent on gathering the reins of state power, and governors from opposition parties were in the firing line. 'It's not like they made it known to me,' Mikhailov explained when I asked how he realized the way things were headed. 'I surmised from their behaviour that it would be impossible to continue as we had been working up until that point.' So, Mikhailov quit the LDPR and joined Unity, a political party set up to support Putin. It had little in the way of ideology.

The writing was also on the wall for the LDPR. The early 1990s had been the party's high-water mark, and by the end of the decade it was moving toward irrelevance. As Russia's economic recovery pushed extremism to the fringes, the LDPR became happy to make political deals with the Kremlin in return for money, and political oxygen. Gradually, Zhirinovsky became a buffoon whose outrageous claims generated headlines and little more. 'It was difficult to have to explain this grotesque show all the time,' Mikhailov said of Zhirinovsky's antics.

In lockstep with the country as a whole, Pskov Region embraced Putin. The rise of the former KGB spy to Russia's highest public office was the expression of a yearning for predictability after a decade of turmoil. And it happened with a marked absence of euphoria, public rallies or flag-waving. Putin's dominance was particularly dramatic in Pskov Region, where, in presidential elections in 2000, he got 10 per cent more votes than he did nationally.

Sure enough, proclaiming support for Putin allowed Mikhailov to scrape through to his own election victory eight months later. Voting patterns show he won the support of the elderly, rural population that traditionally backs the 'party of power'. But he also benefited from the first signs of economic revival, a low turnout and electoral manipulation.

Mikhailov's second governorship was less of a steep learning curve than the first: he now had some experience and a fragile normalcy was taking hold. Instead, his main challenge became to convince Putin's political managers of his loyalty. Once president, Putin began eliminating threats, and consolidating power, one step at a time. His most controversial move came in 2003 with the arrest of the oil billionaire Mikhail Khodorkovsky, which finally broke the power of the Yeltsin-era oligarchs.

For politicians like Mikhailov, the direction of travel was clear: governorships were being transformed from political into administrative roles. Mikhailov sought to survive by cultivating allies and shouting his loyalty to Putin from the rooftops. 'I believe we need to support the president even if he is mistaken,' he said in a 2002 interview. 'Like a monarchy – after all, Russia was originally a monarchic country.'

In the Kremlin, Mikhailov's political patron was Vladislav Surkov, the post-modern, mercurial grey cardinal of early Putinism who penned novels, listened to American rap, and sculpted a 'power vertical'. With Surkov's support, Mikhailov managed to avoid becoming another name on the list of governors forced out of a job. 'I wasn't an independent politician, I was part of a team,' said Mikhailov. Even so, his position was not entirely secure, and he became a pawn in fighting between Kremlin factions, or 'towers', seeking to advance their own interests. It was a Kremlin faction opposed to Surkov that created particular difficulties. 'Different towers had different opinions, and one of the towers played against me . . . but in the end I got the support of the Presidential Administration,' Mikhailov said.

Ironically, it wasn't enough. At the time, the Kremlin did not have the same power to swing governor elections that it would later acquire, and Mikhailov ended up losing in 2004 to his long-time rival Mikhail Kuznetsov. The fatal blow was dealt by Pskov Mayor Mikhail Khoronin, who Mikhailov said reneged on a pre-election deal. 'We had an agreement in which I helped him get elected in the spring,' Mikhailov said. 'But then, instead of supporting me like any normal person, he backed Kuznetsov, so I lost. It was stupidity on his part because Kuznetsov then spent four years trying to destroy him.'

This was an election about personal rivalries, not policy. Mikhailov and Kuznetsov were former LDPR colleagues, and

Kuznetsov bankrolled Mikhailov's first successful campaign for governor. But they ended up falling out, with Kuznetsov alleging Mikhailov lied about stepping aside. Mikhailov deployed what is known in Russian political jargon as 'administrative resources' to try and ensure victory: the police were used to take a Pskov television station briefly off air, and the electoral commission pressured to thin the field of candidates. While Mikhailov was a member of the ruling United Russia party (the new name for Unity) and Kuznetsov ran as an independent, they were politically similar and both proclaimed their support for Putin. Even though Mikhailov had the Kremlin's formal blessing, Kuznetsov's campaign posters featured Putin's face. Forced into a second-round run-off, Mikhailov lost by just 7 percentage points. Tellingly, within months of taking office, Kuznetsov joined United Russia.

Suddenly out of a job, Mikhailov was at a loss. His political masters in the Kremlin promised to find something for him, but they were slow to deliver and he was left kicking his heels. This was the most difficult period of his career: suddenly powerless and irrelevant, he was left to brood over how he lost an intensely personal political fight. 'I missed it a lot,' he said of the governor's job. On top of political defeat, his marriage of thirteen years fell apart.

Eventually, he was offered a minor position in the Kremlin and moved to Moscow. 'It was a sinecure,' Mikhailov said. He left his ex-wife and son in Pskov, where they live to this day. Mikhailov ended up working in the Kremlin for seven years until 2012 when hangers-on and placeholders were cleaned out after Dmitry Medvedev stood aside and Putin returned to the presidency. It was around this time that Mikhailov met his second wife: for their first date, he took her to the Bolshoi Theatre. He recalled how impressed she was when she learned he had been a governor.

When Russia began sponsoring an insurrection in eastern Ukraine following the 2014 revolution in Kyiv, Mikhailov sensed an opportunity. These events were a time of great hope for Russian nationalists, most of whom are also imperialists, and they cheered a face-off with the West and the reclamation of 'lost Russian land'. The Kremlin has traditionally been wary of full-throated nationalism, fearing it can't be controlled. But the conflict in Ukraine required more in the way of public ideology: once marginal cranks were given airtime on state television, millenarian 'Eurasianist' ideas crept into official rhetoric, and arms and equipment flooded across the border to the rebels. Mikhailov was one of the Russian volunteers – a collection of nationalist ideologues, misfits and imperial dreamers – who headed west.

After arriving in Donetsk in May, Mikhailov was introduced to rebel prime minister Alexander Borodai, a former spin doctor, who made him a minister in the Russia-sponsored government. Mikhailov's ex-political overlord Surkov, now coordinating the Kremlin's work in eastern Ukraine, approved his appointment. As the conflict escalated that summer, the rebels went from success to the brink of military defeat.

'I wouldn't say that I enjoyed it there, but I did my work, and I consider it to have been good work,' said Mikhailov. In a chaotic situation, he tried to restrict himself to civilian affairs. But his brand of pragmatism was out of place in a rebel statelet run by soldiers, shadowy financiers, criminals and intelligence officers. In October, as the Kremlin continued publicly to claim this was a Ukrainian rebellion, Mikhailov was told his former roles in Russia made him a liability. 'I tried not to stand out, but, in reality, I had been a governor and an assistant in the Presidential Administration. I was the "hands of Moscow!" And the highest-ranking Russian official there,' he said. Shortly after leaving Donetsk, he was sanctioned by the EU and banned from travelling. He was forced to cancel a holiday to Croatia.

Mikhailov's experience on the frontline of the so-called 'Russian Spring' was a watershed moment: not only did it strengthen his identification with Russian nationalism, it made him feel politically relevant again. But his time in Donetsk did not restart his career. Despite predictions the Kremlin would not be able to put the genie of nationalism back in the bottle, that is exactly what it did. As the military situation in eastern Ukraine reached a stalemate, tempers cooled, the story faded from the headlines, the most independent-minded rebel commanders were removed and the nationalist dog-whistles from the Kremlin ceased. There was no nationalist resurgence.

For Mikhailov, the Kremlin did not go far enough in Ukraine. He was disillusioned and out in the political cold, far closer to a nationalist quasi-opposition than the corridors of power. Just over a year later, he decided to run for office again. 'I needed to prove myself,' he said. 'Just take part. Simply doing nothing would be worse.' The place he chose was his Pskov Region home town, Velikie Luki.

Mikhailov stood in elections to the regional parliament, a significant step down for a former governor. Initially, he sought a nomination from United Russia and arranged a meeting with Andrei Turchak, the influential governor of Pskov Region, to discuss whether this would be possible. When Turchak made clear that the candidates were already chosen, Mikhailov decided to quit United Russia. 'I had been thinking of leaving anyway,' he said.

What happened next is hard to disentangle from Mikhailov's difficulty accepting his political insignificance. First, he reached an agreement with the nationalist party Rodina to be nominated as their candidate without joining the party, and, when Rodina ditched him, he came to a similar agreement with the Party of Pensioners. They, too, dropped him. Mikhailov claimed that both parties were pressured by Turchak. Eventually, A Just Russia, a declining centre-left political party, agreed to nominate him. Ahead of election day in 2016, posters in the red and yellow of A Just Russia appeared around Velikie Luki with a photo of Mikhailov, arms crossed, and his slogan: 'I know what to do.' Although he said he had no chance of winning, he clearly hoped for a comeback. It was not to be: Mikhailov finished fourth with just 10 per cent of the vote. The following year, he made another attempt, this time in Pskov city council elections. Once more, the Party of Pensions agreed to put his name forward and then dropped him at the last minute.

Listening to Mikhailov describing these abortive efforts to re-enter the political fray, I couldn't help thinking how his career had come full circle: he was again a fringe nationalist seeking election in Pskov Region, just like the early 1990s. But Russia is a very different place, and not one where an independent politician, even one as unthreatening as Mikhailov, can hope for an electoral breakthrough. The Kremlin's iron grip on politics at all levels means strangling political threats in the cradle is second-nature.

Unsurprisingly, Mikhailov wholeheartedly backed Russia's full-scale invasion of Ukraine. 'It's my personal opinion that, of course, it would have been three times more simple to do this in 2014,' he said in an interview on the day Russian tanks rolled across the border. With age, he has become more outspoken about his nationalism and he often uses ethnic slurs to refer to Ukrainians. The war put Mikhailov on the map as a nationalist commentator and he appeared frequently on the YouTube show of the former FSB officer Igor Girkin – also known as Strelkov – who was a ruthlessly effective rebel commander in Ukraine in 2014. Strelkov was jailed in 2023, apparently because of his criticism of Russia's military leadership.

Already in his sixties, time is running out on Mikhailov's career. Perhaps inevitably, he looks back on the 1990s with nostalgia. 'Unfortunately, Russia has not managed to create a multi-party system. There are proto-parties like the Communists and the LDPR. But the others are nothing to write home about, they're just interest groups,' he said. 'What's the point of having a party anyway if nothing is decided in the Duma?' After leaving United Russia in 2016, Mikhailov has been without a party affiliation. When I asked if he would ever join another political party, he paused. 'I don't intend to,' he replied. 'But I don't want to rule it out. Not at the moment.' He paused again. 'Maybe.'

13

iPhone Artist

I first met Dima Markov on a train heading to Pskov Region. It was July 2007 and we were travelling overnight from Moscow with about thirty other volunteers to take part in the month-long summer camp at Belskoye Ustye. I was a university student at the time, and had flown into the Russian capital a few days earlier. As the train rolled through north-western Russia, Dima was swilling from a can of beer. He was stick-thin, lanky and had closely cropped hair. He introduced himself to the volunteers, and recounted anecdotes from other orphanages he'd visited. He told me that he was a photographer, and, as if to prove the point, got out his camera and flicked through his photos.

Summer camp would be a life-changing experience for many of the volunteers on that train, but none more so than Dima, who was then twenty-five. Each of us had different reasons for being there: some were training to be speech therapists, psychologists or teachers and needed work experience; some had lofty ideals; some just wanted an adventure. I was there to practise my Russian, and do something I thought would be useful. Dima was there, first and foremost, to take photos.

Every volunteer was allocated to a group of children at the orphanage, and Dima was placed with a group of older boys. He quickly became a hit. His easy eloquence, honesty and empathy made him instantly popular with the muscled and sometimes intimidating teenagers. Instinctively, a few of the volunteers adopted schoolteacher-type personas with the kids, chiding them for scuffles, or not washing their hands. But Dima was never like that: he remained himself. With the older boys he smoked incessantly and peppered his conversation with expletives. For group performances, he taught them to break-dance.

Among the volunteers, opinion was divided about Dima – some idolized him, others were irritated by his tendency to do his own thing. Every evening, we would gather to prepare activities for the coming day, but Dima had little interest in making costumes, planning lessons or trying out board games. He was loud, provocative and seemed to enjoy argument for argument's sake. Some said primly, albeit fairly, that Dima was more concerned with taking photos than contributing to summer camp. Others that his style of photography came dangerously close to exploitation.

There was no disagreement, however, about the quality of Dima's photos. He accompanied his charges everywhere, and took thousands of pictures of them as they washed in the *banya*, fought, smoked, swam and climbed the scaffolding of the Church of the Holy Ascension. Ordinarily, orphanages like the one in Belskoye Ustye were extremely difficult for outsiders to access, but being a volunteer gave you a special status. And Dima took full advantage, using his camera to hack a visual window onto this secretive world.

A few years later, Dima made a short film about summer camp that he called 'Volunteers'. Exhausted but undaunted, volunteers were shown embracing kids, organizing games and, generally, bringing a ray of light into otherwise bleak lives. It captured something of the naïve essence of summer camp, but I always thought it teetered on the brink of glamourization. The film was overlaid with a track, 'Restless', by British electronic group UNKLE, which included the refrain: 'Gotta follow the light to the love.'

Most volunteers were deeply affected by the plight of the orphanage children, and became convinced of the need to do something – *anything* – to help break the vicious cycle of institutionalization. Some went on to become teachers, found charities and children's villages, and a couple even adopted orphanage kids. Many returned repeatedly to summer camp, and a few – like Dima and me – ended up moving to Pskov Region. Later, Dima described the desperate feeling that arose after leaving Belskoye Ustye the first time: 'I told everyone about it – those I should have told and those I shouldn't. Some looked at me like I was a madman. Which, at that moment, I was.'

Soon after our first summer camp, Dima left Moscow and moved to live permanently in Fedkovo, a village near Porkhov, where, under the auspices of a charity, he helped to set up a halfway house for orphanage kids. The young men who came to live in Fedkovo were the most physically and mentally able. At first, they would come for short spells, and then, if they adapted successfully, would relocate permanently. While the majority had lived in Belskoye Ustye, Dima also sought out teenagers from other local institutions. He spent his time doing fostering paperwork, as well as dealing with orphanages, social services and courts.

Initially Dima funded his life in Fedkovo by occasional trips to Moscow where he'd photograph parties at elite nightclubs attended by Russia's super-rich. The contrast with the orphanage was devastating. 'It was really difficult for me to comprehend what I saw in those two places. And I was not only seeing it, but also taking part,' Dima said. 'It was difficult not to start judging. I don't think rich people are bad, swindlers, or thieves. They were intelligent people . . . It was just difficult to observe such a difference.' As soon as he could afford to, he gave up the work in Moscow.

It was while living in Fedkovo that Dima managed, for the first time, to successfully combine the two things he felt most passionately about: photography and social activism. It was a delicate balance. While he'd use his photographs to publicize causes, raise money and attract attention, he did this through intimate portrayals of those under his care.

Every twist and turn of Fedkovo life was documented in detail on Dima's page on then fashionable blogging site LiveJournal, where he built a large following by posting photographs and articles. He created a whole world for his readers, often comparing Fedkovo to a fictional village called Prostokvashino from a beloved Soviet cartoon. Dima – who'd never been to university but was now responsible for looking after several vulnerable young men – was particularly influenced by a famous Soviet pedagogue and theorist, Anton Makarenko, who set up homes for orphans in Ukraine in the 1920s. Dima's evocation of Fedkovo unashamedly echoed Makarenko's novel, *The Pedagogical Poem*, which recounts the exploits of the gangster-like teenagers in his care, who were fiercely loyal, brave and bound by their own honour system. Gradually, Makarenko wins the trust of the boys, and manages to fashion something resembling a functioning community.

When I spent time with Dima in this period, I always found him intimidating. Partly, I was in awe of his raw talent, and his growing celebrity. But he could also be fierce, and unforgiving. He didn't suffer fools gladly. I was never able to keep up with his drinking, which could be unrelenting, and his swearing which was non-stop. He enjoyed arguments, attention, and shocking his interlocuters. As he got drunk, Dima's lanky body seemed to turn floppy, and he would become even more conflict-prone, and sometimes aggressive. Eventually, he fell out with the orphanage staff so dramatically that he was banned from entering the building. In one incident while living in Fedkovo, he asked a confectionary shop in Pskov to bake a cake decorated with two reindeers having sex, and created a mini-media storm with outraged blog posts when they refused. And in 2012, he went along to the trial of Pussy Riot in Moscow with a sign reading: 'Have you lost your fucking minds?' He was immediately detained by police.

At the same time, though, Dima seemed to be able to charm almost anyone – from an alcoholic on the streets of Pskov, to the curator of a prestigious Moscow art gallery. He was also empathetic, and deeply kind. He helped me find somewhere to live when I first moved to Moscow. And I remember one time arriving in Fedkovo in the dead of winter, several hours before dawn. Dima had ensured there was a freshly made bed and hot stove.

For many years, I knew nothing of Dima's childhood, or why and how he started taking photos. But not long before he died of a heroin overdose in 2024, we had a long conversation about his childhood. Dima was born in 1982 in Pushkino, a commuter town just outside Moscow. His early years were defined by the collapse of the Soviet Union and the economic and social upheaval of the 1990s. His father was an artificer, who mostly made tin pipes and ventilation systems, and his mother – like her mother before her – stitched sacking in a nearby factory. Dima remembered ration cards, queuing for food, and how the scarcity of meat made it the subject of endless conversations. He remembered his excitement in the 1990s when the first yoghurts appeared on shop shelves. And when Russian troops loyal to Yeltsin shelled the White House in 1993, he remembered being envious of the older boys who'd gone to see the burning building.

Violence was never far from the surface. Trying to evoke Pushkino in the 1990s, Dima described how he once got caught up in a police raid when buying a cigarette – they were sold individually – at a kiosk. 'Suddenly, fuck, out of nowhere, a car appears and people jump out and start shouting loudly and swearing, like: "Bitch, whore, get on the floor, we're police detectives! Fuck you, whores!" They were armed. Everyone falls to the floor and two men were arrested and taken away. I stood there, shook myself down, bought a cigarette and went on to school.' He also described his father's reaction when his mother came home in tears saying she'd been attacked on the street. 'My father grabbed an axe – his axe was always by the door because fucking alcoholics occasionally got the wrong door and tried to get into our flat – and took my mother by the scruff of the neck and went to find the fucking guy who did it.'

There was no refuge from the violence at school, where teachers would turn a blind eye to kids with bloody noses, or who had obvious problems at home. Dima recounted a strict hierarchy among the boys, and constant fights behind an old greenhouse. 'When a group of people is trapped in a cycle of violence it needs to be constantly maintained,' he said. 'All those fights were necessary to keep the cycle going and ensure no-one escaped. You have to maintain the level of violence otherwise everything falls apart. Everything ended badly for those boys. I think they're all dead.'

The district where Dima's family lived was divided into less prestigious two-storey blocks, and newer, five-storey blocks. Their flat on Factory Street was in a pastel-yellow, two-storey block with a corrugated roof. 'You can't imagine how envious I was of kids who lived in five-floor houses,' Dima recalled. 'I was ashamed to have people around.'

Dima's father drank heavily, sparking frequent arguments, and would pass out most evenings. When Dima helped carry him to bed, he could knock his father's head against the door frame without waking him. Dima's mother took refuge in God, becoming a devout Orthodox Christian when he was twelve. Seeking to avoid home, Dima would climb an apple tree in the vicinity to read, or spend hours playing in building sites and on garage roofs. He and his friends would collect bottles for resale, and sometimes went to the petrol station to wash cars for a few roubles. Once, they were told about the corpse of a woman in a ravine, and went to get a look before it was collected by the police.

Dima was still in school when he started taking drugs. Initially, it was marijuana given to him by his cousin (who had bought it from police officers selling seized drugs). Dima tried heroin for the first time when he was eighteen. He studied for a few years in college, before buying a fake school-leaving certificate, which allowed him to enrol at a university. But this was just a ruse to avoid military service: he never attended classes, and was eventually kicked out when caught with drugs. After that, he worked in a video store. 'At that time I was using anything that I could get my hands on and, at that time, you could get your hands on everything,' he recalled.

In one of several breaks with the past, Dima suddenly decided to move to Moscow in his early twenties. He talked his way into a reporting job at national newspaper *Argumenti i Fakti*, where he spent four years learning the craft of journalism. Only then did it occur to him to try his hand at photography. With a digital SLR camera bought on credit, Dima gravitated towards Moscow's Three Stations Square, a gritty terminus of three railway lines, and a hub for bootleg goods, homelessness and petty criminality. Looming over the square was one of the capital's Stalin skyscrapers. 'It was covered in stalls selling everything from fucking Czech porn to clothes and gifts for kids,' Dima recalled. 'There were many different types of flamboyant people around. I also remember that the fucking police were very angry, and very drunk.'

It was about this time that Dima found himself a photography teacher: Alexander Lapin, a prominent, Soviet-trained photographer then in his sixties. Characteristically, Dima emailed Lapin on a whim after reading his book, and was invited to his flat. Lapin did not run formal courses, or give lectures, but adopted photographers in whom he saw potential, setting them tasks and chatting with them for hours in his kitchen.

Above all, Lapin preached the importance of composition. 'Alexander believed photography was a visual language. In a picture, you are imparting a certain mood to someone that's impossible to pin down – you can only feel it,' Dima said. 'A photograph is like a language, and any language works according to rules.' Lapin maintained that any photograph stood on two legs: truth, and beauty. 'You won't get very far on one leg,' he said in an interview.

Dima's decision to set up the halfway house in Fedkovo – another break with the past like his move to Moscow – was likely an attempt to reduce his drug use. Such changes of circumstance appeared to allow him, at least temporarily, to manage his addiction. He later said those few years in Fedkovo helping extricate teenagers from Russia's orphanage system were a second childhood; and one of the happiest periods of his life. Of course, there were failures as well as successes. But there is no doubt Dima's interventions helped several young men escape a life of institutionalization.

It was hard adapting to rural Pskov Region, and Dima felt torn between Fedkovo and his previous life. 'I find it hard to live in the countryside and, after everything that's happened, impossible to live in the city. It's with horror that I realise it will probably be like this forever,' he wrote to me in an email in the autumn of 2010.

The end of Dima's time at Fedkovo was precipitated by tragedy. One of the young men in their care – a blonde, kind-hearted teenager called Fyodor who suffered from kleptomania – died from a seizure. The exact reason was never established. Perhaps inevitably,

Dima and others at Fedkovo pointed the finger at the orphanage (where Fyodor still attended school). The orphanage staff blamed Fedkovo. Fyodor was buried alongside Sasha, whose funeral I had attended, at the far end of the cemetery in Belskoye Ustye. While the death was a catalyst, it was not Dima's only reason for moving on: he was also burnt out. Either way, his departure pushed him into a spiral of drug use in which, at one point, he injected with a man whose child was locked in the next room. Eventually, Dima was hospitalized, and diagnosed with HIV.

In yet another bid to reinvent himself, Dima moved to Pskov. This was the moment when he abandoned traditional cameras, and switched to using an iPhone that allowed him to get closer to his subjects, and dispense with the paraphernalia of prints, exhibitions and galleries. He became an early user of Instagram, and quickly amassed a large following. Some said, half in jest, that Dima's Instagram page was the sort of page Dostoevsky would have run if the social network had been around in the nineteenth century. And his feed filled up with perfectly composed images from the Russian regions, usually taken on the edge of towns or cities, among crumbling blocks of flats, muddy rivers and old garages. His subjects were the most marginal in society: alcoholics, the homeless, addicts, orphans, the very old and dying, shaven-headed conscripts and children. While most Russians would, instinctively, turn away from such people, Dima imbued them with beauty, glamour and even eroticism.

Street photography allowed Dima to give free rein to his ability to capture fleeting moments of symmetry, and emotion. When he arrived in a new town, he would look online to find out where the biggest concentrations of people were likely to be – markets, railway stations or shops. Sometimes, he would roam the suburbs listening to electronic music, and looking for something to photograph. I never saw him on one of these walks (he said being in the company of other people made photography impossible), but he had a distinctive gait, with all his weight pitched forward, and I can imagine him striding around, earphones in, searching for the perfect image.

While Dima's photos can often seem unbearably sad, he humanized his subjects – whether they were bored shop assistants, scared soldiers, beggars or children playing in the street. One of Dima's friends, the journalist Aleksei Pivovarov, who I spoke to in the weeks after Dima's death, compared Dima to the painter Caravaggio. 'He saw the light inside nondescript people, and shone his love onto them. And they become the centre of the universe,' said Pivovarov. 'Dima was a great humanist who followed directly in the footsteps of the best artists of the Renaissance.'

Taking pictures helped Dima manage his addiction, and he often said that, without art, he would have been dead long ago. For Dima, finding and creating the perfect image was akin to a religious experience – a prayer – or, perhaps, a substitute for a chemical high. 'As an addict, I can tell you that, when you see that a photo is coming together, the feeling is . . . the highest, most satisfying thing life has to offer,' he told one interviewer, going on to compare the process to an expression of divine grace.

Photography was also a means for Dima to process his past. 'Viewers see some of my subjects as bleak if not, let's be honest, depressing. But I feel the opposite: peace,' he wrote in his 2018 book *Draft*. 'When I manage to express this bleakness in a text or photograph, I feel as if it becomes a little less inside me.' This was perhaps why he was drawn again and again to scenes of urban marginality – in other words, back to the people, emotions and aesthetic of his childhood. 'I don't know why I'm so drawn to the past! It's a fucking affliction that our country suffers from. And so do I! It's some sort of fucking hankering after the past, and not the future,' he told me. 'But, fuck it. I'm a person of my country. I've got the same affliction as everyone else.'

After a few years of renting, Dima bought himself a flat in Pskov on the edge of the city centre, where he lived alone. An old shop, the flat had high ceilings. On one wall was a map of Russia marked with all the places Dima had visited; on another hung an expensive-looking bike with flat tyres that Dima said he'd only ever used to retrieve drugs. Dima was not one for saving money, and he liked to spend what he had on expensive electronic gadgets, watches and branded clothing (one article about him after his death dubbed him 'an intellectual in Adidas'). Latterly, he bought a *dacha* near the Velikaya River, where he said his parents could stay when they visited.

When I asked Dima whether he was religious, he had difficulty formulating an answer. Eventually, he said 'yes'. But immediately qualified this by adding he knew religion was used by people, including his mother, as a crutch, and that nothing could replace therapy and medical treatment when it came to managing addiction. He said he only went into churches to take photos. 'Sometimes I think there are . . . higher laws according to which day-to-day life is organized. And that they're above our understanding. At other times I think there's nothing else but the fucking theory of relativity.'

Despite his professional success, Dima continued to volunteer and remained involved with different charities: devising joint projects, taking photos and raising awareness of causes through stories, interviews and images. Such was his online following that, with a single post on social media, he could generate thousands of pounds of donations. The charities he supported included orphan integration programmes, drug rehabilitation centres, homeless shelters, human rights groups and hospices. He said he saw something biblical in the way staff at such organizations would work long hours caring for people despite there being no end to the suffering. 'Justice is the realm of the devil; the realm of God is charity and forgiveness,' he said in one interview.

Dima attributed his popularity to the fact that most Russians – even if they were high-flying professionals in Moscow – retained a nostalgia for the Russia he photographed; the Russia of their childhoods. Some said Dima's greatest service was how he packaged the provinces in such a way as to make them fashionable in Moscow's fancy bars, restaurants and cultural centres.

When it came to politics, Dima was evasive. While he had seen first-hand the gulf between Russia's disadvantaged and its most privileged, he had no problem with untrammelled consumer capitalism. While most of those who praised his photographs were from Russia's liberal intelligentsia, he was also proud of having online followers who backed Putin. Dima's nationalism ran deep. He was a public supporter of Navalny, and I guessed that included Navalny's anti-immigrant rhetoric. Even amid the war in Ukraine, Dima was uninhibited about expressing patriotism. 'It's easy to love the Russia of postcards with cupolas, churches and beauty. But you try loving it with people who are wrong, or who don't think like you,' he told me. 'I love my country, and I love the people that I meet on my travels. I love Russia a lot.'

The last time I saw Dima was in Pskov in early 2023. We hadn't been in touch for a while, and I'd forgotten how intense and impatient he could be. As we spoke, he sat on a kitchen stool, and wrapped his spindly limbs around his thin body: legs crossed, and arms twisted behind his back. Occasionally, he'd stop to crack his neck. He repeatedly ran the palm of his hand over his shaven head and, when he got particularly agitated, he paced the room.

Mostly, we talked about the war in Ukraine. After Russia launched its full-scale invasion, Dima had a major relapse, disappearing into drugs and doing little work for almost a year.

He overdosed three times, and told me he no longer had any veins in his arms. Amid the fires of war, he felt as if nobody needed his photos. And he admitted that he'd been blindsided by the level of support for the invasion in Pskov. 'Even with all my experience, I was fucking shocked by the appetite for war,' he said. 'Of course, I'd noticed it in some of my friends and protagonists. Hypothetically. Before it all started. But I was surprised by the scale.'

As Dima spoke, I had no doubt he was disgusted by the killing in Ukraine. He thought it would end badly for all involved. But I found myself wondering about the nature of his opposition to the war. Did he really want to see Russia humiliated on the battlefield? It dawned on me that he drew a substantial moral equivalence between the two sides. And that his sympathies lay, first and foremost, with the victims he could see in Pskov: the traumatized and injured Russian soldiers, and grieving families.

After Dima's death, I was contacted by a Russian journalist collecting testimony from those who had known Dima. When he told me he'd spoken to pro-war friends of Dima's who believed Dima supported Russia's cause in Ukraine I was taken aback. In my mind, there had been no doubt Dima was against the war. However, I reasoned, Dima liked his celebrity status, and it's perfectly possible that he told people – including me – what they wanted to hear. Perhaps he was scared for his safety. Perhaps he still harboured the idea that, as an artist, he didn't have to take a side. Perhaps I'd projected my own views onto him.

After all, his lifestyle meant Dima was very close to those fighting in Ukraine. He'd taken photos of Pskov's famous paratrooper division, lived for a time with a paratrooper, and several of the young men he'd helped over the years were serving in the army. As news of the invasion broke on the morning of 24 February 2022, Dima said he messaged the Pskov paratroopers he knew: 'Take care.' Their phones were already turned off.

When I asked him how he explained the willingness of Russian men to go and fight, he pointed to how they lived. 'When you don't value your own fucking life, when there's fucking nothing from which you can draw strength, and there's no interest in life, of course you'll fucking go off to war without a second thought,' he told me. 'In normal fucking life, you have to think about where to live, about making sure your fucking woman doesn't scream at you, and solving everyday fucking problems, which are boring and, fucking uninteresting. Fucking debts, all that sort of thing. But out there, there is only one question: either you remain alive, or you die. This simplifies everything. It's easier for you. I have experienced this myself. It's easier because you only have one problem, and it fucking makes life understandable; what you have to do becomes clear.' Russia was a deeply traumatized country, he added. 'You need to relate to Russians as sick people.'

Dima was often asked why he didn't leave Russia following the invasion, but, in truth, it was difficult to imagine him moving abroad. He would have been cut off from his subjects, and unsure how to handle himself – the kiss of death for his type of photography. When I put this question, his reply was: 'Who needs me there?' Nor was he able to abandon the Russian people and places to which he felt so attached. Theatre director Kirill Serebrennikov, a friend of Dima's who had the meeting with Father Tikhon, told me Dima was bound to Russia through good or ill. 'People like him can't be outside Russia. Of course, it's hard for them to be inside Russia, distressing even. And painful. But they stay in the country that they can't live without.'

Dima said he felt sorry for amputee veterans he encountered on trains between Pskov and Moscow, for the conscripts rushed to the front with little idea of the horror that awaited them, and for returning Russian soldiers who had witnessed the death of their friends. They were victims, too, Dima seemed to be saying: victims of Russia's pitiless war machine that had so little regard for human life. One of the last photos Dima posted on Instagram was of an alcoholic veteran back from the front covering his eyes as he sobbed.

In the end, Dima chose to stay in Russia while the war in Ukraine raged – and he embraced that choice, making the compromises it required. To avoid jail, he stopped publicly expressing his political opinions, and referred to the war by its official term of a 'Special Military Operation'. Even in private he was more cautious. For a time, he stopped using Instagram (which was banned by the authorities at the beginning of the fighting), and posted more content to Telegram, as well as Russia's Facebook equivalent, VKontakte.

His position, and his compromises, though, clearly caused him some anguish. Just ten days before he died, he addressed his critics – real or inside his own head – in a blunt post. 'I understand that, having moved abroad, it's easy to stifle your urge to pity,' Dima wrote. 'But I am here. I can't just stop loving those close to me and start hating them . . . I don't know how to act correctly in this situation and be a good person for everyone, or whether, indeed, that is even possible.'

In the last year of his life, Dima became heavily involved with Survivor, a charity that helps drug users, and was part of a project to set up a rehabilitation centre in the city of Nizhny Novgorod for teenage addicts. He was even planning to leave Pskov, and move back to Moscow.

At the beginning of 2024 he was living in one of Survivor's centres and writing a book. When he went back to Pskov for a few days, he stopped responding to messages, and Survivor's founder, Maksim Uryadov, raised the alarm. One of his friends in Pskov went round to his flat, where, through the window, she could see him on the floor. Eventually, the police arrived and broke down the door. There were several syringes on the table, and Dima was dead. He was forty-one.

The news of his death was reported by *Pskovskaya Guberniya* on 16 February, 2024, just a few hours after the death of Navalny in an Arctic prison colony. For many, including myself, it was a haunting coincidence. It seemed as if two of the brightest lights left in Putin's Russia had been snuffed out simultaneously, leaving little but darkness. Dima's family were strongly opposed to a public funeral, so the only guests who attended the remembrance services – one in Pskov, one in Moscow – were those on a pre-approved list. A few days after the second anniversary of Russia's invasion of Ukraine, Dima was buried in Pushkino.

In his last years, Dima was frank about his drug use, and whenever he'd told me the details, I'd been left with the uncomfortable thought that he was unlikely to live to an old age. He was always extremely thin, but latterly became almost translucent, the skin drawn so tightly you could trace his skull. One time we met in Pskov, his face was bloodied and bruised – he waved away a question about what had happened. Nevertheless, his death was still a shock. In the following days, much was written about his talents as a photographer, which would have pleased him. Some compared Dima to Henri Cartier-Bresson, and said his photos would be studied for many centuries to come. Others placed him in a Russian tradition of socially orientated artists, like the writer Maxim Gorky or painter Ilya Repin, who made the 'invisible' people of Russian society 'visible'.

Re-reading Dima's last posts on social media, I was struck by one I found on Telegram just a few months before his death. 'One day, the happy moment will come along when, at last, I'll die,' Dima wrote in a few paragraphs of philosophizing as he reflected on seeing a pile of his books ready to be shipped to buyers. 'My few neurons will stop firing, and, along with them, all the mistakes that have piled up over the course of my tormented existence will dissipate. But, when all the dross is forgotten, my photos will remain. That's the part of me for which I feel no shame, and which can be thrown into the future as little paper planes.'

14

War

Svetlana pleaded with her husband not to go and fight in Ukraine. 'I tried everything: "What about the children? How will it affect the kids? And what about us?" But nothing worked,' she said. 'What else could I have done? Should I have threatened to slit my throat with a knife if he left? Or what? If words didn't help, what could I have done? Maybe I should have fought him, or tied him to the bed with handcuffs?'

After visiting a Pskov military recruitment office in late 2022 to put his name forward as a volunteer, Mikhail, a thickset thirty-one-year-old with mousy brown hair, got a phone call on Svetlana's birthday to report for active service. He bought himself some equipment, including a sleeping bag, and left for training at a military base north of St Petersburg two days before New Year. While still at home, Svetlana recalled Mikhail talking about his own death: 'He even said to a friend as they were saying goodbye: "Well, that's it then, we'll probably never see each other again." As if it was their final meeting!'

Svetlana and Mikhail's last encounter before his deployment was a month later when she took the two children to visit him at the base. They spent five hours together. A photo taken that day shows the four of them in a café: Mikhail in a military jacket and tight-lipped, Svetlana smiling slightly at the camera. The following day, he was put on a train to Belgorod, the closest Russian city to the Ukrainian border.

It's hard to miss the military in Pskov Region. One of the first associations most Russians not from Pskov have with the city is that it's home to the 76th Guards Air Assault Division. Paratroopers in their sky-blue berets are a common sight on the streets, and the transport planes they use for practice jumps circle endlessly overhead. One summer, I rented a fourth-floor flat in the centre of the city, and, on warm afternoons, the distant crackle of small-arms fire from the 76th's ranges wafted through the open windows.

Considered an elite force with a reputation for brutality and bravery, Russia's paratroopers mark their professional holiday on 2 August, which is notorious for its displays of brawling, violence and drunkenness. It's an excuse for ex-paratroopers, now mostly balding and sporting beer bellies, to don their berets, consume large amounts of vodka, jump in fountains and roam the streets looking for trouble.

At the forefront of almost every major conflict in Russia's post-Soviet history, the 76th saw action in both Chechnya and Ukraine. As exposed by Pskov opposition leader Lev Shlosberg, they were one of the units secretly sent across the border into Ukraine in 2014. In Pskov, the 76th has two large bases: at the entrance to one there is a large poster with a picture of planet Earth alongside a tank, helicopter, plane and several masked soldiers. It reads: 'Russia's borders have no limits.'

The wider region is also home to plenty of other military infrastructure, including airfields and radar installations. While driving near the town of Ostrov on a winter afternoon, the blue sky dusted with tufts of clouds, I remember seeing several Ka-52 'Alligator' attack helicopters skimming above the distant treeline. When one of the helicopters approached us head-on, just a few hundred metres above the road, it dipped its nose as if lining up to open fire.

Mikhail was raised on the edge of Lake Peipus to the north of Pskov, and the Russian armed forces would have been part of the backdrop to his day-to-day life. He would certainly have been familiar with the 76th. And he would have known about Pskov's martial traditions in which the city guarded Russia's western flank against invaders – whether Polish Catholics, Lutheran Swedes or Nazi Germans. The Russian medieval leader Alexander Nevsky famously defeated an army of Teutonic knights in the 1242 Battle on the Ice just a few kilometres from the village where Mikhail was born and raised.

As the war raged in Ukraine, I found the profile of Mikhail's wife, Svetlana, on social media. Fearing official reprisals, the relatives of Russian soldiers are usually reluctant to talk to Western journalists. So, I turned for help to an old friend and journalist, Katya Fomina, who did groundbreaking reporting on Russian atrocities in Ukraine. Katya agreed to be an intermediary, and contacted Svetlana to set up an interview.

A short woman with large, black glasses, Svetlana appeared on the video call that Katya conducted in a T-shirt decorated with pineapples, and her youngest daughter in her arms. Her hair was straight, and, as she spoke, she moved around the house doing odd jobs.

Svetlana said she was not the only one who had argued with Mikhail over his decision to go to war – his mother and friends also begged him to reconsider. Apart from the obvious danger, there were plenty of reasons to stay: Mikhail's job in a cement factory made him the family's sole breadwinner, and the couple had two young daughters. The eldest, Dariya, was seven when Mikhail joined up. The younger, Yevdokiya, just six months.

It's true that Russia offers significant financial incentives for contract soldiers, which can mean men like Mikhail receive the equivalent of almost a year's salary as a sign-on bonus. But Mikhail was not in debt, he was not prone to drinking binges, and, while the family was undoubtedly poor, they were not poverty-stricken. Nor was he motivated by ideas. At least according to Svetlana, Mikhail did not believe he was defending his family, or liberating the oppressed people of Ukraine from a mythical 'Nazi' regime. He didn't watch the news, and had no interest in developments on the battlefield. He'd never been to Ukraine. The closest he came to an ideology was professing a desire to kill *khokhli*, an ethnic slur for Ukrainians. Svetlana recalled him saying: 'We'll kill all the *khokhli*.'

Instead, his decision seems to have been wrapped up in how he understood his masculinity; a child-like fascination for guns and explosions; and the traditional appeal of the armed forces as a social elevator.

Mikhail first told Svetlana he was interested in enlisting after Putin announced partial mobilization in September 2022. Over the course of several weeks, mobilization hoovered up a few hundred thousand men for the army, which was then on the backfoot as Kyiv reversed some of the gains Russia had made in the first weeks of fighting. Mikhail's younger brother, Alexander, was one of those who received his call-up papers. 'When mobilization started, he said it would have been better if they'd taken him instead of his brother,' said Svetlana. Perhaps Mikhail thought it was wrong that his younger brother was in danger while he was safe at home. Perhaps he was jealous to be missing out.

Either way, the war appeared to make Mikhail start thinking about what it meant to be a man. The pull of traditional masculinity is a powerful one, immediately understandable to most Russians, and has been used extensively in army recruitment campaigns. In one slickly made, viral recruitment video from 2023, which also plays on the insecurities of those in low-paid jobs, a taxi driver, gym trainer and security guard are shown transformed into soldiers. 'You're a real man!' flashes up on the screen. Followed by: 'Be one!'

Svetlana believes that – 'like all men' – Mikhail was interested in 'running around with a gun, grenades, mortars, and riding on a tank'. Apparently, he told her shortly before departing that he'd 'always wanted to do some fighting'.

Indeed, joining the army was one of Mikhail's few life ambitions. He had enjoyed his year-long military service a decade earlier near Moscow when he was likely regaled with stories about how professional soldiers were well paid, had a steady career, and got financial perks, including a heavily subsidized mortgage. In other words, for a young man from a poor, rural community in Pskov Region, the army was a prestigious job that offered material, educational and social opportunities – and could imbue life with some obvious meaning.

Mikhail twice tried to enlist once he returned to civilian life after his military service, but was knocked back both times. Svetlana said he failed 'psychological tests', suggesting he was deemed unfit by a doctor, possibly because of some sort of mental illness, learning disability or because he was judged to be a suicide risk. The extent of his disappointment can only be imagined. However, with Russia suffering a desperate shortage of manpower in Ukraine, all such checks were scrapped – there were no longer any obstacles. Mikhail, of course, knew he was destined for the front lines. But it's difficult to guess what he was expecting to find there, or whether he quite realized the level of physical danger to which he would be exposed. Perhaps he thought little beyond having a break from the humdrum reality of work, young children and family responsibilities.

If he'd known soldiers who'd already fought in Ukraine, he might have been more wary. Those serving in Pskov's 76th had been at the centre of some of the most intense battles of the early phase of the war. And, like other paratrooper units, they'd taken heavy casualties. After just six months of fighting, some estimates put Russia's total paratrooper losses as high as 50 per cent killed or wounded from a pre-invasion force of some 45,000.

The 76th was at the spearhead of Russia's over-ambitious initial plan. In particular, they were due to take part in the seizure of Hostomel airfield outside Kyiv on the first day of the war. If successful, this would have allowed Russia to fly troops and heavy equipment to just outside the Ukrainian capital, paving the way to a quick victory. Some analysts believe the outcome of the battle of Hostomel altered the course of the war. About 1,000 soldiers from the 76th actually took off on the afternoon of 24 February and were en route to Hostomel when their mission was aborted because Ukrainian artillery rushed to the area had managed to damage the runway.

Instead, the 76th was deployed to the north of Kyiv as part of the Russian attempt to seize the city. The fighting was extremely fierce: what Russian generals had thought would be a cakewalk became a bloody struggle. Incompetence was rife. Some units of the 76th were even issued with out-of-date maps from 1989. Under-prepared, and facing fierce Ukrainian resistance from all sides, Russian soldiers engaged in widespread lawlessness and looting, and committed numerous war crimes.

I vividly remember the day Ukrainian troops liberated Bucha, and news emerged of the worst Russian atrocity to date. At least 500 people, the vast majority civilians, were killed in the Kyiv suburb during its month-long Russian occupation, which saw mass graves, summary executions and torture. Of several horrifying images to be beamed around the world that day, one showed the contorted bodies of seven Ukrainian men lying among rubbish, including Russian army ration packs, by a grey-brick building. All were in civilian clothes: three were topless, their skin greying, and the head of one was flung in the direction of the photographer, his eyes rotted away. The hands of another, slumped face-down on the muddy concrete, were tied behind his back.

Members of a poorly equipped Ukrainian militia unit, the men had been captured and executed in cold blood thirty-one days earlier. Their bodies had been lying there ever since. It subsequently emerged in statements by Ukrainian officials and investigations undertaken by media outlets that the men had been murdered by soldiers from Pskov's 76th.

Events in Bucha were the most flagrant evidence of Russia's disregard for human life in Ukraine. But brutality has been a hallmark of the invasion since its beginning. We don't know whether Mikhail would have been capable of meting out the sort of violence inflicted by the 76th in Bucha. His words to Svetlana about wanting to kill *khokhli*, as well as the fact he volunteered to fight, suggest, at the very least, that it's possible. By the time Mikhail got to Ukraine, however, the situation on the battlefield had changed. After the Russian army withdrew from around Kyiv, it suffered a series of reversals during Ukrainian autumn counter-offensives in Kharkiv Region, and around the city of Kherson.

In a bid to regain the momentum, and buoyed by an influx of freshly mobilized men, Russia launched a winter offensive at the start of 2023. At this point in the war, a major breakthrough for either side already seemed a distant prospect, with the fighting gradually becoming an attritional struggle. Nevertheless, Russia committed tens of thousands of poorly trained troops and large quantities of armour to frontal assaults on eastern Ukrainian towns like Vuhledar, Marinka, Avdiivka and Bakhmut. The offensive began in late January with an unsuccessful attack on Vuhledar. According to a tally kept by independent journalists, the first week of February saw more reports of Russian military deaths than any other week of the war up to that point.

It was at this moment that Mikhail arrived in Ukraine. Svetlana does not know when exactly he crossed the border, nor to what unit he was assigned – although it was nothing as prestigious as the 76th. She does know he was separated from those alongside whom he'd trained. We can guess that, as commanders became frustrated by a lack of progress, new recruits were dispatched piecemeal to wherever they were needed.

The last time Svetlana spoke to her husband was on 4 February, the day before Dariya's eighth birthday. Mikhail phoned from an unknown number to wish Dariya a happy birthday and say he was OK. They only chatted for a few minutes before the conversation was cut short because of a bad line. 'I think he phoned before they departed for an attack,' said Svetlana.

Mikhail was killed four days later.

Svetlana never received any official information about the circumstances of Mikhail's death. But she tried repeatedly to ring the number from which he'd contacted her that final time and, eventually, a man picked up. When she asked what had happened, he told her Mikhail was sleeping in a shelter when it was hit by a shell. Three others died alongside him. It's not clear whether, by that point, Mikhail had taken part in an attack, or if he'd even fired his weapon in anger. 'It seems that was his fate,' said Svetlana. 'He'd only just arrived, and then it was all over.'

The authorities made all the arrangements for the funeral, which was well attended by family, friends and local well-wishers. It took place in a church near where Mikhail had grown up, and he was accorded military honours, including a flag-draped coffin, the Russian national anthem and a military guard who discharged their rifles over the grave. 'Thank God he was in an open casket,' said Svetlana. 'The only thing was that it looked like he didn't have any legs. So, I didn't try to touch his legs. He had some burn marks on face. But it was him – he was recognizable.'

A few days after the funeral, one of Mikhail's sisters posted a photoshopped image of him on VKontakte in which he is wearing military camouflage and holding two rifles. She captioned it with crying emojis and the words: 'You are always in our hearts.' Mikhail's younger brother, then fighting in Ukraine, also posted photos as a sort of online memorial, including several of Mikhail and Svetlana from a night in the village when they were much younger. They show Mikhail's large, calloused hands embracing Svetlana while she grips him tightly by the lapel, as if afraid he's going to get away.

The speed of events made everything seem particularly unreal, and Svetlana said she struggled to process what had happened. 'We'd seen him less than a month ago, and now he was . . . in his grave. I still don't believe it – it feels like he's simply gone away for work and will be back again.'

When he died, Svetlana had known Mikhail for a total of twelve years. While the two had been teenage sweethearts, their time together appeared marked by ambivalence and an acquiescence in the face of more powerful forces. They got to know each other while studying together at a school in Slantsy, a town a few kilometres north of Pskov Region. 'Slantsy' is the Russian word for shale, and the town was founded in the 1930s to mine shale oil deposits. All the mines are now closed.

Born in St Petersburg, Svetlana was removed from her family by social services aged five, and grew up in Russia's orphanage system. She lived in several different orphanages, latterly in Slantsy, before 'graduating' at the age of eighteen. Mikhail was raised in the countryside in a large family – he had seven brothers and sisters. His mother worked in a shop, and remarried after the death of Mikhail's father.

In Svetlana's telling, their relationship was not one of great passion. She messaged Mikhail while he was doing his military service, and they kept in touch over the phone. After he returned, they began seeing each other. He was her first serious boyfriend. She said she was drawn to his air of responsibility, which made him seem adult beyond his years. 'I thought he was already mature,' she said. 'He was serious about life even though he was only twenty.'

After leaving the orphanage, Svetlana moved to St Petersburg to study to be a nurse. Mikhail would come and see her in the city, and she would travel to visit him in the countryside. Unexpectedly, Svetlana got pregnant, and it's here that their lives appear to bow to circumstance, and the inexorable weight of social expectation. Svetlana said neither of them wanted a child, nor were they planning to marry. But that's exactly what happened.

'His relatives were like: "Come on, come on – this is what you have to do. Let's put on a wedding and have some fun." And that was how it was decided,' Svetlana said. 'Of course, all little girls dream about getting married, but, even so, I think you shouldn't get married when you're young . . . [But at that moment] all my girlfriends had already gotten married. It was happening faster and faster. And you looked at them and thought: maybe I want this as well.' Svetlana was twenty-one when they tied the knot; Mikhail twenty-three.

When talking on the video call, Svetlana was business-like, almost emotionless. She spoke loudly, as if she was shouting over someone, a trait I recognized from other children I'd known from orphanages. Raising your voice is a way to stand out; a way to be heard.

After the wedding, Svetlana abandoned her studies and moved to Gdov, a town near Lake Peipus, so they could live together.

Mikhail had various farming jobs, including as a tractor driver, and she worked in a nursery. In 2020 they returned to Slantsy and, with the money from the sale of a flat Svetlana inherited, they bought a house. Mikhail was hired by the town's cement factory, and Svetlana became a full-time mother.

Of course, nothing special had ever been expected of Mikhail or Svetlana when they were growing up – not by their teachers, family, nor orphanage staff. Staying out of trouble, getting married, and starting a family was likely the most anyone could imagine for an orphanage girl, and a boy from a remote village. Still, the absence of ambition in Svetlana's life with Mikhail was striking.

Svetlana recounted how she took Dariya on holiday to resorts on the Black Sea, and occasionally visited St Petersburg. 'I wanted my child to go places, travel and see things,' she said. But Mikhail always stayed at home. He wasn't interested. According to Svetlana, one of his favourite phrases was: 'Not at the moment.' He'd use it when she wanted something, and he didn't. Mikhail's only interests appeared to be holding down a nine-to-five job and joining the army. Occasionally, Svetlana said he'd daydream about setting up a business – opening a garage or a timber-felling firm – but he never came close to getting such ideas off the ground.

Svetlana's daily life has not changed significantly since Mikhail's death. She receives benefit payments of 44,000 roubles (£390) a month, which is enough to get by in Slantsy. 'All the same it's difficult when you're alone,' she admitted. '[But] what else is to be done? If I get drunk, would it be any easier? It would not be easier for the kids. And social services would be set on me because I was boozed up and the kids were feral. For what? That wouldn't make anyone's life easier. So, what can I do? You cry and cry.'

One friend urged her to move to St Petersburg to be nearer her mother, with whom she now has some contact, and to give the children more opportunities. She demurred. It was too scary, too complicated, too stressful and too much of a leap. Anyway, she was used to life in Slantsy.

While she said she didn't blame herself, Svetlana repeatedly came back to her role in Mikhail's death in a way that suggested she did feel some guilt. This seemed to stem from a widely held understanding that men are infantile beings, passed from the care of mothers to dutiful wives. A good wife, the logic runs, should have been able to rid Mikhail of the notion of going to war. His departure for the front and subsequent death implied that Svetlana was a bad wife – and a failure as a woman. Svetlana said she was often asked by others: 'How could you have let him go?'

Svetlana also downplayed her grief, as if she was somehow unworthy. After the interview was over, my friend Katya told me she thought Svetlana was someone who took everything on herself. 'I think no one has loved her in her life – not her mother, and not in the orphanage. Nor did her husband show much love,' Katya said. 'That's why she runs herself down so much.'

Pskov Region has been targeted by Ukrainian attacks several times since the beginning of the war. Most spectacularly, six months after Mikhail was killed, Pskov's dual-use civilian and military airport was struck by several waves of what appeared to be drones, resulting in explosions at a petrol dump and the destruction of at least four Ilyushin-76 transport aircraft used by the 76th. Despite the death of her husband and such strikes, the war for Svetlana was something that remained very far away: or, as she put it, 'on another part of the planet'. She said news bulletins on state-owned television were full of lies, and, like Mikhail, she had no time for propaganda stories about the oppressed Ukrainian people, reconquering 'Russian' land, or a Nazi regime in Kyiv. Nor did she mention another common official justification for the invasion – that Russia was threatened by NATO (even though she lives just fifteen kilometres from Russia's border with Estonia, a NATO country). In fact, Svetlana struggled to see any meaning in what was unfolding.

'No one understands where it's happening, no one understands how it will end, and it's unclear what they're trying to achieve. We don't need that land. We live here quietly, peacefully and calmly. And out there, they're just killing one another for reasons that are baffling,' she said. 'If we were under fire it would be different. But there are no tanks here, no bullets flying, no drones in the air, and we're not yet cowering, terrified, in the cellars.' Even Russian soldiers in Ukraine don't know what they're fighting for, according to Svetlana. 'Many even say that it's . . . just for kicks,' she said.

Yet, Svetlana wasn't angry, and didn't blame anyone for Mikhail's death. She levelled no accusations at the Russian state, which had been her guardian as she was shuttled between orphanages as a child, and then took away her husband. Fatalism saturated everything she said. Tragedies were something to be endured; your lot in life was preordained. Maybe, she wondered, Mikhail had been drawn to go off and fight by a 'higher power'?

At the same time, like Mikhail, she expressed absolutely no empathy for Ukrainians who continue to suffer from Russian aggression. 'I don't have a drop of pity for anyone,' she said. Wartime Russia is alive with fantasies about the ghastly things Ukrainian soldiers apparently did to Russians, and Svetlana explained her indifference by referencing oft-heard rumours: how Ukrainian soldiers took drugs, mutilated the bodies of dead Russians, or tortured prisoners of war.

The families of Russian soldiers killed in Ukraine receive compensation and, occasionally, gifts from the local authorities. Svetlana described hers as 'blood money'. But she did go to a ceremony in which the head of Gdov District presented her with Mikhail's posthumous Order of Courage. In photos of the event, the diminutive Svetlana stands stiffly on a stage wearing a bright red dress, clutching the medal in one hand and a large bunch of flowers in the other. Dariya is next to her in a pale green dress.

A few months later, Slantsy updated a local war memorial, adding the names of Mikhail and other Russian casualties from Ukraine. At the ceremony, a group of uniformed kids from Russia's Youth Army held up placards with photos of the dead as relatives laid flowers and officials made speeches. Svetlana, who was in the crowd, said she 'cried and cried'. Of the 23 men commemorated on the memorial, nine died in the decade-long Soviet invasion of Afghanistan and separatist wars in Chechnya in the 1990s and early 2000s. Fourteen had been killed in less than two years of fighting in Ukraine.

There is no memorial to Mikhail in Gdov District where he grew up, but Svetlana said she would like to see one erected. 'That way it would be written into history,' she said. 'It's true he only fought very briefly and wasn't there for very long – but even still! It would have made him happy.' She visits Mikhail's grave every few months, but it's ninety minutes in the car to the cemetery, and she can't drive. She doesn't take the children.

Despite its crippling losses in the first months of the war, the 76th has been gradually reconstituted with mobilized men, volunteers and even a punishment battalion of criminals used for the most dangerous missions. In Russia's badly mauled and depleted army, it has retained its reputation for effectiveness. When Ukraine's 2023 counter-offensive came close to breaking Russian lines in the south, it was the 76th that was deployed to stop them.

In wartime, there are very few blue-beret paratroopers to be seen on the streets of Pskov. But the high casualty rates mean there are thousands of men with permanent mental and physical injuries, and hundreds of widows like Svetlana. Funerals are a regular occurrence, and few cemeteries in Pskov Region lack the graves of dead soldiers. In 2023, the local authorities granted a request for a daily bus service from Pskov to Vybuty, the cemetery most heavily used by the 76th that lies close to the ancient ford.

Svetlana seemed to have few plans for her future. She said she had not thought about remarrying. Apart from dreaming of a holiday at a Turkish resort or going on a cruise, there was nothing she wanted. With the two children, she existed from one day to the next, avoiding decisions that might disturb their routine. 'Time flies,' she said, speaking, not for the first time, as if her life was already drawing to a close. If you didn't know Svetlana was only thirty years old, listening to her would make you think she was twice that age.

Even for Dariya and Yevdokiya, Svetlana's hopes were rudimentary. 'I don't know why, but in my head I'm already giving them away to be married,' she said. 'I would like them to grow up to be decent people, who don't drink themselves into an early grave, get involved with bad company, or go to prison.'

15

Brother Priests

Father Raphael loved taking risks. In his late teens, he terrified a girl riding a motorbike with him when he turned around and tried to kiss her. Later in life, as a parish priest, he would scare passengers with his reckless driving along battered, pot-holed earth roads. He preferred not to use the brakes of a car unless intending to come to a complete standstill, and was known to remove the steering wheel while in motion to fine-tune the mechanism below.

For much of the 1980s, Father Raphael worked as a priest in far-flung parishes in Pskov Region. His third such posting was to Porkhov, where his parish church, the Church of the Nativity of John the Baptist, was an unremarkable, whitewashed nineteenth-century building. It was across the road from an empty field that, decades earlier, had been used as a runway for light aircraft.

Unlike most priests in the atheist Soviet Union, Father Raphael would wear his black cassock everywhere. His two favourite activities when not conducting church services were tinkering with his car – a Soviet-made Zaporozhets – and drinking tea. He cared little for material possessions. One young Muscovite, who would go on to write his biography, recalled the squalor in which he lived: 'Behind the priest's house was a boiler room and the smoke from the chimney was carried into the courtyard, and sometimes into the house itself. There were a lot of flies – Father

Raphael never killed them, preferring to brush them away with a dishcloth. There was so much dirt that had been brought in from the street. Rats ran around the kitchen at night, chased by the cats.'

Despite his eccentricities, or perhaps because of them, Father Raphael, then in his mid-thirties, attracted a group of devoted acolytes. These people were not only local outcasts and elderly parishioners; they included luminaries from Russia's intelligentsia, who would take the overnight train from Moscow. Many adored Father Raphael to the point of obsession. All were drawn to his charisma, deliberate obtuseness and spiritual clarity.

The trajectory of Father Raphael's life is impossible to understand without his elder brother, Alexander Ogorodnikov. They both ended up becoming devout Christians in their early twenties, and undergoing severe trials because of their faith.

In photographs from his youth, Alexander Ogorodnikov has long, thick black hair, which he often wore in a ponytail. When I met him on a February afternoon in his flat on the edge of Moscow, he still had the ponytail, except it was grey. He was softly spoken, had a slight stutter and wore rectangular glasses. His left eye drooped slightly. It had taken me months to find Alexander and get him to agree to an interview, and I'd wondered if he was suspicious. But when we met, I realized what I had taken for reticence was absent-mindedness. As he told stories, he often got sidetracked, leaving his original tale unfinished. Occasionally frustrated by his inability to recall names, he would click his fingers in irritation. The flat was dirty and sparse, filled with papers, books, icons and religious paraphernalia. On a white sofa in the room where we sat drinking tea, a New Testament lay next to a pile of bank receipts.

Alexander and Boris – the future Father Raphael – were born fourteen months apart in the town of Chistopol about 1,000 kilometres east of Moscow. Chistopol was a monotown: almost all its residents, including Alexander and Boris's father, Iol Ogorodnikov, worked in the enormous Vostok watch factory. While Alexander was a keen boxer, Boris trained as a cyclist at the velodrome run by the watch factory. 'He followed me everywhere,' Alexander said of Boris. Far from being religious, both boys were leading members of the Komsomol. Alexander even helped to set up a commando group within the Komsomol that won plaudits for seeking out Chistopol criminals and beating them up; a form of radical Communism that pitted teenage idealists against anti-social, counter-revolutionary elements. Boris also came along. The group followed a number of rules – no weapons, no leaving unconscious people in the streets, no pressing charges – but their opponents were less principled, and several of their friends were killed.

'You didn't need a lot of strength. Just speed and a bit of abruptness,' said Alexander as he described the brawls. 'Particularly when you were in a crowd and everyone could see, it worked out very nicely. It was a lesson.' Eventually, the group came to the attention of the national press, and a full-page article on them appeared in the *Komsomolskaya Pravda* newspaper.

Prestigious Soviet careers looked to be opening up for both Alexander and Boris – but it was not what they wanted. Asked to set up another commando group in a nearby city, Alexander understood he was being offered a foot on the first rung of a Communist Party career, and he refused. Similarly, Boris backed out of a possible cycling career just as he was poised to join the national team. 'He said he realized he was gradually becoming nothing more than a machine for processing food,' Alexander said.

Even as teenagers, it was clear the two young men were repelled by the conventionality of an ordinary Soviet existence, and the emptiness of post-war Communism. They were seeking something more. 'We talked about things together,' said Alexander. 'It was natural that, if I had some thoughts, or doubts, I would share them with him. And that he would share them with me. There were questions to which we were looking for answers.'

In 1971, Alexander enrolled at Moscow's VGiK – the same prestigious film school attended a few years later by Father Tikhon. Alexander was soon joined in the capital by Boris, who had worked for a year in Chistopol's watch factory, and then completed his military service in the Far East. They lived together in Alexander's student dormitory that was filled with young men and women discussing culture and ideas. It was a journey of self-discovery for the two brothers. 'He took after me in most things,' Alexander said of Boris. 'We could disagree about things, of course, and not see eye-to-eye, but to argue? I just don't remember any arguments.'

As if in tandem, the two brothers began to be drawn to Christianity. One milestone on Alexander's journey was watching Pier Paolo Pasolini's *The Gospel According to St Matthew* in a closed Moscow archive (studying at VGiK meant having permission to watch banned films). He found Pasolini's Christ – as much an advocate for social justice as spiritual leader – instantly appealing. In another milestone, he attended a service led by the famous Bishop Anthony Bloom, who he was convinced could see right through him. 'I simply realized he knew everything about me,' said Alexander. 'I was physically convinced he knew who I was, what I was, where I had come from and what tormented me.'

Boris went even further than his brother, and, after embracing Christianity, he enrolled in a Moscow seminary in 1974. Although he easily passed the final exams, the authorities blocked him from graduating – standard practice if the candidate was deemed likely to be too independent-minded. Undeterred, Boris decided, instead, to become a monk. Knowing his friends and family would seek to dissuade him from such a drastic step, he secretly quit his job as a nightwatchman in Moscow and took a train to Pskov Region, where he joined the Caves Monastery. Both Alexander and his mother were shocked he'd made such a big decision without consulting them and they tried to persuade him to reconsider, or just take things slower. But to no avail.

Just as for Father Tikhon, the Caves Monastery played a central role in bringing Alexander and Boris into Orthodoxy. Both travelled there regularly prior to accepting Christianity, and it was there that both men had some of their first, most intense, spiritual experiences. Alexander told me about one of his early trips to the Caves Monastery where he had a vivid encounter with a demon. He'd hitchhiked from Moscow, and the driver dropped him by the side of a deserted road a few kilometres from the monastery entrance. There was forest on either side. 'It wasn't twilight yet, but it was getting dark,' he recalled. 'Suddenly, I saw a girl in a white dress. And this girl started walking toward me. I saw how the dress billowed around her legs as she came closer and closer. And I realized she wasn't walking, but floating. And I was seized with horror.' At this point, Alexander was not a fully-fledged Christian, but he knew about the power of the sign of the cross – so, he crossed himself. The effect was instantaneous. 'She didn't simply vanish. She twisted and turned and gave out a demonic laugh and then disappeared,' he said.

Becoming a monk in the Soviet Union was not straightforward, and accounts differ about how Boris came to be accepted as a novice at the Caves Monastery. Alexander told me local officials were bribed to turn a blind eye to the admission of this former sporting champion and once model Communist. Others claim it was an act of defiance by the abbot at the time, Father Alipiy, who was seriously ill and would soon pass away. Either way, Boris was tonsured as a monk and given his new name – Raphael – in 1975. Less than a year later, he moved up the monastic hierarchy when he was made a hieromonk (a monk who is also ordained as a priest).

By this point, Alexander and Boris' lives were diverging. Even as both were defined by their new faith, they took very different paths. Alexander travelled to the Caves Monastery when he had the time, but the two brothers saw less and less of each other. While Boris immersed himself in monastic life, Alexander was drawn into the Soviet dissident movement. After being arrested at a gathering of a Christian-hippy group called 'Jesus People' he'd organized in a forest in Estonia, Alexander was expelled from VGiK. He began keeping company with famous dissidents, including the nuclear physicist Andrei Sakharov.

Most significantly, Alexander helped found the Christian Seminar – a discussion group about religious life that spread to cities across the Soviet Union. The ideas of its members were bottom-up, and they believed in the importance of the laity in revitalizing the Church. Groups like the Christian Seminar, which gathered in strict secrecy, were one of the few ways for people to find out about Christianity, and they helped shape a whole generation of clerics and influential religious thinkers. Those who came to the discussions broadened their understanding of religion, met like-minded people, and slowly built a new, democratic Christian community.

This was a direct challenge to Soviet ideology, and eventually, perhaps inevitably, Alexander was arrested and jailed. In total, he was kept behind bars for nine years, including a stint in the infamous Perm-36 camp. He experienced the full, brutal force of the late Soviet prison system – a system that was adept at breaking dissidents. Alexander, though, did not submit tamely to incarceration – and fought prison officials for more humane conditions, spending almost two years on hunger strike, and over 400 days in solitary confinement. He attempted suicide several times; was subjected to 'fake releases' in which he was freed and then immediately re-arrested; deprived of letters and parcels from the outside world; and was badly beaten on several occasions. Worst of all, though, was the force-feeding, an ordeal he underwent hundreds of times. This involved prison guards forcing a rubber tube down his nose and pumping scalding liquid-food into his stomach. It was so hot that he would be left in agony from internal burns.

When I met Alexander, I struggled to see the core of steel he must have possessed to survive such violence and despair. Occasionally, as he got into his stride, he was more forceful, but he was still soft-spoken, hesitant and retained an air of helplessness. The answer, I surmised, lay in his faith. 'My heart was burning when I was in prison. I understood that it was not an ordinary imprisonment – it was a kind of mission,' he said in one interview.

Astonishingly, Alexander did win some small victories in his battles with prison staff: notably, he was allowed to keep a Bible in his cell. Gradually, he became the most famous religious dissident in the late Soviet Union – and one of the country's last political prisoners. His case was something of a cause célèbre, particularly in the West. Sakharov, by then a Nobel prize-winner, regularly drew attention to Alexander's plight, and Prime Minister Margaret Thatcher asked Gorbachev about him at one of their encounters.

Finally, in 1987, came the day of his release. After listening to the governor read the formal pardon from Gorbachev, Alexander was led through the prison corridors. News had already spread, and prisoners called out to him as he passed: 'Alexander, do not forget us!' When the prison gates clanged shut, Alexander turned to the blank walls and yelled a line from Corinthians: 'Death! Where is your sting?! Hell! Where is your victory?!' In his telling of the story, his words were answered by the whole prison, 'as if with a single, thousand-strong voice', shouting back at him: 'Alexander, do not forget us!'

While Alexander was behind bars, a great tragedy took place in his brother's life. Boris – now Father Raphael – left the Caves Monastery with a group of other monks in 1982 as a result of a dispute with the authoritarian abbot, Father Gavriil, who also presided over Tikhon's stint at the monastery. The exact reasons for the falling out are not entirely clear, but it's likely there was something of a generational disagreement in which younger monks rebelled against Gavriil. Alexander despised Gavriil, and described him to me as a 'dictator'. Either way, Raphael ended up leaving a place that he loved. Instead, he was appointed to a distant parish in Pskov Region.

In his last years at the Caves Monastery, Raphael had befriended a Moscow student called Grigory Shevkunov, who was increasingly interested in Christianity. A few years younger than Raphael, Shevkunov looked up to the older monk, describing him as an 'elder brother'. Shevkunov is, of course, better known under his monastic name – Tikhon.

For the moment, though, Tikhon's meteoric career was in the future. When he first met Raphael, he was studying at VGiK in Moscow, just like Alexander had been a few years earlier, and inhabiting a world once very familiar to Raphael. Perhaps that was what drew them together. In surviving photographs they make an odd pair: Tikhon is small, thin and fashionable with styled hair and an immature moustache; Father Raphael is at least a head taller, with the beginnings of a paunch, looking stern and dressed in his black cassock.

They were, of course, bound by a shared love of the Caves Monastery, which was a catalyst for both men's religious awakening. And they shared the same *dukhovnik*: Caves Monastery monk Father Ioann Krestiankin. A famous Church elder, who had spent seven years in the gulag for his religious belief, Father Ioann cultivated a grandfatherly appearance, and was wildly popular for his spiritual advice and clairvoyance. Long lines would form outside his monastic cell, and the list of his visitors includes both Yeltsin and Putin. The bond between Krestiankin, and his 'spiritual children' like Tikhon and Raphael, was intense, and he played an oversized role in their lives.

The depth of this attachment was illustrated by one story Alexander (who also had Father Ioann as a *dukhovnik*) told me about the first time he went to the Caves Monastery after he was freed from prison. Barred from entering by Gavriil, Alexander waited until nightfall when a monk on the inside threw down a rope so he could scale the fortified walls. When he went into Father Ioann's cell for the first time in a decade, the revered monk told Alexander, without hesitation, that Alexander had 'suffered for Christ' in jail. As Alexander recounted this moment to me over thirty years later, he paused repeatedly, struggling to control a wave of emotion, his eyes reddening. 'For him to say that to me was very important,' he stammered. It was clear the blessing had been an essential validation of his immense suffering.

Even after he left the Caves Monastery, Raphael would send men and women seeking his help to talk to Father Ioann. One of those dispatched in this way was a teenager from Moscow called Yevdokiya Pozdnyakova, who remembered Father Ioann referring to Raphael as 'Angel Raphael'. Pozdnyakova had met Raphael one Sunday in Pskov after a service in the Trinity Cathedral when she was contemplating suicide. He invited her to Porkhov for a cup of tea, and she ended up staying for several weeks. Pozdnyakova became deeply attached to the charismatic priest, and her memoirs of that time are a fascinating glimpse into how Raphael lived, his character and the influence he exerted over those around him.

Perhaps most surprisingly, Raphael was not given to long lectures about religion, or even talking much about God. Instead, people looked to him as an example, finding inspiration in his simple religious instructions, or in gnomic requests that turned out to have profound meaning. He was not placid, or predictable, and could be quick to anger. Tikhon's anecdotes about Raphael include one in which he assaulted a group of men who attacked him and a group of other monks in Pskov, and another in which he gave his only pair of shoes to a beggar despite the freezing slush of early winter.

As well as a passion for cars, Raphael was obsessed with the ritual of tea drinking. He was particular about how the tea should be made: when boiling the water, he turned off the lights in the kitchen so as to see when the water turned white in a multitude of bubbles. At that exact moment, it had to be taken off the heat. If the person responsible for the tea made a mistake, Raphael would force them to pour everything away and start again.

Visitors would spend hours gathered around the table in his house in Porkhov, drinking tea and conversing. 'When talking with him, every word entered my heart,' recalled one acolyte. 'In crisis situations, I didn't remember what I had read, but only

Father Raphael's words . . . my coming-of-age as a person, and as an Orthodox believer, took place because of him; and him alone.'

Reading Pozdnyakova's memoirs, I was struck by Raphael's cruelty. Pozdnyakova worshipped the ground he walked on – she was likely in love with him – yet his strictness frequently reduced her to tears. He would accuse her of things she had not done, only relenting when she asked for forgiveness; he would jokingly call her his 'whore'; or treat her like a servant in front of guests, ordering her to stand by the table with a towel to mop up spilt tea. Even with hindsight, Pozdnyakova showed no anger about this treatment. She believes it helped break her pride, gave her an opportunity to show humility, and taught her about obedience – a value very important for Raphael, Tikhon and most of those who lived in the Caves Monastery in the 1970s and 1980s. 'Raphael told us so many times that we have to respect the hierarchy,' she wrote. 'If you're told off by your boss, you mustn't say anything to justify yourself.'

Still protective of their mentor thirty years later, several of Raphael's protégés declined to talk to me when I contacted them. However, I did manage to speak to one of Raphael's most famous acolytes from the Moscow intelligentsia – Olga Okudzhava, wife of poet and singer Bulat Okudzhava, the Bob Dylan of the Soviet Union. Olga Okudzhava now runs the Okudzhava museum near Moscow in memory of her dead husband, and when I asked at the ticket office if she was around, she emerged, bustling and self-important, protesting she had only agreed to talk to me because it was about Raphael. Her blonde-silver hair hanging in long plaits, Olga told me repeatedly that Raphael was 'exquisite' and a 'dreamboat', before cutting short the conversation. Raphael only met her husband, an atheist, a couple of times in Moscow. There is an oft-repeated legend that Okudzhava gifted Father Raphael a red Mercedes – but Olga denied this outright.

Alexander said his brother's appeal lay in his straightforwardness and 'extreme' modesty. Raphael was marked by 'simplicity, a lack of artifice, and a lack of spiritual swagger,' Alexander told me. 'With him you didn't have to try and . . . conduct yourself in a certain way, but just behave as came naturally to you.'

When Tikhon wrote *Everyday Saints* many years later, he made Raphael one of the book's heroes. In Tikhon's telling, Raphael was a devout and gentle priest with unique spiritual gifts who could see the path to God in routine situations. However, not all agree. There are those who think Tikhon unjustifiably elevated his friend to a status of near-sainthood. One Orthodox priest and historian of the Caves Monastery I spoke to told me that some of the monks believed Raphael was simply a 'good-for-nothing' who resented the authority of the abbot. Others have said that Raphael's pride was all too evident when it came to cars.

With his brother locked away in prison, the KGB kept a close eye on Raphael. Those who visited him in Porkhov were followed, and a police car would sometimes drive past his house in the middle of the night for no reason. Pozdnyakova recounted how Raphael was once called in by the KGB, who suggested he turn collaborator in exchange for a promotion. Raphael, however, accepted all this unsought attention with humility – and humour. Sometimes, he would even prank KGB officers by deliberately inflating baptism figures, or making reference to non-existent underground printing presses when talking on his tapped phone.

On the morning of 18 November 1988, Raphael collected his newly repaired car from a garage in Moscow and set off on the 700-kilometre journey to Porkhov. A few hours later, shortly after midday, his car collided head-on with a truck south of Velikiy Novgorod. He was killed instantly.

The death was a deep shock to his friends and followers. But it was a particular tragedy for Alexander, who had been out of prison less than a year. 'It was such a blow,' he said. 'I had so many plans.' Alexander has alleged repeatedly over the years that the KGB staged the fatal car accident, but there is no conclusive proof. Given Raphael's love of reckless driving, it's easy to believe he made a fatal mistake on that Moscow–Leningrad highway.

Even in death, Father Raphael was not allowed back to his beloved Caves Monastery. Instead, he was laid to rest in Porkhov. The church was packed for the occasion, stuffy and hot, with those in attendance including Raphael's parents, his brother Alexander, and friends from Porkhov, the Caves Monastery, Moscow and Leningrad. Twelve priests led the service. In the coffin, Raphael's face was covered, but his bare hands were still visible, scarred by the glass cuts he had received in the crash. When the work of the gravediggers was complete, mourners watched as a single dove landed on the wooden cross.

Just over three years later, the Soviet Union collapsed, turning relations between the Church and State on their head. From a persecuted movement, the Orthodox Church returned to the mainstream. In subsequent decades, it became a huge, sprawling institution with a level of wealth, power and confidence unthinkable in the 1980s. No one personifies the new, thrusting Orthodox Church more than Raphael's once-skinny friend, Tikhon, who forged a friendship with Putin.

If Tikhon has flourished in modern Russia, Alexander has slipped into obscurity. In the 1990s he was involved in abortive attempts to establish a Christian Democrat political party before setting up a shelter for homeless teenagers outside Moscow. But he was always more comfortable when there was something to struggle against, and he seems to have been cut adrift by the arrival of religious freedom. Perhaps also, the torture he suffered in prison has left more indelible marks than simply physical scars. An English-language autobiography of Alexander published in 2013 was aptly titled: 'Dissident for Life'.

In many ways, Alexander's failure to make a mark in post-Soviet life was typical of the generation of men and women from the intelligentsia who embraced Christianity in the 1970s and 1980s. They had learnt about religion in democratic seminar groups, suffered for their faith, and thought deeply about the meaning of spiritual truth. But they were crowded out by an, emboldened Church and the masses who flooded into Orthodoxy in the 1990s, many of whom understood little more than when to cross themselves and which icons to kiss. Those like Alexander could have become the foundation of a post-Soviet Orthodox Church that was less fixated on acquiring buildings, money and power – and more on people's souls.

Instead, the progressive Christian thinkers and priests of Alexander's generation have been sidelined. While Alexander was trying, and failing, to found a Christian political party in the early 1990s, Tikhon was given the task of ejecting a reform-minded priest, Georgiy Kochetkov, and his followers from the Sretensky Monastery – a job for which he hired a group of thugs.

Whenever he can, Alexander travels to Porkhov for the anniversary of his brother's death. On one such trip, he told me that he and a few friends were surprised to hear birdsong as they were leaving the cemetery. 'It was the middle of the night. The end of November and there was snow everywhere. Suddenly, an astonishing birdsong broke out,' he said. 'It was happy, full of life, spring-like. We heard it, but we couldn't see the bird. It was joyful, Easter-like, life-affirming. We all understood that he [Raphael] was saying to us: "Be happy for me". It was so clear what was happening.'

Alexander and Metropolitan Tikhon have little contact, but they occasionally meet when Tikhon, too, visits Raphael's grave on the anniversary of his death. Alexander prefers it when Tikhon is absent, as the powerful prelate is inevitably accompanied by a crowd of hangers-on. When Tikhon turned up in 2018 to mark thirty years since the fatal car crash, he gave a sermon in which he said the example of Father Raphael's life was 'so strong, so compelling, and so obviously pleasing to God that hundreds, if not thousands, of people have been led to faith by him'. Photographs from the evening service show the golden-robed Tikhon wearing his bishop's crown and flanked by two priests holding candles. Alexander, in black, looks on from the crowd, his face stained by tears.

16

The Jews of Nevel

As the invading Nazis approached the town of Nevel in 1941, there were agonized conversations in Jewish families about whether to flee east, or sit tight and hope for the best. Many of the older generation remembered the benign German occupation of nearby areas during World War I and believed there was nothing to fear. Others worried about abandoning their houses, or livestock. Liliya Shtykan, then aged eleven, witnessed her family split down the middle. 'Grandma Hana-Riva said the Germans were a refined, cultured nation and that she didn't trust the Soviet authorities. She refused point-blank to leave and relinquish the house,' Liliya recalled. Her distraught father, who was already resolved to leave with his wife and Liliya, fell on his knees and begged his parents to reconsider. They refused.

The Wehrmacht entered Nevel on 15 July without facing any resistance, seizing control of the main road connecting Kyiv to Leningrad. Normal life quickly resumed as the fighting moved east. However, five days later, the Jews who stayed were ordered to register with the new authorities, and wear white armbands and a yellow star on their back. Soon after, most were moved to a ghetto constructed near a light-blue *dacha* owned by one of the town's senior police officers in the gently rolling land around Nevel. Some Russians helped the Germans identify Jewish households.

There are several accounts of the subsequent mass murder of Nevel's Jews, but the most detailed comes from a German motorcyclist. On 6 September, hearing that killings were underway, he and some friends went to have a look. When they arrived, a crowd of about 600 women and children were being guarded by SS soldiers. 'They would take groups of five women from the crowd to an anti-tank ditch about two hundred metres away,' the motorcyclist recalled. 'The women were blindfolded, and supposed to hold onto a stick to be guided to the ditch by an SS man. When they got there, they were expected to get completely undressed, apart from a few old women who only had to go topless. Then, several SS guys pushed them into the ditch and shot them from above. When the women heard the order to undress, they cried out loudly because they realized they were about to be executed.'

In total, about 800 men, women and children, including Grandma Hana-Riva and her husband, were killed at the site, which has since become known as Blue Dacha. Similar terrible scenes were repeated over and over again as the Nazis advanced into the Soviet Union, but Nevel's location near the Belarusian border meant the Nevel ghetto, and the Nevel executions, were among the first atrocities of the Holocaust in Russia.

After the war, Liliya Shtykan wanted nothing more to do with Nevel. A few relatives returned in order to sell the house, noticing that neighbours had taken many of Grandma Hana-Riva's belongings. Liliya was haunted until her death about how they left her grandparents behind. 'She dreamt of that image of her father on his knees,' Liliya's daughter recalled. 'It persecuted her for her whole life, and that's why she never went to Nevel.'

But some Jews did return. One of those was Miron Maksimovsky, who was raised in Nevel in the 1920s, and came back to the town after his wartime service. There, he met and married a gentile schoolteacher, Valentina, who'd been sent to the town from Leningrad after university. Their daughter, Lyudmila, was born in 1952.

When I got to know Lyudmila seventy-one years later, she was living with her husband in the house where she had been raised. A short woman with cropped grey hair, she met me in Nevel's Karl Marx Square, elegantly dressed in a long blue coat and mittens. Polite and attentive, she had the air of a teacher-cum-tour guide, and, if left to talk, would slip into repeating speeches she had given many times before. After showing me some of the buildings, her eyes watering in the wind, we walked across a bridge to her house, which backed onto the Yemenka River.

When Lyudmila was growing up in Nevel, there were still some traces of Jewish life. Minyan, the quorum for certain religious obligations, could still be met, and worship continued in some private properties. Many of those with Jewish heritage used both Russian and Jewish names: Lyudmila's father, Miron, was also Yankel-Meer; and her uncle, Mikhail, was Mendel. Occasionally, you would hear spoken Yiddish, particularly in the market, and at the well. 'Sometimes the adults forgot about their fears,' Lyudmila wrote later. 'And they sat around the table singing "O-o-o, Nevel, mein *shtetl*, Nevel . . ." We listened to this singing as if it was the call of our ancestors, and we were seized by some sort of difficult-to-describe feeling that made us want to be a part of a life about which we knew nothing.'

The Holocaust, and Soviet repression of organized religion, meant many adults in Nevel who remembered Jewish traditions – even if they were not believers – avoided passing on anything to their children so as not to endanger themselves, or their families. Lyudmila was not told that two of her uncles, Haim and Mendel, and their mother, Zina, were among those executed at Blue Dacha. When she was a child, another uncle would take Lyudmila to the memorial erected on the site of the killings to keep him company while he cut the grass. It was not until 1993 that he told her some members of their family were buried there.

Nevel is in southern Pskov Region, less than twenty kilometres from Belarus. There are few border controls between Russia and Belarus, and it's just a ninety-minute train ride from Nevel to the Belarusian city of Vitebsk, which is famous as the home town of painter Marc Chagall. It takes twice as long to get to Pskov. Originally founded as a fortress to protect Muscovy's western flank, Nevel was fought over repeatedly by Poles and the Russians until it was eventually incorporated into the Russian Empire's Vitebsk governorate in 1772. Only in the 1920s did it become part of Pskov Region, and Russia proper. 'When it comes to mentality, Pskov is a foreign town,' Lyudmila told me. 'Like Nevel is foreign for those from Pskov.'

Perhaps more significantly, Nevel was on the eastern fringe of the Russian Empire's Pale of Settlement, the enormous area covering much of modern-day Belarus, Ukraine, Moldova, Lithuania and Poland, where Jews were confined for more than a century before the 1917 Revolution. This was the region of Jewish *shtetls*, which have come to be associated with Chagall's colourful and fantastical paintings, and films like *Fiddler on the Roof*. They nurtured a quintessentially Jewish way of life that was almost entirely obliterated in the fires of the Holocaust.

The number of Jews in Nevel crept slowly upward during the nineteenth century, particularly after the opening of the Kyiv–St Petersburg road. By 1915 it was home to 12,333 Jews

– more than 70 per cent of the town's population. Jewish merchants traded leather, sheepskins, bristle and flax. There were Jewish schools, a Jewish theatre, a Jewish library, a Jewish club and 15 synagogues and prayer houses. Most of Nevel's Jews were Hasidic Jews who belonged to the Chabad-Lubavitch movement that was centred in Lyubavichi, not far to the south. 'In Nevel, not a single table stood smoothly' was a local saying about the enthusiasm with which religious holidays were celebrated.

Of course, *shtetls* were not exclusively Jewish, and Nevel was also home to Russians, Belarusians, Poles, Lithuanians and Gypsies. There were occasional tensions, and the town suffered a pogrom in 1905, but the community was generally tolerant, and tight-knit. 'The specialness and atmosphere of Nevel came from this co-existence and respect for difference,' wrote Lyudmila in her memoir, *Keys From the Old House*. The philosophers Mikhail Bakhtin and Matvei Kagan, who lived briefly in Nevel after the revolution, recalled celebrating both Jewish and Russian festivals.

At first glance, Nevel's Karl Marx Square was typical for small towns all over Pskov Region: large, windswept and grey. But Lyudmila explained this was only its modern iteration: in the nineteenth century there had been an Orthodox monastery on one side, while on the other, instead of a block of flats, a Catholic church. The nearest synagogue had been just around the corner. The churches survived the longest – they were only dynamited in the 1960s, their remaining icons and books burnt in the square.

Lyudmila lived in a part of Nevel formerly nicknamed 'America' because it was a poverty-stricken world apart from the rest of the town, and because it was from where Jews left for the New World. The other Jewish district in Nevel was called 'Amur', after the Siberian river, a combination that led to an oft-repeated joke that Nevel was a huge town – stretching from Amur to America.

It was cosy inside Lyudmila's unpainted wooden house, which had low ceilings and high thresholds. She ushered me past the stove, which she still used for cooking, into her pine-panelled study that had a single bed, bookshelves and a window looking down to the Yemenka past bare fruit trees. 'Life in this corner of the world took place between the road and the river,' Lyudmila wrote of her childhood in this house. 'The river was everything: a beloved view, swimming pool, water for the garden and washing, and a source of fish.'

While the 1941 killings were the most dramatic, and violent, episode in the disappearance of Nevel's Jewish community, decline had set in many years earlier. The Pale of Settlement suffered badly from fighting and pogroms during the First World War, and it was abolished by the Provisional Government that came to power in 1917. No longer restricted in where they could live, many Jews from the Pale of Settlement moved to big cities. Later, the Soviet Union cracked down on organized religion, banning religious education, requisitioning synagogues, suppressing practices like kosher and arresting Jewish leaders. In the 1930s, Communists in Nevel staged a parody Passover Seder, called a 'Red Seder', in which they mocked Judaism and extolled the power of socialism. Outside, crowds of observant Jews passed by in silence, appalled by the sacrilege.

A generational divide emerged between those Jews – like Lyudmila's father – who received a secular education, and their parents, who strove to observe religious practice and uphold tradition. Some young Jewish revolutionaries even took their prayer shawls, and tefillin, and publicly burnt them on Karl Marx Square. A Jewish member of the Pioneers, a Soviet youth organization, remembered taking part in a round-the-clock guard of their headquarters, a former synagogue, to stop older, observant Jews burning the now desecrated building to the ground.

Inevitably, many simply worshipped in secret. Prayer services took place in private houses, and traditions were upheld as far as possible. When the *mikveh* – a small pool used for ritual cleaning – was filled with rubble in 1921, it was replaced by a secret one in a basement that functioned until 1935. After that, at least in summer, local Jews used rivers for ritual cleaning. Even though religious schools were banned, some teaching continued on the sly. One Jewish boy who attended illegal classes remembered his instructor's fear. 'The *melamed* who taught us was terrified of the authorities. It wasn't just the police, even if a postman turned up, he'd tell us all to get under the table. It was a long table covered with a long tablecloth. If someone came into the house, all eleven of us were told to get under the table and be silent.'

Under pressure, the number of Jews in Nevel dropped steadily: from over 12,000 on the eve of the Russian Revolution, it fell to about 6,000 in the mid-1920s. By the start of World War II, there were just a few thousand left. Opinion differs on how many functional synagogues there were when the Nazis entered Nevel – some maintain there was just one in a private house, others as many as three.

There was no slackening of Soviet repression when Nevel was liberated from the Nazis, and assimilation continued apace. It was a process replicated in all the other Pale of Settlement towns that run in a swathe across the south of Pskov Region. When I visited a local museum in nearby Sebezh, the director expressed bafflement when I asked whether there had been many Jews living in Sebezh after the Holocaust. Who, he asked in return, would want to identify as Jewish when just a few years earlier that had been a reason for extermination?

Even the echoes of Jewish culture – a snatch of Yiddish, songs around the table or the presence of a tzadik (a Jewish religious leader) at funerals – that Lyudmila had witnessed as a child, gradually faded. The final blow was the start of the mass emigration of Soviet Jews to Israel and America that began in the 1970s.

Boris Neplokh, whose Jewish-born father left Nevel in the mid-1930s, recalled going back in 1978 and being unable to find any remnants of *shtetl* life. 'In the morning we got off the train at the station Nevel II. Nearby was the wooden bus station, and the market. There were horses pulling carts. People dressed in village clothes. Men in caps lined with cardboard, women in headscarves. A smell of dung. In the small market, an elderly woman selling apples told us: "Almost no Jews remain in Nevel. Some were shot by the Germans during the war, others left to live in various different towns. Have you been to Blue Dacha? You must go there."' From being a living, thriving entity, Nevel's Jewish culture had become a piece of history that was of interest only to occasional tourists, and family history enthusiasts.

Lyudmila moved to Leningrad for university when she was seventeen. And that's where she remained for most of her adult life, teaching Russian literature at schools and universities. Unreligious, and with no particular interest in Jewish culture, almost the only reminder of her Jewish heritage was when she came up against anti-Semitism. In one incident she was almost refused entry to an MA programme. In another, a man on the street told her that she 'belonged in Israel'.

Nevel, however, drew Lyudmila back. A few years before the collapse of the Soviet Union, her parents bought a house in a village not far from the town. Lyudmila, her husband Sergei (a mathematician) and their three children began to use it as a *dacha*. But they liked living in the countryside so much that it became their main home. Gradually, Lyudmila got interested in *kraevedenie*, a Russian term that is hard to translate, but which means, loosely, the study of local history. In a country where history has been erased, manipulated and marginalized, *kraevedenie* is a powerful bulwark against forgetting. *Kraevedi* – those who practise *kraevedenie* – can be extraordinary repositories of knowledge.

What began as a hobby soon became an obsession. First, Lyudmila opened a museum in the village where they had their *dacha*. Then, in the mid-1990s, she was invited to become the director of Nevel's museum. 'Life was full of happiness because I discovered new things every day,' she said of these first years. The museum was a new venture set up after the end of the Soviet Union, and there were numerous blanks she wanted to fill. 'No one had ever paid much attention to Nevel's history,' she said. 'It had been studied by Belarusian historians, but when Nevel ended up in Russia, Russians weren't interested because it was a

Belarusian town, and Belarusians stopped being interested because it was Russian.'

Above all, though, it was Jewish history that was missing. In the Soviet period, there had been an unofficial ban on all Jewish history: almost nothing was written or published, and it was absent from museums. In a Soviet-era tourist guidebook about Nevel that I found in a second-hand bookshop in Pskov, which included a detailed overview of the town's history, Jews were not mentioned once. Of course, the history of Judaism, the Pale of Settlement and Yiddish culture was preserved within families, but there was no collective memory. 'When it came to Blue Dacha and Jewish history,' said Lyudmila, 'I was the very first.'

Boris Zvyagin, who was born in Nevel and later became a leading Soviet physicist, described the town's predicament eloquently in a 1993 letter to Lyudmila: 'Of course, time changes everything, and modern Moscow doesn't look like the Moscow of the 1930s. But the changes Nevel has seen are on a different scale. Everything that existed prior to 1941 was wiped from the face of the earth by those tragic events; continuity was broken; all traces vanished. The world of Nevel as it once was is only kept alive in the fading memories of people, who are fewer and fewer with each passing year.'

Under Lyudmila's stewardship, the museum worked at a feverish pace: staging exhibitions, putting on talks, interviewing the town's elderly residents, organizing trips and guided tours, and running conferences and events. As well as Jewish history, they also focused on Nevel's so-called 'Renaissance' – a period of two years after the Russian Revolution when philosopher Bakhtin, pianist Maria Yudina and a handful of other intellectuals lived and worked in the town. In a similar way to how Semyon Geichenko popularized Pushkin Hills, Lyudmila went about acquiring items for the museum's collection, including books in Hebrew and Yiddish, Jewish prayer shawls and tefillin. She appeared on television and radio programmes, and wrote hundreds of newspaper articles. In total, she's authored 14 books, mostly about Nevel.

Although Lyudmila found a calling in her work, and clearly took pleasure in her lonely fight for historical justice, it was not a glamorous existence. To this day, the museum, which is funded from the town's budget, has no running water, and only an outside toilet. The pay was terrible, and Lyudmila sometimes did not have enough money to make ends meet. 'I sold my engagement ring,' she wrote in a diary entry in 1995. 'We have enough food for a week, but what comes after that?' It didn't help that she occasionally put her own money into museum projects, and book print runs.

Nor was the museum universally welcomed. There were a series of bitter conflicts with Nevel's mayor, who periodically tried to slash the museum's already meagre budget. In her memoirs, Lyudmila described how the museum was visited one day in 1996 by the mayor and his deputy in charge of culture (a former dentist). They were deeply unimpressed by what they saw. 'What sort of museum is this?' Lyudmila quotes them as saying afterward. 'They've got three Jews working here, and all they talk about are three Jews' (a reference to Bakhtin, Kagan and Yudina). Nevertheless, Lyudmila had, by this time, acquired enough friends and supporters, including in Moscow, St Petersburg and even abroad, that she was able to resist efforts to shut her down. The museum survived.

When I asked whether locals had responded to efforts to popularize their history, a flash of anger passed across Lyudmila's face, and I realized that, for her, I must have unwittingly sounded a bit like one of those ignorant town officials. 'This question always irritated me,' she replied. 'If you've read Brodsky, you'll know that Brodsky wrote about how poetry resonates with only one per cent of the population. But that doesn't mean it shouldn't exist. I could say the same about cultural history.'

In today's Nevel, the sole physical remains of the Jewish past are cemeteries: the memorial at Blue Dacha, and a Jewish graveyard. When I visited Blue Dacha before meeting Lyudmila, the footpath was not cleared, and I had to walk about half a kilometre through deep snow, sinking up to my knees. But a giant, black menorah, erected under the auspices of the museum when Lyudmila was in charge, and the old Soviet memorial, which sit in a natural depression in the land, were well maintained and marked with stones according to Jewish practice. Regular commemoration events take place on the anniversary of the killings.

The town's Jewish cemetery, though, is in a dire state: overgrown, abandoned and with many of the nineteenth-century Yiddish-inscribed headstones toppled. After World War II, part of it was turned into a football pitch. The situation was the same for the Jewish cemetery, on a sandy slope dotted with pine trees, in the nearby town of Sebezh – a particularly uncomfortable contrast given its proximity to the well-tended cemetery for World War II German soldiers that I'd visited with Sergei.

The Jewish cemeteries in both Nevel and Sebezh, however, are not just dilapidated, they are being actively destroyed. A need for new burial space means that the next-door Orthodox Christian cemeteries are gradually consuming the historic Jewish graves, the remains removed and broken headstones tossed to one side. There have been sporadic protests about this practice – including an intervention from Lev Shlosberg – but it continues. Lyudmila held out no hope. It seemed certain that the last physical traces of Jewish culture in southern Pskov Region would not exist for much longer.

Lyudmila never really overcame the official hostility to her way of running the museum and, eventually, it became too much. After the appointment of a new mayor, there was another round of criticism, threats to cut funding, and political interference. 'I realized it was impossible to go on,' she said. 'After all, I'm not young and I can't waste my strength on pointless battles. So, I resigned.' Since her departure in 2019, many of the displays have been removed, and some of the items she collected put into storage. Her successor is thirty years younger, a member of the United Russia party and, Lyudmila said, presiding over a 'combination of ignorance and cheap glamour'. She was scathing about the new approach: 'They said that the museum should be for the people. Now it's for the people, and you can go and you can take a photo of yourself with a big, blue bunny.'

With more imagination from officials, and a bit more funding, Lyudmila believes Nevel could have established a Bakhtin centre that would have attracted interest from academics and researchers all over the world. Or it could have been turned into a bustling university town full of students like Tartu in nearby Estonia. But these high-culture projects were pipe dreams. 'It all turned out to be an illusion,' said Lyudmila.

Lyudmila now yearns for the cultural and social opportunities of St Petersburg. But her son lives in Nevel with his wife and four children, and they need Lyudmila and Sergei to help out. 'We have become stuck in Nevel,' Lyudmila said. She no longer spends much time writing history books, having switched to fiction.

Even though the fate of the museum remains a source of bitterness, Lyudmila finds some comfort in how she helped Nevel rediscover its past. She acknowledged that, while the physical record of Jewish culture will disappear, the historical record she has created will endure. Thirty years of work was not in vain. 'If I'm honest, I feel like the most important things have now been articulated,' she said. 'The things for which Nevel will find its place in history, […] have been said; they have been fixed in time. If you were to continue this work, you could only add details.'

17

Divided Lives

Tiina Süvaorg's eyes were a washed-out blue, a few shades lighter than her dress. As we sat in the dappled sunlight outside a café in southern Estonia, gusts of wind spun her dyed blonde hair in all directions and she toyed with the pink plastic slip-on shoes dangling from her feet. Born in a small village in Pskov Region, Tiina moved to neighbouring Estonia in the 1990s and built a life, raising three children who are now in their late teens and early twenties. But her ancestors are all from Russia, her husband grew up in Russia and, until a few years ago, her parents lived in Russia.

Just a few kilometres away from us was the Estonia–Russia border that has marked the eastern edge of the EU and NATO for more than two decades. Heavily patrolled and monitored, this border has become increasingly militarized amid the dramatic collapse of relations between the West and Russia, looming ever larger in the lives of those who reside in its shadow. Hard borders erase ambiguity. But Tiina is one of a fast-dwindling number of people who would be equally comfortable on either side.

Tiina is neither Russian nor Estonian. She is Seto. A tiny ethnic group of some 10,000 people, the Setos have inhabited these borderlands for centuries, retaining their own distinctive traditions, beliefs and culture. Like the Russians to their east, Setos are Orthodox Christians (distinguishing them from the largely Lutheran Estonians). At the same time, they are a Finno–Ugric people like the Estonians and their language, written in Latin script (not Cyrillic), is closer to Estonian – making it incomprehensible to Russians. Historically, some referred to the Seto as 'Pskov Estonians'. Many believe it has been their location on the 'edge of the world' that allowed them to survive. If fate had dropped them a hundred kilometres further to the west or the east, the reasoning goes, they would have been assimilated long ago.

The Seto call their historical homeland *Setomaa*. Comprising some 17,000 square kilometres of forest, marsh and cultivated fields, *Setomaa* abuts the reed-choked banks of Lake Pskov in the north and Russia's border with Latvia in the south. The capital, what the Setos call the 'town of heaven', is Pechory on the Russian side. The Caves Monastery is their most holy site.

The Seto are perhaps best known for their choirs, which preserve a polyphonic, multipart singing tradition, and the enormous conical silver brooches worn by women when in national dress. As part of the Seto 're-awakening' in the late 1980s and early 1990s, the community invented a number of traditions including the election once a year of a *ülembsootka* – a 'king' or 'regent' – in a joyous, day-long festival in southern Estonia that includes a spoof military parade and cheese-making competitions.

For hundreds of years, *Setomaa* has been a border zone: a place where ethnicity shifts from Slav to Finno–Ugric; the language goes from Russian to Estonian; Estonian homesteads replace Russian villages; and religion switches from Orthodoxy to Lutheranism. Over the centuries, it was contested by Russians, Germans, Estonians, Poles and Swedes, and control has passed like a baton between different political masters, tugging the Seto first eastward, then westward, then back again.

But *Setomaa* was never physically split in two by a hard border until Estonia emerged as an independent country following the Soviet collapse. The modern frontier – with its razor wire, CCTV and crossing points – is a man-made barrier between villages, tearing at the fabric of Seto communities. It has even been referred to as the 'Seto Wall', a reference to the Berlin Wall. Above all, it has caused a corrosive imbalance of opportunity. Better economic and educational prospects in Estonia – not to mention access to the EU – have fuelled a Seto exodus from Russia.

The decision to move westward was a simple one for many Setos, because almost all were eligible for Estonian citizenship. Most young Setos also spoke Estonian. Moving to Estonia was the path taken by both Tiina and her sister, Marika. Listening to Tiina talk about her poverty-stricken upbringing in Russia, where the family relied on a horse and cart well into the 1990s, it was easy to understand her striving for a better life. Tiina went to university in Estonia's second city of Tartu, and now works in a customs post on the Russian border; her husband is a long-distance lorry driver. They live in a large house outside Obinitsa, the centre of Seto life in Estonia. While we spoke, the keys to Tiina's black BMW lay on the table between us.

The outflow to Estonia means that many Seto families have been split along generational lines. While young Setos and their children reside in Estonia, their elderly parents live out their days in Russia. There are no exact numbers, but about 4,000 Setos are believed to live in the 25 per cent of *Setomaa* controlled by Estonia. In Russian *Setomaa*, there are just a few hundred, mostly very elderly. This is not a process that happened overnight. Even twenty years ago, Father Yevgeny, a legendary priest among Setos who served in a Pechory church, told a documentary film crew that Russian Setos were dying out: he was conducting just one Seto baptism a year, and no weddings.

The day before meeting Tiina, I'd visited Saatse, which sits on a bit of Estonian land jutting into Russia. The patchwork of Russian, Estonian and Seto villages in this area flummoxed Stalin's post-war planners, who could not find a logical way to draw the border. The result is a tourist curiosity called the Saatse Boot, where an Estonian road briefly runs through Russian territory. But I wanted to visit Saatse because I knew you could walk right up to the border. Despite spending so much time in Pskov Region, I had rarely glimpsed its international borders: Russia enforces buffer zones along all its frontiers and individuals require a permit from the FSB to enter (unless you are arriving in, or leaving, the country).

A five-minute walk from Saatse through an airy pine forest dotted with yellow chanterelles brought me to the demarcation line. The smell of pine rose in the morning sun, and it was quiet apart from a light breeze and the chirp of birds. While the Estonians mark the edge of their territory with black-and-white posts, the Russians use striped red-and-green ones with silver-imperial eagles. In places, Estonia has constructed large, green interlocking fences with spiked tips along the border. Here, however, there was just a single coil of razor wire and a jeep track. Locals told me that, when the war in Ukraine began in 2022, Estonian border guards stopped waving hello to their Russian counterparts on the other side.

Estonia has invested more and more in tightening security along its eastern border as relations between the West and Russia have collapsed. For much of the 1990s, large sections were mostly a symbolic boundary, with stories of people slipping across to visit friends and enjoy picnics, and a flourishing trade in smuggled vodka and cigarettes. Russia's invasion of Georgia in 2008, Ukraine in 2014, and then its full-scale war on Ukraine, however, made small, former Soviet states like Estonia nervous. And in recent years, Tallinn has ramped up its monitoring of what Russia is up to – and beefed up its border defences. While it is rare to see an Estonian patrol, the CCTV coverage is comprehensive enough that, I was assured, if you lingered at the border for too long, officers would quickly arrive on the scene.

As tensions rise, there have been a growing number of incidents. In 2014, Russia snatched an Estonian security officer, Eston Kohver, in what appeared to be a brief foray into Estonian territory near the Seto village of Miikse. He was freed the following year in a spy exchange at a border crossing on a bridge over the Piusa River for Alexei Dressen, an Estonian security official jailed in Russia on espionage charges. Three years later, another carefully choreographed spy-swap reminiscent of the Cold War took place on the same bridge, men in balaclavas and vans with blacked-out windows waiting on either side. Estonia and Russia also probe the other's defences: in 2022, for example, a Russian military helicopter flew at low altitude above *Setomaa*, deliberately violating Estonian airspace for a few seconds.

Over the years, Tiina has crossed the border hundreds of times. Perhaps most symbolically, she and her husband crossed it on their wedding day: they had a religious ceremony and exchanged rings in Russia's Pechory, and then married at a registry office in Estonia. But the occasions on which she was blocked from entering Russia are the ones she remembers most. Once in the 1990s, when Russia was allowing entry according to pre-submitted lists of those with family ties, Tiina was turned back on her way to visit her parents in Russia because of an administrative error.

After Tiina phoned home in tears, her mother drove to the border, crossed into Estonia, and they sat together eating still-warm pancakes in a car park.

Eventually, Tiina renounced her Russian citizenship, meaning she needed a visa to enter Russia. Putting together the visa applications for herself and her children to visit her parents was a 'nightmare', she said. And nor was passing the checkpoints straightforward. 'You had to wait in queues at the border. Maybe the kids were sleeping, maybe not. Maybe they were crying, maybe not,' she said. 'Often we got to the border and there was such a long queue that we turned around and went home. Sometimes we crossed on foot.'

But the border is more than simply an administrative hindrance for the Seto – it complicates access to their ancestral homelands. The Seto have a traditionally close relationship with the land, and they maintain pagan beliefs that include attributing power to certain stones, trees and springs; the worship of non-Christian gods, like Peko, the king of the Setos, who they believe sleeps beneath the Caves Monastery; and a vibrant cult of ancestors.

The Setos' strong attachment to their dead is expressed through visiting the graves of relatives, and by eating and drinking with the headstones. This ritual, according to Tiina, is not one of mourning for those who are gone. 'Mourning happens at funerals,' she said, looking straight at me, her sunglasses perched on top of her head. 'We laugh, we talk, we cry. It's not mourning. It's more like a festival.' Visiting with the dead always take place on certain days, like Pentecost, when the whole community is to be found in cemeteries, as well as the anniversaries of deaths, which are believed to replace birthdays. Seto graves, always accompanied by benches, are cleaned and tended at these gatherings, which means the cemeteries are spotless. 'We would sit there with sandwiches, pies and eggs – grandmother would always boil eggs – and when friends, or people that our relatives knew, walked past we'd always invite them over,' said Tiina.

The hardening of the border and tightening of visa rules means it has become more and more difficult for Setos in Estonia to visit the graves of their relatives on the Russian side. Many simply can't afford the visas. During the coronavirus pandemic, travel was forbidden for long periods of time. And the war in Ukraine and increasing repression in Russia has added a new element of fear. As an employee of Estonia's border guard service, Tiina was banned from visiting Russia after the 2022 invasion.

Being cut off from their ancestors is a source of visceral sadness for Setos, which they find difficult to explain with words. It's like a hidden wound; a link broken across time and space. When Tiina was talking to me about the inaccessibility of her ancestors' graves in Russia, she suddenly gave a half-sob and stopped short. She did not brush away the tear that gathered in her right eye.

The Russian–Estonian border in *Setomaa* – like all the international borders of post-Soviet states – follows the Soviet-era dividing line between the Estonian and Russian republics that was in use from World War II until 1991. Except in the Soviet Union, of course, it was nothing more than a line on a map. This period of the twentieth century was one during which Estonians, Russians and Seto were far more intertwined than today. Interacting on a daily basis, they often felt closer to each other than they did to outsiders from big cities like Moscow, Leningrad or Tallinn.

'My parents always said that a bad peace is better than a good war,' wrote Nadezhda Kataeva-Valk in her touching memoir of growing up in the 1950s and 1960s as an ethnic Russian in *Setomaa*. Throughout her book, she calls the Seto *poluvertsi* – half-believers – a reference to their quasi-pagan beliefs. 'Of course, the *poluvertsi* were different from us: they spoke in their own language, wore their own clothes and the women even gave birth differently – squatting – but that didn't stop us from valuing peace and good neighbourly relations. We were, after all, baptized in the same baptismal font, given the funeral rites in the same church and buried in the same land,' she wrote.

There were also strong economic ties between Russians and Estonians, with those in Estonia reliant on selling livestock and food to the Russian market. One Seto man living near Saatse told me that his grandfather regularly took birch baskets, cucumbers and cabbages to sell in Pskov; in winter he travelled to the city by horse along an ice road on Lake Pskov. Most of these connections were killed off by the modern border, but Russians and Estonians with visas or dual citizenship continue to cross to the other side. While Russians seek Western brands in Estonia, Estonians stock up on cheap petrol and vodka in Russia. Some Estonians even cross over to buy sugar: the sugar available in Estonia is made from sugar cane, whereas the sugar sold in Russia – like that consumed in the Soviet Union of their childhood – is made from sugar beets.

At the same time, of course, there was always enmity. The Seto have long been looked down on as uneducated country bumpkins by Estonians, while the Russians saw them as quislings. Tiina told me how, at school in Pechory in the 1990s, she was mocked for her Seto accent and strange name, occasionally being called a 'fascist'. And at university in Estonia, she was mortified whenever Russian or Seto words slipped into her speech. 'They teased me in Pechory, and they teased me in Tartu,' she said. 'In Tartu, they could hear my Russian accent and in Pechory they could hear my Estonian accent.'

Suspicion and hostility between Russians and Estonians has risen in recent decades as cross-border ties have been cut, and Estonia's fears of Moscow's revanchist aggression grow. On several occasions in Pskov, I heard people referring to Estonians as *kuradi*, an ethnic slur that comes from the Estonian word for 'devil'. In Estonia many view ethnic Russians – even those with Estonian passports – as a security risk. Tiina recounted her son's deep disappointment when he wasn't accepted for police training in Estonia, apparently because of his Russian roots. 'He couldn't understand it,' said Tiina. 'I don't know for how many generations we will have this stigma.'

Inevitably, the Seto get caught up in this animosity, with both Russians and Estonians claiming the Seto are better off on their side of the border. Russians allege that the Seto language is being destroyed by Estonian cultural policies and the Estonians point to how few Seto choose to remain in Russia. There is truth in both allegations.

While Tiina's age means she has only vague memories of life before the appearance of the Russian–Estonian border, her parents spent most of their lives in the Soviet Union. So, after speaking to Tiina, I asked if she could introduce me to her mother, Helju Tsopatalo, and she agreed to arrange for us to meet the following day in the same café.

When Helju arrived, my first impression was of severity. Wearing a tightly bound headscarf, she seemed to be a caricature of a village librarian (her job before retirement). Although she had the same pale-blue eyes as her daughter, she was more restrained, and her guarded smiles contrasted with Tiina's light, carefree laughter. The fitness tracker on her wrist, and her New Balance trainers, were, I guessed, gifts from her daughters, or grandchildren.

Helju, now in her mid-seventies, lived almost her entire life in the Russian village of Podlesye, a mixed Seto and Russian settlement some eight kilometres from Estonia. Her mother survived the Nazi occupation, burying her Seto jewellery in a field during the war, while her father fought for the Red Army. Seto culture was in the doldrums in the post-war period, unfashionable and widely considered to be backward, but Helju made surreptitious visits to church, ran a Seto choir in her library, and donned national costume on special occasions. She twice moved to live in Estonia, but was pulled back both times by family ties. The first time, as a young girl, her parents returned to Russia to care for her sick grandfather; the second time, after working in Tartu for several years, she went back to marry her husband, who was a local. 'It was my fate to return to my motherland,' she said.

As we spoke, Helju relaxed, taking an obvious pleasure in reminiscing. The appearance of the modern border in the 1990s had required her to do bureaucratic somersaults, particularly when it came to her six grandchildren who usually came to stay for the summer holidays. Helju smiled at the memory of the ridiculousness. As foreigners, the grandchildren would need to be registered at her apartment if they stayed in Russia for more than five days in a row – so, to avoid this complicated procedure, Helju would take them across the border once a week, entering Estonia for just a few seconds, to reset the registration requirement. The kids crossed over so often, it inspired a game. 'They built a sort of frame and threw a rug over to make it look like a border checkpoint. And then they checked passports. They all had pieces of folded up paper. My oldest granddaughter was already able to write at this point and she would write who they all were on pieces of paper. They would have a sign saying "STOP" in Russian and pretend to lift the barrier,' she said.

Seto children have particularly close relations with their parents, which made pandemic-era border closures very difficult. There was something particularly distressing about Tiina's parents being so close, yet completely inaccessible. 'You could reach out to touch them, but couldn't get to them,' she said.

When Tiina was finally able to visit, she didn't tell her parents she was coming in case something went awry. 'As I was driving, I thought the road would never end. That it would go on forever!

When I reached the lake, I opened the window because there was nothing to breathe. My heart was beating so fast. The adrenalin! I can't explain it to you. I don't know what speed I was going, but it seemed as if the road would never end.'

The experience of the pandemic worked as a catalyst for a long-delayed family decision, and Tiina told her parents they had to move to Estonia. Helju said she and her husband agreed with barely a moment's thought. By that point, there was little for Helju in Russia – she was retired and her only remaining relatives were her dead brother's family. 'There was nothing keeping us,' she said. So, after fifty years in Podlesye, she and her husband packed up and moved across the border to a flat in Obinitsa, near both their daughters, leaving behind most of their furniture and their cat.

Helju fretted about how she would be received in the local community on the Estonian side, fearing she would be seen as Russian, not a Seto. But she needn't have worried. Invited to a local Seto gathering, she said everyone was so kind that she burst into tears. She has planted a new garden in Estonia with vegetables and flowers, and at least one of her daughters visits every day. Tiina said her mother had found a new lease of life.

Even when Helju went back to Podlesye for a visit and saw the overgrown grass around her old apartment, which she had kept in pristine condition, there was no tug of sadness. 'I drove past, I saw. But I didn't feel upset or anything. I just went past,' she said. 'I don't miss it.'

However, the move to Estonia does mean Helju is now estranged from the graves of almost all her relatives, including her parents. She has asked her niece to make sure the graves are well looked after, but it's not enough. Helju's uncle is buried in her new home of Obinitsa and, on the most recent anniversary of her mother's death, she walked down the road to her uncle's grave. 'I went to light a candle. But I also lit another candle: one for my mother and one for my brother,' she said, her voice breaking and her eyes filling with tears. 'I sat there and cried. Because you can't go to Russia every time.'

Tiina, Helju and their immediate family are trilingual – speaking fluent Russian, Estonian and Seto. While they identify as Seto, keep Seto traditions, and mostly speak Seto among themselves, they are also firmly rooted in both Estonian and Russian culture. Helju told me that, after a lifetime of dealing with Russian books in the library, she was now only reading Estonian novels. The family celebrates some religious festivals, including Christmas, twice: once according to Western Christian tradition and, again, thirteen days later when they are marked by the Orthodox Church. Although Tiina is part of a Seto choir, she also enjoys Soviet and Russian songs. 'When my heart is crying, I listen to Russian music,' she said.

However, these sorts of polycentric families are increasingly rare as the hardening border destroys nuance, and forces people to make an allegiance clear. With Estonia and Russia more and more seeing one another as enemies, the pressure to pick a side has intensified.

This process has been dramatically accelerated by the war in Ukraine. Following the invasion in February 2022, Estonia closed a consulate office in Pskov, halted the issuance of visas to most Russian citizens, and enforced an EU ban on allowing entry to Russian cars. Some Seto in Estonia told me Russian visas were now harder to obtain, and they recounted interrogations by Russian border guards – a not-so-subtle message that they were seen as potential spies. At the time of writing, Tallinn was considering permanently closing the Koidula border crossing with Russia, which is the most convenient route for Setos to reach Pechory and has been used extensively by Tiina and her family over the last three decades. A large rail terminal on the Estonian side of the border at Koidula lies almost deserted.

While Tiina's family may preserve Russian culture and language, they have made an unequivocal choice in favour of Estonia. With time, they will gradually lose their Russian identities. Even Helju, who lived in Russia for more than seventy years, said she now disliked going back. 'I don't want to go often,' she said. 'It's scary. I don't know what the Russian state is thinking. You could go there in the morning and, when you come back in the afternoon it's all changed. Who knows? It's nerve-wracking. When I went there in the spring, I breathed a sigh of relief when I passed the Russian border post and entered Estonia. It immediately became easier. Like a weight had slipped from my shoulders.' When Helju's Russian passport expires, she said she won't renew it, leaving just an Estonian passport. 'When I don't have a passport, then there's nothing to be done. I can't go,' she said. 'That's it.'

The day after speaking with Tiina, a local guide who worked at the Seto Institute took me to see an elderly Seto woman who lived alone in the Estonian village of Serga that was just a few hundred metres from the Russian border. Eevi Liname was in her eighties and had three children, eight grandchildren and six great-grandchildren. Like Russia, Estonia has seen rapid depopulation in recent decades – with many young people moving to other EU countries after Estonia's 2004 accession – and Serga was a shadow of its former self. Eevi said 170 people lived in the village before the 1917 Revolution; now there were just 19. I couldn't help thinking about Nina and Nikolai in Baranovo.

Eevi was waiting for us inside a small, wooden chapel. In anticipation of our visit, she'd lit a clutch of candles and, as we spoke, they began to gutter, the smell of smoke wafting across the room. Outside, wind chimes clunked in the breeze. Eevi wore a floppy beige hat and her skin reminded me of thin paper.

For the last thirty years, the border in Eevi's back garden has become steadily more impenetrable. Mature trees now grow through the beaten earth of the road she used to bike down. Four kilometres away, on the Russian side, is the once-Seto church of Tailovo – where Eevi was baptized and where most of the graves of her family lie. Eevi had not been to Russia since the start of the pandemic. When I asked how she felt about being cut off from parts of *Setomaa*, she replied it was a cause of 'sadness', and looked at the floor.

For Eevi, the inability to visit Tailovo – her family's church and the resting place of her ancestors – amounted to something close to physical pain. It was scant consolation that Tailovo's bells can sometimes be heard from Serga. Nevertheless, on Sunday mornings in autumn she goes down to the village well, where the distant tolling of bells is carried on the crisp, still air.

Epilogue

After knocking, I could hear Fyodor shuffling toward the front door of his red, clapboard house. It opened to reveal a man in his sixties wearing grey dungarees. His white, bushy hair and beard would have given him a passing resemblance to Father Christmas if not for the scowl. A fisherman, Fyodor said he no longer plied his trade because of EU laws that made fishing a farce. When he discovered I was from the UK, he was unimpressed: despite Brexit, I was an emissary of his hated Europe.

'I turned on the TV and saw the most amazing prophecy,' he told me, low cunning flitting across his face. 'To cut a long story short, your England will soon be underwater. It will stop existing . . . Norway, Sweden and Finland will also be swimming with the fishes. But the Baltics will not be underwater like the rest. Instead, they will return to Russia.'

We were on the small Estonian island of Piirissaar on Lake Peipus, a few kilometres from the Russian border. And Fyodor, an ethnic Russian, looked to Russia, visible yet inaccessible, as a better model – politically, economically and culturally. Not only were we speaking Russian, but the programme he referred to had been broadcast by a Russian state channel banned in Estonia. It was covertly accessible on Piirissaar, though, because of the proximity to Russia, as long as you tuned your antennae correctly.

Just down the road was an enormous tower of metal struts with an ever-turning radar that Estonia used to monitor Russian activity. But radars and cameras also help Estonian border guards catch poachers from their own side. 'They've hung a lighthouse – excuse my language – on your arse,' said Fyodor.

During the Soviet Union, fishermen from Piirissaar like Fyodor were free to roam the whole lake, setting their nets to catch bream, zander, burbot, perch, vendace, pike and the sought-after Peipsi whitefish. But when Estonia regained its independence, the Russian half of the lake became off-limits. Then Estonia joined the EU and, according to Fyodor, the fishing industry fell victim to environmental regulations, quotas and red tape. Like others on the island, the span of Fyodor's lifetime has bracketed the slow-motion implosion of his remote community. I found myself wondering if he was one of a tiny number of Estonians who would actually welcome Russian troops if they ever dared to launch an invasion across the lake.

Earlier that day, I'd taken a boat to Piirissaar from a small harbour on the Estonian mainland, about an hour's drive north of *Setomaa*. The squat car ferry with a handful of day-trippers chugged along a narrow channel marked by red and green buoys. It was a sunny August afternoon, just a few tufts of cloud floating over the distant Russian shore. To the south, the forested banks on either side narrowed toward Lake Lämmi, which led to Lake Pskov.

Piirissaar was visible from the moment we left the harbour. A thin strip of green drowning in reeds and marshes, it looked like a place it would be hard to scrape a living. As we approached, a couple of brilliant white egrets stalked slowly along the edges of the reed beds. The ferry seemed to have nowhere to go, but, at the last minute, it did an S-shape manoeuvre through the reeds into a man-made canal, which led to the heart of the island.

In the summer, Piirissaar's population swells to several hundred, including children packed off to stay with their grandparents for the holidays. In the winter, surrounded by ice, and with freezing winds whipping across the lake, there are just a few dozen people.

All three villages – Zhelachek, Toni and Mezha – are on the island's eastern side. There are no paved roads, and everywhere you go there is evidence of the lost fishing industry: nets recycled to serve as fences; crude floats stacked in a corner; discarded fishing equipment piled in abandoned houses. The western side of the island, mostly marsh, is uninhabited. In the warm evenings when I was there the air filled with huge clouds of lake flies – non-biting midges – twisting and turning like a murmuration.

Piirissaar has always been a place of borders and frontiers, with liminality embedded in its language. The name for the village Mezha, for example, which first appeared in the eighteenth century, comes from the Russian word for 'boundary' – 'mezha'. In Estonian, Mezha became 'Piirikyula' – literally, 'border village' – from which arose the island's modern name. Even after absorption into the Russian Empire, the official border between the governorate of Livonia and the governorate of St Petersburg ran right through the middle of the island.

Its location on the fringes meant that, in the late seventeenth century, Piirissaar became the adopted home of religious dissidents fleeing repression in Russia for their opposition to liturgical reforms. Known as Old Believers, these men and women ended up scattered across remote areas all over the Russian Empire. In time, they settled even further away, including Bolivia, Canada and New Zealand. Today, there are a few thousand Old Believers on the western edges of Lake Peipus, including on Piirissaar. They include fisherman Fyodor. Linguistic scholars believe the ancestors of local Old Believers came mostly from Pskov Region, travelling across the frozen lake to escape persecution, or working their way around the southern shore.[1]

Old Believers have always rejected modernization, and are known for their conservatism, patriarchism and millenarianism. Their communities tend to be tight-knit, secretive and self-sufficient, and they are sometimes compared to the Amish in America. Famously, Old Believer men refuse to shave and are easily recognizable by their long, flowing beards. Women dress modestly, with ankle-length skirts and headscarves.

Those living around Lake Peipus are 'priestless' Old Believers, who accept only three of the seven Orthodox sacraments. Baptisms that must involve three full immersions (not a sprinkling of water) were traditionally done in the waters of Lake Peipus.[2] There were even some beliefs peculiar to the area. On Piirissaar, for example, Old Believers held that an unbaptized child who died would be blind in the afterlife, able to see only when there was simultaneous sun and rain on earth.[3]

Ever since they arrived on Lake Peipus, Old Believers – like Fyodor and his ancestors – have been known as accomplished fishermen. But the Old Believer communities supplemented their income from fishing with the sale of vegetables, including the famous Peipus onions, which are planted in raised earth beds and prized for their tartness. Cultivation of onions is labour-intensive, though, and, like fishing, it has collapsed as a commercial prospect in recent decades. Today, small amounts of Peipus onions are grown for locals and tourists.

While Piirissaar was dominated by Old Believers from the end of the seventeenth century, it was also home to smaller communities of Estonians and Russian Orthodox Christians. As I wandered through the island's cemeteries, the civilizational gulf became very clear: in the Estonian cemetery, names on headstones had a German-Baltic-Scandinavian feel, including Karl, Jaan, Elmar, Adolf, Juulie, Oskar, Hendrik, Peeter, Mari, Eliisabeth and Johannes. Graves in the Old Believer cemetery were very different, with the unmistakably Slavic-sounding Yeladiy, Yevdokiya, Yefroseniya, Marfa, Agafiya, Iraida, Stefanida, Karp and Muuga. Although Piirissaar's communities lived apart from one another, worshipped separately and were buried separately, Pavel Umbleja, an amateur historian who showed me around, said there was no record of any ethnic or religious strife.

Perhaps it was the daily struggle for survival that bound islanders together. Lake Peipus, known locally as 'the sea', could be a dangerous place, with storms rising in a matter of minutes. 'You think the lake is very small,' fisherman Fyodor told me. 'But it's not

. . . storms can be so powerful that the water becomes mixed with sand and earth all the way to the bottom.'

Even more treacherous was the ice. Winter was a good time for fish, so fishermen would travel dozens of kilometres over the frozen lake and live in improvised houses on the ice for days at a time.[5] The risks rose exponentially in the spring and autumn when ice was either forming or melting. Black ice was the most unpredictable.[6] 'If the weather's clear and quiet and you see fog in front of you, that means there is open water, not ice. And you shouldn't go in that direction,' Fyodor told me. In spring, fishermen would never venture out alone – for fear of being unable to extricate themselves if they fell through thin ice.

Given the danger, it's no surprise there were a lot of superstitions: it was considered bad luck to whistle, to think about hares,[7] or to encounter people with dubious reputations prior to going out on the lake – in fact, any sort of argument or disturbance was to be avoided.[8] If you met a woman with an empty bucket while walking to your boat, you were likely to return empty-handed.[9] The most unlucky wind was considered a westerly, which fishermen believed would blow all their catch to the Russian shore.

Fyodor was not exaggerating when he said that Piirissaar's fishing industry no longer existed. All that remains are a handful of amateurs, and some poachers who evade border guards. In the last years of the Soviet Union, 'there were eighty-six professional fishermen on the island and 250 retirees who could also catch fish,' said Fyodor. 'Now, there are two.' Above all, this collapse was caused by the emergence of a hard border between Russia and Estonia that gradually cut off locals from their main market for fish and vegetables – the region's biggest city, Leningrad. The economic blow was compounded when Estonia joined the EU, further decoupling the economy from Russia. Unsurprisingly, most people on Piirissaar voted against EU accession in Estonia's 2003 referendum, which returned a nationwide result of 66 per cent in favour. Those who remain on Piirissaar today seemed embittered and, perhaps inevitably, obsessed with past glories – both real and imagined. The Russian ethnicity of the majority, the economic blows of the last three decades, and the legacy of the Soviet Union, meant they were consumed with nostalgia.

Pavel, who came from a mixed Estonian–Russian family, had also witnessed Piirissaar's decline and decay. While his fixation with the past was channelled into an all-consuming interest in local history, he was also bitter. I lost count of how many times he repeated the phrase 'all this is disappearing' as we strolled around the island. His childhood memories, he told me, were of a bustling place far removed from today's reality. 'Even when I visited in Soviet times, there was always something going on,' he told me. 'During the holidays, there were many people and loads of kids running around. There was a racket until midnight. Today, it's nothing like that. If you went out naked, no one would notice you.'

Even for a visitor like me, it felt as if life on the island was being squeezed from all directions. Piirissaar's only school closed in the 1980s and never reopened; the ferry does not run some days, making it impossible to hold down a regular job on the mainland; food, wood and building materials are eye-wateringly expensive; and it takes hours to get to the nearest hospital. Until I arrived on Piirissaar, I'd not realized the sole shop was only open for a few hours each week (there are no restaurants or cafes), and I got very hungry. When I confessed to the founder of a local Old Believer museum that I had barely eaten for several days, she very kindly cooked me a meal.

One evening, I walked to a small beach on the eastern edge of the island where there was a gap in the reeds. There was no one else around, and I could see all the way across the lake. With the sky a deep azure, the rays of the setting sun lit up everything in front of me. Less than a kilometre away the border was marked by a series of buoys glowing golden in the dying light. The Russian shore was close enough to make out dotted pine trees, sandy cliffs and red and white houses.

Gazing across the lake, I realized I was looking at the stretch of water where Russian medieval leader Alexander Nevsky defeated an army of Teutonic knights at the Battle on the Ice in 1242. Although I couldn't see it, I knew there was a huge monument of Alexander Nevsky and his soldiers trampling their – Western – enemies underfoot on the Russian bank. Its lavish opening ceremony in 2021 was attended by Putin, and Father Tikhon.[10] I also realized that Mikhail – the Russian volunteer killed in Ukraine – grew up in a village just a few kilometres inland from the Russian shoreline.

In my mind's eye, I traced the road running south on the Russian side, which I knew would pass by the Yelizarov Convent, where the idea of Moscow as a 'Third Rome' was developed by Philotheus of Pskov, and which I'd visited with Artyom on our walk across Pskov Region. A little further on would be the turn-off to the psychiatric hospital at Bogdanovo. Then, you'd enter the outskirts of Pskov, and glimpse the cupolas of the Trinity Cathedral.

As I stood there in August 2023, I knew this was likely to be the last time I would see Pskov Region for many years. The dangers for journalists in Russia had become too great to justify a visit, and there seemed little chance of that changing anytime soon. Even if Putin dropped dead, a democratic restoration in Russia was no more than a pipe dream.

My feelings were mixed: in some ways, I'd come to see Pskov Region as a sort of second home. It was a place where I had a lot of friends. But it was also a much darker, more disturbing and less welcoming place than it had been fifteen years earlier when I'd arrived for the first time on the night train from Moscow.

The confrontation between Russia and the West means Pskov has again taken on its medieval role as watchtower on Russia's western border. It guards against enemies, and, if needed, would be a jumping-off point for military expansion. But such a stand-off cannot last forever. One day, the pendulum will swing back, and this part of Europe will again become a place of intermingling, compromise and trade – rather than suspicion and war.

The afternoon ferry that took me back to the Estonian mainland from Piirissaar was busy with holidaymakers enjoying the sun. As the buoys marking the Russian border slipped out of view, a dozen Estonian women drank prosecco out of plastic cups. They sang 'Happy Birthday' to one of their group.

I bumped into Pavel, the amateur historian, at the harbour, and he kindly offered me a lift to Tartu. As well as myself and three other passengers, Pavel's car was packed with a summer's worth of home-grown goods: string-sacks of Peipus onions, large jars of honey and improvised containers overflowing with tomatoes, carrots and cucumbers. On my lap, I balanced my rucksack on a rusty supermarket shopping basket full of vegetables. Although Pavel turned on the air conditioning, it got increasingly hot as we sped westward under a cloudless sky. The smell of onions filled the car.

Image Credits

Page xv: Pskov's *kremlin* and the Trinity Cathedral (2017) © Dmitry Markov

Page 2: Nina and Nikolai, supplied from family archive

Page 5: Church of the Holy Ascension in Belskoye Ustye (2009) © Howard Amos

Page 19: German army cemetery in Porkhov (1942), unknown photographer, from the collection of Sergei Yegorov

Page 26: Sergei Kirin in the *Volksbund* cemetery outside Sebezh (2021) © Dmitry Markov

Page 34: Flax growing near Rodina in Pskov Region (2021) © Howard Amos

Page 44: © Illustration by Roger Amos

Page 52: Doves circling over outhouses in Nikandrova Monastery (2020) © Howard Amos

Page 55: Krypetsky Monastery (2020) © Howard Amos

Page 64: Pskov's fourteenth-century Church of Cosmas and Damian on Gremyachiy Mound (2021) © Dmitry Markov

Page 72: Lev Shlosberg (2018) © Dmitri Beliakov

Page 78: Semyon Geichenko in Pushkin Hills (1977) © Yuri Belinsky/TASS

Page 82: Visitors to Mikhailovskoye in Pushkin Hills (1989) © Yuri Belinsky/TASS

Page 85: Geichenko statue being repaired in Pyotr Bystrov's workshop (2021) © Howard Amos

Page 92: Copy of Pushkin death mask hanging on the wall in Vyacheslav Kozmin's *dacha* (2021) © Howard Amos

Page 99: Pskov Caves Monastery (2015) © Jérémie Jung

Page 103: Pskov Caves Monastery during the annual Feast of the Dormition of the Mother of God (2015) © Jérémie Jung

Page 107: Vladimir Putin and Father Tikhon at the Pskov Caves Monastery (2018) © Mikhail Klimentyev/Russian Presidential Press and Information Office/TASS

Page 116: Corridor in the Belskoye Ustye orphanage (2007) © Dmitry Markov

Page 139: A Pskov Region born Russian Trotter named Aleko being ridden in Kyiv in 1976 © Photograph of image by Howard Amos

Page 143: Workers at Volyshovo's stud farm in 1984 (Lyudmila is on the far right) from the collection of Lyudmila Yakovleva © Photograph of image by Howard Amos

Page 150: Volyshovo manor house (2015) © Clive Boursnell

Page 159: The iconic "Raising a flag over the Reichstag" photo by Yevgeny Khaldei (2 May 1945). Source: 1st title page (not on cover) of "Ogoniok" magazine (No 19, 1945) © mil.ru

Page 163: Mikhail Minin © Photograph of image by Howard Amos

Page 170 (left hand-side image): Yevgeny Mikhailov in Pskov (1993), provided by Yevgeny Mikhailov, unknown photographer

Page 170 (right hand-side image): Yevgeny Mikhailov in Pitsunda, Abkhazia (1989), provided by Yevgeny Mikhailov, unknown photographer

Page 176: Vladimir Zhirinovsky (1995) © Yuriy Zaritovskiy / Sputnik / SIPA PRESS

Page 191: Dima Markov (2017) © Aleksei Golovshchikov

Page 199: Paratroopers from Pskov's 76th Guards Air Assault Division (2010) © Vasily Ilinsky

Page 203: Bodies of men dressed in civilian clothes killed at close range in Bucha, Ukraine, during its occupation by Russian forces (3 April 2022) © Associated Press/photographed by Vadim Ghirda/Alamy Stock Photo

Page 209: Conscript soldiers outside a military base in Pskov (January 2023) © Nanna Heitmann/Magnum Photos

Page 220: Father Raphael (right) © courtesy of Pokrov Publications

Page 226: Damaged tank on the streets of Nevel (1941), WikiMedia Commons, unknown photographer

Page 234: Lyudmila Maksimovskaya giving a presentation (2008), supplied by Lyudmila Maksimovskaya, unknown photographer

Page 239 (left hand-side image): Tiina Süvaorg at Kingdom Day (2023) © Harri Sundell

Page 239 (right hand-side image): Tiina Süvaorg with her mother (Helju Tsopatalo) and father in Izborsk (1986), supplied by Tiina Süvaorg, unknown photographer

Page 243: A road connecting Riga (Latvia) to Pskov that runs along the symbolic border of *Setomaa* in Estonia (2015) © Jérémie Jung

Page 248: A Seto women's choir from Obinitsa (2015) © Jérémie Jung

Page 258: Looking east toward Russia from the ferry to Piirissaar (2023) © Howard Amos

A Note on Sources

The research, interviewing and writing for *Russia Starts Here* took place between 2019 and late 2024. The process was interrupted twice: by the coronavirus pandemic, which made travel to Russia impossible, and then by the war in Ukraine. I have only been to Russia once since leaving the country immediately after the full-scale invasion (for a month in early 2023).

The individuals you encounter on these pages are all real people and the quotes attributed to them are exactly what was said to me (not inventions, or imaginative reconstructions). Descriptions of thought processes, or feelings, are based on what I was told by those involved. Where possible, I have made every effort to corroborate the accounts I was given.

With the exception of a couple of conversations that took place in Estonian, or Seto, all the interviews for *Russia Starts Here* were carried out in Russian. The translations from Russian are my own.

The risks of speaking openly and honestly to journalists, particularly foreign journalists, have increased steadily since I first started working as a reporter in Russia in 2010. While I have used the real names for most of those identified in *Russia Starts Here*, in cases where I judged publicity might be dangerous, or inappropriate, I have altered names, locations and small details. Occasionally, for the same reasons, I have chosen to identify people only by their first names.

A Note on Language

At the risk of being erratic, I have tried to use the most meaningful translations for English speakers, prioritizing comprehension.

Translation was particularly tricky for some topics (like disabilities and social care) when the choice was sometimes between a literal translation, holding little meaning; and an equivalent English term, which could be misleading. I selected throughout the translation I thought best conveyed reality. For example, I used the term 'orphanage' even though the literal translation of the Russian 'детский дом' would be 'children's home'.

Writing about border areas throws up its own linguistic complexities. I have courted inconsistency by being led by context – when the events I described took place Estonia, I have used the the English word transliterated from Estonian; when in Russia, the English word transliterated from the Russian.

In some cases, to avoid the confusion of using multiple names for a single place place, I opted for the one that made the most sense in the overall context of the book. For example, I chose to refer to the large body of water near Pskov as Lake Pskov rather than its Estonian name of Lake Pihkva; and I called the larger lake to the north Lake Peipus (its Estonian name), rather than by its Russian name, which is Lake Chudskoye.

Finally, many towns and cities in modern Russia had different names during the Soviet period (for example, St Petersburg was known as Petrograd from 1914 to 1924, and as Leningrad between 1924 and 1991). I have used the names that were current during the period about which I was writing.

Notes

EPIGRAPGH

vi 'Water' by Philip Larkin, from *The Whitsun Weddings* by Philip Larkin © Faber and Faber Ltd.

PREFACE

xiv **territories that make up the Russian Federation:** Russia has 83 internationally recognized regions. The current regime believes that it has permanently annexed six regions of Ukraine, and would claim, therefore, that Russia is made up of 89 regions.

xv **new and unfamiliar atmosphere:** Saki, *The Penguin Complete Saki*. London: Penguin, 1982, p. 557.

xvi **about 10 per cent of Russia's international trade:** '"РОСТЭК-Терминал" предупредили выстрелом в затылок' ['ROSTEK-Terminal was warned with a shot in the head'], *Delovoi Peterburg*, 12 September 2001, www.dp.ru/a/2001/09/12/ROSTJEK-Terminal_predupr2

xvii **giving the town a wonderful brilliance:** G. Lind and A. L. Khoroshkevich (eds), Якоб Ульфельдт: Путешествие в Россию [Jacob Ulfeldt: Journey to Russia]. Moscow: Yaziki Slavyanskoi Kulturi, 2002, p. 297.

xviii **any other region in western Russia:** Olga Ivshina, 'Пропасть между Тувой и Москвой: что известно о потерях разных российских регионов в Украине' '[The gulf between Tuva and Moscow: what we know about the losses of different Russian regions in Ukraine]', BBC Russian Service, 24 November 2023, www.bbc.com/russian/articles/cmmpo4mz53po

CHAPTER ONE

8 **killings of World War II:** In addition to killings, the Nazis rounded up tens of thousands of civilians from occupied territories, and shipped them off for forced labour in Western Europe. One writer who travelled around

Pskov Region in the 1960s recounted how his wife's mother, who lived in Porkhov, was taken to France and used as a forced labourer on Hitler's 'Atlantic Wall' designed to prevent an Allied landing in France (Sanin, *We Are From Pskov!*, p. 15).

8 **pre-war population of 9,562:** These are the figures given in a report issued on 11 May 1944 by a Soviet commission investigating Nazi war crimes.

9 **rural areas of Pskov Region has halved:** Data from Russia's official statistics agency, the State Statistics Service.

9 **contained no people at all:** Cited in Yulia Orlova and Svetlana Popova, '"Выжженная спинами победителей". Псковская область – лидер по вымиранию' ['Scorched earth in the rear of the victors. Pskov Region is a leader when it comes to dying out'], Radio Free Europe/Radio Liberty, 19 May 2023, www.severreal.org/a/vyzhzhennaya-zemlya-za-spinami-pobediteley-pskovskaya-oblast-lider-po-vymiraniyu/32415411.html

9 **fell 40 per cent in the 1990s:** Nefedova, *Ten Pressing Questions*, p. 80.

10 **boar and brown bear are enjoying a renaissance:** Viktoriya Odissonova and Yelena Racheva, 'Волчье место Репортаж из Псковской области, где звери теснят людей с обжитых мест' ['Wolf places: A report from Pskov Region where animals are pushing out people'], *Novaya Gazeta*, 26 March 2017, www.novayagazeta.ru/articles/2017/03/26/71899-volchie-mesto and Lyudmila Savitskaya, '"Это последняя собака на улице"' ['"It's the last dog left on the street"'], Takie Dela, 5 April 2021, www.takiedela.ru/2021/04/yeto-poslednyaya-sobaka-na-ulice

10 **kill farm animals and pets in Pskov Region:** 'Без разрешения не стрелять. В Псковской области сообщают о нашествии волков' ['Don't shoot without permission. Reports in Pskov region about an invasion of wolves'], *Argumenti i Fakti*, 5 February 2020, www.pskov.aif.ru/incidents/bez_razresheniya_ne_strelyat_v_pskovskoy_oblasti_soobshchayut_o_nashestvii_volkov and Anastasia Tarasova, 'Санитары леса или безжалостные убийцы: псковичи осудили охотников за и стребление волков' ['Forest orderlies or ruthless killers: Pskov residents condemn hunters for killing wolves'], *Komsomolskaya Pravda*, January 2021, https://www.pskov.kp.ru/daily/27228/4354742

10 **hissing like a frying pan:** Senkin-Tolstoy, *Ferdinand, or the New Radishev*, p. 5.

10 **patchy in rural Pskov Region:** 'Доступ к мобильному интернету имеют только 78 процентов жителей Псковской области' ['Only 78 per cent of the residents of Pskov Region have access to mobile internet'], *Pskovskaya Guberniya*, 3 July 2023, www.gubernia.media/news/dostup-k-mobilnomu-internetu-imeyut-tolko-78-procentov-zhiteley-pskovskoy-obla/?fbclid=PAAaYd1R3noawHbQDofA_33nnuG01FILWg-Maj1Ol5iXTK_dVvgKKy7ayXoco

14 **their populations are wobbling:** 'За пять месяцев численность Пскова сократилась на 1105 человек из-за миграционного оттока' ['Over the course of five months, the population of Pskov has fallen by 1,105 people because of migration outflow'], *Pskovskaya Guberniya*, 17 August 2022, www.gubernia.media/news/za-pyat-mesyacev-chislennost-pskova-sokratilas-na-1105-chelovek-iz-za-migracion

CHAPTER THREE

30 **the 'wings of a moth':** Hans Christian Andersen, *The Complete Fairy Tales*. Ware: Wordsworth Editions, 1997, p. 404.

30 **for at least 900 years:** Abu Hamid al-Gharnati, an Arab traveller who visited what is now Russia in the twelfth century, described locals who wore linen 'despite the cold' (*Ibn Fad.lān and the Land of Darkness: Arab Travellers in the Far North*. London: Penguin Classics, 2012, p. 73).

31 **the further you rode, the taller the flax:** Gadlo, *Historical-Ethnographic Sketches*, p. 90.

31 **a third of the country's flax exports:** Gadlo, *Historical-Ethnographic Sketches*, p. 89.

31 **leaving the peasants destitute:** Vladimir Lenin, *The Development of Capitalism in Russia*. Moscow: Foreign Languages Publishing House, 1956, p. 298.

31 **It's my favourite profession:** Vinogradov, *The Stories of Former Flax Workers*, p. 9.

31 **or an oil worker in Baku:** Vinogradov, *The Stories of Former Flax Workers*, p. 12.

35 **it looks like I was wrong:** Zvontsov and Geichenko, *How's It Going in Mikhailovsoye?*, p. 176.

36 **allowing companies to pay next to no tax:** Clifford Gaddy, 'Russia's Virtual Economy', Brookings Institute, 11 February 2008, www.brookings.edu/articles/russias-virtual-economy

37 **worsened the mill's financial situation:** Svetlana Prokopyeva, 'Льноволокита' ['Red tape flax'], *Pskovskaya Guberniya*, 27 November 2002, www.gubernia.media/number_117/17.php

38 **capacity of flax mills is being used:** Mikhail Sheludyakov, 'Валюту за пределы области' ['Currency outside the region'], *Pskovskaya Pravda*, 20 January 1996.

38 **estimated to be making a loss:** Ponomarenko, *Pskov Region Flax Workers*, p. 15.

39 **stable and functioning enterprise:** Smirnov, *The Colour and Salt of Dedovichi Lands*, p. 108.

39 **ruins would be exactly what she left behind:** I contacted Antonina and requested an interview about her experience as a flax mill director, but she declined.

39 **Soshikhinsky Flax Mill should have a future:** Shershneva and Tikhonova, *A Small Town in Big Russia*, p. 296.

CHAPTER FOUR

53 **lying around that had been blown up:** Petrova, *Monks Are God's Beloved Children*, p. 396.

53 **Of a world forgotten, but familiar:** This poem was written by Bunin during a stay in Pskov Region for a month in the summer of 1912. (Ivan Bunin, Стихотворения [*Poems*]. Leningrad: Sovetksy Pisatel, 1961).

56 **you feel its wholeness:** Morozkina, *Pskov Lands*, p. 79.

56 **without the slightest chance of restoration?**: Yelena Shiryaeva, 'До основанья' ['To the foundations'], *Pskovskaya Guberniya*, 3 October 2007, www.gubernia.media/number_357/10.php

CHAPTER FIVE

59 **fallout from a scoop:** Aleksei Semyonov, 'Война спишет всё' ['War writes off everything'], *Pskovskaya Guberniya*, 25 August 2014, www.gubernia.media/number_705/00.php

61 **the events of the previous night:** Maksim Fyodorov, 'В больнице у Шлосберга' ['In hospital with Shlosberg'], *Kashin*, 2 September 2014, www.kashin.guru/2014/09/02/lev-2

63 **'our Jewishness ended with that,' he said:** Soviet passports had the notorious 'fifth line' that specified the nationalities of their bearers. 'Jewish' was one of the nationalities.

65 **unforgettably beautiful in its severe and solemn greatness:** Quoted in Cothren, *Outcast Visionary*, p. 44.

66 **like a sleight of hand, or a cruel trick**: One of the best depictions of the many subtle transformations that take place during the shift from a planned economy to the free market is Lea Ypi's memoir about growing up in 1990s Albania (Ypi, *Free*).

68 **on the floor of the Pskov parliament:** 'Grazhdanin TV, Лев Шлосберг Андрею Турчаку о подлинных врагах Псковской области' [Lev Shlosberg to Andrei Turchak on the real enemies of Pskov Region], 2014, www.youtube.com/watch?time_continue=215&v=oYjZX9WBs-Y&feature=emb_logo

73 **sight of desperation and powerlessness:** 'Супруги из псковской "Открытой России" получили больше 10 лет по делу о наркотиках'

['Married couple from Pskov's Open Russia given over 10 years in a drugs case'], 12 August 2021, www.bbc.com/russian/news-58161584

73 **as a 'civilizational choice':** 'Varlamov Talks, "Путин может править пожизненно" | Шлосберг про Украину, Навального, дело Яшина и ошибки Ельцина' [Putin could rule for life | Shlosberg on Ukraine, Navalny, the case against Yashin and Yeltsin's mistakes], 2022, www.youtube.com/watch?v=yZbA8GkKsr8

CHAPTER SIX

74 **"Danger" and "No access":** Geichenko, *In Lukomoriye*, p. 154.

75 **'unique manifestation of the Russian spirit':** Quoted in Binyon, *Pushkin: A Biography*, p. xxvii.

76 **they had two children, Fyodor and Natalya:** *Семен Гейченко и Любовь Сулейманова. Больше, чем любовь* [*Semyon Geichenko and Lyubov Suleimanova. More than Love*], Anna Epshtein, 2010, GTRK, www.smotrim .ru /video /232736.

76 **Although released in 1943:** There is some evidence Geichenko was released early because he cooperated with the NKVD, but it is impossible to say with any certainty because the relevant archive is closed. According to Geichenko's biographers, in later life he hated talking about the camps, and refused to meet with people he had known there.

77 **Geichenko later told a journalist:** Ageeva and Lavrov, *Custodian*, p. 108.

79 **Dryads, in pensive mood immersed:** Alexander Pushkin, *Eugene Onegin*, Chapter II, Verse 1, p. 34 (Penguin Classics, 2008).

79 **after those of Lenin:** Yandex (a Russian equivalent of Google), which has a popular online map service, tallied up the number of monuments in Russia to named individuals in 2018. After Pushkin, the only other writers on the list were Maksim Gorky (4th place), Mikhail Lermontov (13th place) and Lev Tolstoy (15th place), https://yandex.ru/company/researches/2018/monuments

79 **dozens of Pushkin statues in Ukraine were toppled:** Charlotte Higgins, 'Pushkin must fall: monuments to Russia's national poet under threat in Ukraine', *The Guardian*, 5 May 2023, www.theguardian.com/world/2023/may/05/monuments-to-russia-national-poet-pushkin-under-threat-in-ukraine

79 **Pushkin's remains were akin to relics:** Geichenko, *In Lukomoriye*, p. 134.

79 **dreaming about Pushkin was widespread:** Ageeva and Lavrov, *Custodian*, p. 279.

79 **status of demi-gods:** Thomas De Waal, 'Taking Pushkin off his pedestal'.

80 **'Pushkin became our religion':** Ageeva and Lavrov, *Custodian*, p. 280.

81 **bring him any 'old village stuff'**: This was recounted to me by Anatoly – Tolik – who I met when I visited the Dovlatov Museum in Pushkin Hills. Dovlatov immortalized Tolik by making him a character (a drinking partner for the narrator) in his book *Zapovednik*.

81 **'don't trust what they hear in conversations':** Geichenko, *In Lukomoriye*, p. 219.

83 **'can allow itself 3,000 hectares!':** 'Советское телевидение. ГОСТЕЛЕРАДИОФОНД, Семен Гейченко. Встреча в Концертной студии Останкино (1987)' [Semyon Geichenko. A meeting in the concert studio in Ostankino (1987)], 2019, www.youtube.com/watch?v=4BnD5S3_nYQ&t=3161s

86 **'to come out from around the corner':** Dovlatov, *Pushkin Hills*, p. 13.

86 **'create an enormous amusement park here':** Dovlatov, *Pushkin Hills*, p. 68.

87 **'I myself am happy to be deceived!':** These are the last two lines of Pushkin's 'Confession' written in 1826. (Alexander Pushkin, Избранное [Selected Poems]. Moscow: Pravda, 1978, p. 130).

90 **'afterwards we sat spellbound':** Peter Pears and Philip Reed, *The Travel Diaries of Peter Pears, 1936–1978*. Woodbridge: Boydell & Brewer, 1999, p. 132.

91 **'to experience the past as living reality':** Ageeva and Lavrov, *Custodian*, p. 33.

91 **did not double-check Geichenko's stories:** Larissa Ageeva, 'Уроки Семена Гейченко' ['The lessons of Semyon Geichenko'], in O. Bakhtina (ed.), *'Дай оглянусь . . .': материалы Февральских музейных чтений памяти С. С. Гейченко* [*'Let Me Have Look Around . . .': Materials of the February Museum Conference in Memory of S. S. Geichenko'*, Seltso Mikhailovskoye Pushkinskoye Zapovednik, 2019, pp. 164–83.

CHAPTER SEVEN

95 **one in seven of all Russians:** 'Парк "Россия – моя история" принял 20 млн посетителей' ['Russia – "My History Parks" have received 20 million visitors'], TASS, 3 November 2023, www.tass.ru/obschestvo/19198697

95 **film star Russell Crowe:** Clover, 'Putin and the monk'.

95 **could be the next Patriarch:** Zoya Svetova, a journalist who has interviewed Tikhon Shevkunov, told me: 'It's obvious that Shevkunov would like to be patriarch.' Others believe this is very unlikely to actually happen, or, at the very least, a long way off.

96 **homosexuality is a 'cross to bear':** eter the Great St Petersburg Polytechnic University (SPbPU), Архимандрит Тихон (Шевкунов):

о любви, вере и мире [Arkhimandrit Tikhon (Shevkunov) on love, faith and peace], 9 February 2015, YouTube, www.youtube.com/watch?v=DoRlPQteGD8

97 **Tikhon officiated at the funeral of Putin's father:** Zholobova, 'A propagandist from God'.

97 **dubbed 'Putin's *dukhovnik*' for the first time:** 'Путин и его семья – христиане. Это главно' ['Putin and his family are Christians – that's the most important thing'], *Izvestia*, 7 December 2001, www.web.archive.org/web/20120206131228/http:/www.izvestia.ru/news/255666

97 **'one of the most important encounters of my life':** Dimitro Sevastopol, Первая пресс-конференция Тихона Шевкунова в Крыму (РИА новости Крым) [The first press conference of Tikhon Shevkunov in Crimea (RIA Novosti Crimea)], 23 November 2023, www.youtube.com/watch?v=tbTPuj7x6DY

97 **'Putin likes this combination very much':** 'Миллиардер Пугачев. Умер ли Путин и гей ли он, вербовка Пригожина, Зеленский, что будет в 2024 году' ['Billionaire Pugachyov. Is Putin dead? Are you gay? Prigozhin's recruiting, Zelensky, and predictions for 2024'], V Gostyakh u Gordona, www.youtube.com/watch?v=o_S67zRiNQg

100 **a thousand monasteries in the Russian Empire:** Marite Sapiets, 'Monasticism in the Soviet Union', *Religion in Communist Lands*, 4 (1), 1976, pp. 28–34, www.doi.org/10.1080/09637497608430750

100 **the site of his spiritual 'birth':** Kashevarova, 'Metropolit Tikhon: If a Russian stops being a statist'.

100 **apart from empty ritual:** Martin, 'Startsy, Samizdat and underground seminars'.

101 **Caves Monastery by a university friend:** Author interview with Andrei Dmitriev (17 January 2024). A prominent Russian fiction writer who was friends with Tikhon at university, Dmitriev, who grew up in Pskov, was the first person to tell Tikhon about the Caves Monastery.

101 **'something wondrous':** Tikhon, *Everyday Saints*, p. 12.

101 **he would never be the same again:** Tikhon, *Everyday Saints*, p. 22.

101 **became a voracious reader, and excelled:** Author interview with Andrei Dmitriev.

101 **'smiley, soft, and quiet':** Svetova, '"Sechin in a cassock"'.

101 **eventually draw him to Orthodoxy:** Tikhon, *Everyday Saints*, p. 5.

101 **funerals for several of his VGiK teachers:** Andrei Dmitriev, 'Георгий Шевкунов между ВГИКом и РПЦ' 'Georgiy Shevkunov between VGiK and the Russian Orthodox Church', *Ogonyok*, No. 5, 3 February 2008, www.kommersant.ru/doc/2300234

101 **a demon tried to get him to commit suicide:** Tikhon, *Everyday Saints*, p. 9.

101 **loaned the Bible:** Tikhon, *Everyday Saints*, p. 8.

102 **punched an attendant in the face:** From an interview given by a monk at the monastery to a Russian researcher, who passed the transcript to me. Both the monk and the researcher wished to remain unidentified.

102 **Gavriil kicked a monk:** Tikhon, *Everyday Saints*, p. 261.

102 **sending the monk sprawling:** Tikhon, *Everyday Saints*, p. 130.

102 **monitor what was happening in the monastery:** For example, Zuban, *The Pskov Eparchy of Russian Orthodox Church*, pp. 82 and 180. Father Gleb Yakunin, a prominent priest and dissident, refers to Gavriil as the 'chief informer' in Gleb Yakunin, О современном положении Русской Православной Церкви и перспективах религиозного возрожден ия России [*On the Modern State of the Russian Orthodox Church and the Prospects of a Religious Revival in Russia*], *Volnoe Slovo (Samizdat)*, Nos. 35–6, Posev, 1979, p. 12, www.vtoraya-literatura.com/pdf/volnoe_slovo_35-36_1979__ocr.pdf#page=13

102 **'came a deacon from the monastery':** From an unpublished interview with Alexandra Orlova-Model, who emigrated from the Soviet Union in 1972, and returned for a visit – which included a trip to the Caves Monastery – in 1983. Supplied by Oleg Ustinov.

102 **Demons were real:** For example, Tikhon, *Everyday Saints*, p. 102.

103 **'Nobody spoke about Christ himself':** According to the interview with the unidentified monk in the Caves Monastery.

104 **recruited by the KGB:** Famously, Father Gleb Yakunin, a liberal reformer, alleged Pitirim was a KGB asset known as 'Abbot' after he studied the KGB archives in 1992 (Clover, 'Putin and the monk'). Another priest from the liberal wing of the Church, Alexander Men (who was later murdered), said of Pitirim: 'The KGB think he's a believer, but they're mistaken' (Interview of Pavel Men by Anna Kurt, Moscow, 2015. Personal archive of Barbara Martin).

104 **objections from his mother:** Author interview with Andrei Dmitriev. Tikhon has said that, late in life, his mother also converted to Orthodox Christianity.

104 **who worked as a builder in his teens:** Ilya Kolodyazhny, 'Смута Преодолена' ['The time of troubles is over'], *Literary Russia*, No. 43, 2008, www.litrossia.ru/item/3112-oldarchive

104 **'moves on to somewhere else and does the same':** Author interview with journalist Zoya Svetova (16 January 2024).

104 **generals and top FSB officers:** In *Everyday Saints*, Tikhon describes how he called up Russia's prosecutor general after a theft at Sretensky Monastery (Tikhon, *Everyday Saints*, p. 407). His close associates also reportedly include ex-Security Council head Nikolai Patrushev,

Constitutional Court head Valery Zorkin, and prominent talk-show host Andrei Malakhov (Svetova, '"Sechin in a cassock"'). Tikhon reportedly baptized the daughter of oil tycoon Igor Sechin (Pertsev and Reiter, 'An enlightened Russian nationalist').

105 **'impossible to explain rationally':** Author interview with Nadezhda Belyakova (22 January 2024).

105 **far-right politician Jean-Marie Le Pen:** Tikhon (Shevkunov), 'Судьба Северного Человека' ['The fate of a northern person'], Pravolsavie.ru, 5 December 2005, www.pravoslavie.ru/4647.html

106 **publishing sensation:** Anastasia Batmanova, 'Ozon назвал самые покупаемые книги десятилетия в России' ['Ozon names the most-bought books in the last decade in Russia'], *RBK*, 2 December 2020, www.rbc.ru/society/02/12/2020/5fc701e99a7947588oa26occ

106 **Tikhon personally carrying out the baptism:** 'На ночь глядя' ['Looking at the night'], 18 June 2013, Channel One www.1tv.ru/shows/na-noch-glyadya/vypuski/gost-arhimandrit-tihon-shevkunov-na-noch-glyadya-vypusk-ot-18-06-2013

106 (**Tikhon remembers encountering him as a student):** Kashevarova, 'Metropolit Tikhon: If a Russian stops being a statist'.

107 **undoubtedly widely read in Kremlin circles:** For different perspectives on the subject, see: Anton Barbashin, 'Ivan Ilyin: A fashionable fascist', *Riddle*, 20 April 2018, www.ridl.io/ivan-ilyin-a-fashionable-fascist; Marlene Laruelle, 'In search of Putin's philosopher', and *Riddle*, 19 April 2018, www.ridl.io/in-search-of-putins-philosopher; and Denis Leven, 'Иван Ильин – любимый философ Путина, симпатизировавший фашистам. В РГГУ (под руководством Дугина) работает политическая школа, названная в его честь' ['Ivan Ilyin is Putin's favourite philosopher who sympathized with the fascists. In RGGU (under Dugin's leadership) there is a school of philosophy named in his honour'], *Meduza*, 25 April 2024, www.meduza.io/feature/2024/04/25/ivan-ilin-lyubimyy-filosof-putina-kotoryy-simpatiziroval-fashistam-v-rggu-rabotaet-politicheskaya-shkola-nazvannaya-v-ego-chest-ee-vozglavlyaet-aleksandr-dugin

107 **Ilyin as having a 'prophet's gift':** Телеканал Радость моя [Channel Radost Moya], Неравнодушный разговор. Архимандрит Тихон Шевкунов. Несвятые святые. Часть 1 [Not indifferent conversation. Arkhimandrit Tikhon Shevkunov. *Everyday Saints*. Part 1], 27 September 2023, www.youtube.com/watch?v=4pEv_JdBUUc

107 **'just because it is':** 'TIKHON SHEVKUNOV: On Russia, the Church and war'

108 **'bad, vulgar game':** Tikhon (Shevkunov), 'Шенгенская зона' ['Schengen zone'], *Russkiy Dom*, No. 3, 1998, www.russdom.ru/oldsayte/1998/19980310.html

108 **obvious anti-Semitic undertones:** Vladimir Isachenkov, 'Russian probe asks if czar's 1918 killing was ritual murder', Associated Press, 28 November 2017, www.apnews.com/general-news-1ae93c8a88da4ece9f8a71daaa265e83

108 **led directly to the Ukraine war:** SolovievLive, Полное видео беседы с Митрополитом Симферопольским и Крымским Тихоном в студии [Full video of the conversation with Simferopol and Crimea Metropolit Tikhon in the studio], 1 February 2024, Telegram, www.t.me/SolovievLive/237975

108 **being overly harsh:** 'Архимандрит Тихон: приговор девушкам из Pussy Riot суров' ['Arkhimandrit Tikhon: The sentence for the girls from Pussy Riot is harsh'], Vesti.ru, 17 August 2012, www.vesti.ru/article/1998459

108 **denied speculation:** Aleksei Obukhov, 'Венедиктов: Мединский потребовал отменить "Нуреева" после звонка "духовника Путина"' ['Venediktov: Medinsky demanded the cancellation of Nureev after a phone call from "Putin's Confessor"'], *Moskovsky Komsomolets*, 11 July 2017, www.mk.ru/culture/2017/07/11/venediktov-medinskiy-potreboval-otmenit-nureeva-posle-zvonka-dukhovnika-putina.html

109 **as a martyr:** Svetlana Reiter, a journalist who interviewed Tikhon in the Sretensky Monastery, told me his office was filled with portraits of Nikolai II.

110 **Red tsars ruling over a Red empire:** PravoslavieRu, Встреча с архимандритом Тихоном (Шевкуновым) [A meeting with Arkhimandrit Tikhon (Shevkunov)], 8 March 2013, YouTube, https://www.youtube.com/watch?v=lLkouooGHt8

110 **sublimated prayers:** 'На ночь глядя' ['Looking at the night'], 18 June 2013.

110 **directly to the war in Ukraine:** Осторожно: Собчак [Careful: Sobchak], АНДРЕЙ КУРАЕВ: о церкви в военные времена, патриархе и интригах [ANDREI KURAEV: on the Church in wartime, the Patriarch and intrigues], 28 March 2022, YouTube, www.youtube.com/watch?v=O_IeOa4JKKo

110 **dubbed national imperialism:** Andrei Kolesnikov, 'Blood and Iron: How Nationalist Imperialism Became Russia's State Ideology', *Carnegie Russia Eurasia Center*, 6 December 2023, www.carnegieendowment.org/russia-eurasia/politika/2024/07/moldova-opposition-stoianoglo-sandu?lang=ru&center=russia-eurasia

111 **in harm's way:** Patriarch Kirill himself has not made a single public trip to Crimea since the annexation in 2014 – likely in order to avoid being targeted by Western sanctions.

111 **and, perhaps, a seminary:** 'В Крыму рассмотрят идею перевода Таврической семинарии в "Херсонес Таврический"' ['In Crimea they are looking at the idea of moving the Tavrichesky Seminary to "Khersones Tavrichesky"'], TASS, 22 November 2023, www.tass.ru/obschestvo/19357807

111 **'Whether you like it or not':** Архимандрит Тихон (Шевкунов): о любви, вере и мире [Arkhimandrit Tikhon (Shevkunov) on love, faith and peace].

CHAPTER EIGHT

115 **'selective memory of the past':** Markov, *Chernovik*, p. 68.

117 **making you want to cry:** Ilya Zhegulyov, '"Надя шила флаг на Болотной. А я сидела в Луганске" Интервью Марии Алехиной о новых клипах Pussy Riot, театре и психиатрических больницах' ['"Nadya was making flags on Bolotnaya and I was in Luhansk". An interview with Mariya Alyokhina about Pussy Riot's new clip, theatre, and psychiatric hospitals'], *Meduza*, 6 November 2016, www.meduza.io/feature/2016/11/06/nadya-shila-flag-na-bolotnoy-a-ya-sidela-v-luganske

117 **subjected to punitive psychiatry:** Ludmilla Thorne, 'Inside Russia's prisons', *The New York Times*, 12 June 1977, www.nytimes.com/1977/06/12/archives/inside-russias-russian-prisons.html

120 **was pregnant:** Svetlana Burakova, '"У ребенка в системе не может быть ребенка": как беременеют девочки в детских домах' ['"A child in the system can't have a child": How girls get pregnant in orphanages'], *Cherta*, 2 October 2023, www.cherta.media/story/beremennost-v-detdomax

CHAPTER NINE

127 **Chekhov short story:** Admittedly, the name of the ward where Moskalyov worked and the title of the Chekhov short story are slightly different in Russian: Moskalyov was head of an 'otdelenie' (which could also be rendered as 'department'), whereas Chekhov uses 'palata'. However, the usual translation for both words in this context would be 'ward'.

127 ‘***Ward No. 6*** **is everywhere. It’s Russia’:** Quoted in Ilya Vinitsky, ‘Духовный карцер. Н. С. Лесков и “Палата N 6” А. П. Чехова’ [‘Leskov’s spiritual punishment cell and Chekhov’s “Ward No. 6”’], *Voprosi Literatura*, No. 4, 2006, www.voplit.ru/article/duhovnyj-kartser-n-s-leskov-i-palata-n-6-a-p-chehova/

128 **‘only in our hospitals and prisons’:** Chekhov, *Ward No. 6*, p. 30.

130 **‘And so it goes on day after day’:** Chekhov, *Ward No. 6*, p. 40.

131 **sleep, play and work are broken down:** Goffman, *Asylums*, p. 5.

132 **almost 180,000:** Yelena Kostyuchenko and Yuri Kozyrev, ‘Интернат’ [‘Internat’], *Novaya Gazeta*, 30 April 2021, www.novayagazeta.ru/articles/2021/04/30/internat

132 **523 adult institutions:** Yekaterina Drankina, ‘“Смерть там наступает раньше, чем заканчивается жизнь”’ [‘“Death comes before life ends”’], *Takie Dela*, 3 November 2020, www.takiedela.ru/2020/11/smert_ranshe_zhizni

132 **‘death comes before life ends’:** Nyuta Federmesser, ‘“Система ПНИ – это современный ГУЛАГ для п рестарелых и инвалидов” Доклад Нюты Федермессер о ситуации в российских психоневрологических интернатах. Расшифровка’ [‘“The PNI system amounts to a modern gulag for old people and the disabled”: Transcript of Nyuta Federmesser’s presentation on Russia’s system of psychoneurological institutions’], Meduza, 26 June 2019, www.meduza.io/feature/2019/06/26/sistema-pni-eto-sovremennyy-gulag-dlya-prestarelyh-i-invalidov

134 **inflicting it on Ukrainian prisoners:** See, for example: ‘Российские военные опубликовали видео, как кастрируют пленного украинца’ [‘Russian soldiers published a video of the castration of a Ukrainian prisoner’], *Nasha Niva*, 29 July 2022, www.nashaniva.com/ru/296334; and Christina Lamb, ‘She thought she was unshockable, then two castrated Ukrainian soldiers arrived’, *The Times*, 17 June 2023, www.thetimes.co.uk/article/ukraine-soldiers-castrated-russia-war-ohflzhzlv

136 **reminiscent of *Crime and Punishment*:** ‘В Псковской области двое мужчин убили 91-летнюю пенсионерку из-за 3 500 рублей – Источник’ [‘In Pskov Region two men killed a ninety-one-year-old pensioner for 3,500 roubles – source’], VLuki.ru, 21 December 2020, www.vluki.ru/news/2020/12/21/530014.html

136 **buried her body in woods near the city:** Lyudmilla Savitskaya, ‘“Я мастер по самбо, все приемы на уровне автоматизма”. В Пскове преподаватель Академии ФСИН получил 11 лет колонии

за убийство следователя МВД' [“"I'm such a master of Sambo it's automatic”. In Pskov, a teacher at the FSIN Academy was given 11 years in prison for the murder of a MVD investigator'], *Mediazona*, 29 December 2020, www.zona.media/article/2020/12/29/mikhailov

CHAPTER TEN

138 **279 hares and nine foxes were killed:** S. O. Kuznetsov, '"Порядочных собак очень мало". Охотничьи интересы Сергея и Ольги Строго новых в течение 1880-1890-х гг.' ['"There are very few decent dogs". The hunting interests of Sergei and Olga Stroganoff from 1880–1890'], in Lidiya Vasilieva and Tatyana Mednikova, Краеведические чтения*:* материалы научных конференций Порхов-Холомки *2004–2005* [*Local History Conference Materials Porkhov-Kholomki, 2004–2005*]. Pskov, 2006, p. 86.

139 **'everyone was offered gingerbread':** Proskoryakova, *Good Old Days in Volyshovo*, p. 69.

141 **chimneys poking upward like teeth:** In 2020, after my visit, money was allocated to protect the manor house from further disintegration by the installation of a temporary roof, boarded-up windows and a metal fence around the perimeter. As of late 2024, the building was not in danger of imminent destruction.

143 **'wonderful sculptures on the walls and ceilings':** Sanin, *We Are From Pskov!*, p. 22.

144 **'Volyshovo was terribly unlucky,' he lamented:** Yuli Seliverstov, 'Отечество без богатства' ['A fatherland without riches'], *Pskovskaya Guberniya*, 6 October 2010, www.gubernia.media/number_510/04.php

147 **the chances of turning a profit are nil:** 'В 4 млрд рублей оценили эксперты восстановление усадьбы Волышово' ['Experts estimate the cost of restoring the Volyshovo estate to be 4 billion roubles'], Pskovskoye Agentstvo Informatsii, December 13, 2019, https://informpskov.ru/news/312049.html

148 **'reading the Holy Scriptures':** Alexandra Golytsina, Когда с вами Бог [*When God Is With You*]. Moscow: Nikeya, 2017, p. 110.

149 **'take them back':** Yulia Kuzyaeva and Sergei Maiorov (dirs.), *Документальный фильм Строгановы. Елена последняя* [*Documentary Film on the Stroganoffs. Yelena the Last*], Channel One, 2018.

CHAPTER ELEVEN

152 **as darkness fell on 30 April 1945:** The following account is based on Minin's memoirs, *Difficult Roads to Victory*, his writings in Pskov's archive, and interviews that he gave when alive.

156 **'taking me with it':** Minin, *Difficult Roads to Victory*, p. 221.

156 **'On the crown of some German whore!':** This is the phrase given by Arkady Dementyev, a World War II veteran and historian who was the museum curator responsible for the red banner between 1980 and 2011, in a television documentary: Alexander Kasyanov (dir.), *Знамя Победы* [*Banner of Victory*], 2015. Minin gives a sanitized version of the phrase in his memoirs.

159 **wearing a watch on each wrist:** Khaldei gives a detailed version of how the photo was taken in a documentary about his life: Marc-Henri Wajnberg (dir.), *Yevgeny Khaldei, Photographer under Stalin*, Wajnbrosse Productions, 1997

160 **kind heart and a sweet tooth:** Author interview with Karina Smirnova (14 March 2023).

161 **report aired after his death:** 'Настоящий герой, водрузивший знамя Победы' ['The real hero who raised the Banner of Victory'], NTV, 14 January 2008, https://www.ntv.ru/novosti/124378

162 **'first to raise the Red Banner':** Minin, 'Legends and facts about the storming of the Reichstag', p. 18.

162 **never allow his account to be published:** Minin, 'Legends and facts about the storming of the Reichstag', p. 34.

162 **'I simply wasn't allowed to speak out':** Minin, 'Legends and facts about the storming of the Reichstag', p. 34.

162 **'made-up heroics' of Yegorov and Kantariya:** Minin, 'Legends and facts about the storming of the Reichstag', p. 44.

162 **'sells his honour and conscience for money':** Minin, 'Legends and facts about the storming of the Reichstag', p. 29.

163 **undermine the official version of events:** Kasyanov, *Banner of Victory*.

163 **'difficult to be around them':** Kasyanov, *Banner of Victory*.

163 **bonhomie rings painfully false:** The men appeared on a famous Soviet entertainment show on Victory Day in 1975: Советское телевидение. ГОСТЕЛЕРАДИОФОНД [Soviet television. GOSTELERADIOFOND], 'Как водружали Знамя Победы над Рейхстагом. Голубой огонек 9 мая (1975)' ['How the Banner of Victory was raised over the Reichstag. Golubiy Ogonyok, 9 May (1975)'], 11 May 2020, www.youtube.com/watch?v=urHbhpAnc44

164 **Zhukov hated political officers:** Yuri Kalugin (dir.), *Судьба Алексея Береста* [*The Fate of Aleksei Berest*], Dontelefilm, 1995.

164 **two other soldiers:** See, for example, Ivan Zhilin, '"Останетесь в живых и дойдете – получите по золотой звездочке" Рахимжан Кошкарбаев и Григорий Булатов установили Знамя Победы на Рейхстаге вместе. Казахстан признал своего Героя, а Россия – нет' ['"If you Get There and Remain Alive, then You'll Receive Gold Stars", Rakhimdzhan Koshkarbayev and Georgiy Bulatov put the Victory Banner on the Reichstag together. Kazakhstan has recognized its heroes, but not Russia'], *Novaya Gazeta*, 25 March 2020, www.novayagazeta.ru/articles/2020/03/25/84503-ostanetes-v-zhivyh-i-doydete-poluchite-po-zolotoy-zvezdochke

164 **raise the red flag on the Reichstag:** Marina Dokhmatskaya (dir.), *Солдат и маршал* [*Soldier and Marshal*], GTRK, 2001.

165 **re-enactments, including by children:** 'Знамя Победы поднято над Рейхстагом в парке "Патриот" в подмосковной Кубинке' ['The Banner of Victory is raised above the Reichstag in "Patriot Park" in Kubinka near Moscow'], CGTN, 24 April 2017, https://www.youtube.com/watch?v=aC1VunyYmEs

165 **invasion of Ukraine:** Their participation in the fighting has been documented by Russian Telegram channels. For example: Операция Z: Военкоры Русской Весны [Operation Z: Military Correspondents of the Russian Spring], 'Кадры с фронта: 150 дивизия в боях на Донбассе и Украине' ['Images from the front: the 150th Division in battles in the Donbas and Ukraine'], 20 December 2022, Telegram, www.t.me/RVvoenkor/34306; and Форпост [Forpost], 'Бойцы 150-ой дивизии в русском городе Бахмут' ['Fighters of the 150th Division in the Russian town of Bakhmut'], 28 June 2023, Telegram, www.t.me/vorposte/42865

165 **deliberate cosplaying of 1945:** There are dozens of examples of Russian forces using the Victory Banner in Ukraine. For example, this state-owned television report by war correspondent Alexander Sladkov from Marinka in Ukraine's Donetsk Region, which was taken by Russian forces in December 2023: 'Специальный репортаж: Марьинка. Освобождение' ['Special report: The liberation of Marinka'], Rossiya 24, 30 December 2023, www.smotrim.ru/video/2738622

166 **'Sooner or later, the truth will out!':** Minin, 'Legends and facts about the storming of the Reichstag', p. 51.

CHAPTER TWELVE

168 **'stealthy destruction of the Russian people':** Mikhailov, *Burden of an Imperial Nation*, p. 6.

168 **Some in Moscow believed:** Dmitry Kamyshev, 'Либерал-демократическая Псковщина' ['Liberal–Democrat Pskov region'],

Kommersant, 5 November 1996, https://www.kommersant.ru/doc /242601

169 **'Swear words and foul language were the norm':** Mikhailov, *Burden of an Imperial Nation*, p. 9.

171 **'I welcomed perestroika with all my heart':** Mikhailov, *Burden of an Imperial Nation*, p. 28.

173 **2,608 per cent in 1992:** Russia's State Statistics Service (Rosstat).

173 **life expectancy fell by five years:** Russia's State Statistics Service. (Rosstat)

173 **unemployment doubled:** Russia's State Statistics Service (Rosstat).

173 **annual suicides increased by 50 per cent:** Ya. Gilinsky and G. Rumyantsev, 'Динамика самоубийств в России' ['The dynamics of suicide in Russia'], *Demskop Weekly*, Nos. 161–2, 7–20 June 2004, www .demoscope.ru/weekly/2004/0161/analit01.php

173 **economy shrank to half its size:** Marina Moroshkina, 'Исследование различий развития российских регионов на основе динамики и уровня валового регионального продукта' ['Research on the development of different Russian regions based on the dynamics and level of gross regional domestic product'], *Teoreticheskiy I Prikladnaya Ekonomika*, No. 1, 2013, pp. 64–90.

174 **near the ancient fortress of Izborsk:** Prokhanov founded a conservative and nationalist think-tank called the Izborsk Club in 2012. Its members included famous public figures like Father Tikhon and the nationalist–fascist philosopher Alexander Dugin, as well as cabinet ministers, regional governors and Kremlin advisers.

174 **'mysterious roar of Russian history':** 'Священный холм. Реплика Александра Проханова' ['Sacred Hill. Thoughts of Alexander Prokhanov'], Vesti.ru, 3 October 2014, www.vesti.ru/article/1818028

176 **traditionally backs the 'party of power':** Andrei Manakov and Aleksei Finashkin, 'Сравнительный географический анализ губернаторских выборов в Псковской области (1996–2004 гг.)' ['A comparative geographical analysis of Pskov Region's governor elections (1996–2004)'], *Pskovskiy Regionalny Zhurnal*, No. 2, 2006, pp. 43–52.

177 **'Russia was originally a monarchic country':** Alexander Polyansky, '"Президента нужно поддерживать, даже если он ошибается"' ['"You Need to Support the President Even if he's Mistaken"'], *Boss Magazine*, No. 1, 2002, www.cfin.ru/press/boss/2002-01/02.shtml

178 **Mikhailov lied about stepping aside:** Valery Tsygankov, 'Псковская Область' ['Pskov Region'], *Kommersant Vlast*, 7 November 2000, www .kommersant.ru/doc/17942

181 **interview on the day Russian tanks rolled across the border:** 'Евгений Михайлов: Будем надеяться, наши войска не понесут больших

потерь' ['Yevgeny Mikhailov: We hope that our forces will not suffer big losses'], *Pskovskaya Lenta Novostei*, 24 February 2022, www.pln-pskov.ru/politics/439856.html

CHAPTER THIRTEEN

183 **film about summer camp that he called 'Volunteers':** https://player.vimeo.com/video/135572652?fbclid=IwAR1FzPE4cPtG4gVSqebBXr2TmejqCp-f4SuBBFfxz9OIfAuIY_8uUyvjpWs

185 **more conflict-prone, and sometimes aggressive:** A friend of Dima's, Polina, recounted how he once tried to get into a fight when drunk: Редакция [Redaktsiya], 'Жизнь и судьба Дмитрия Маркова, фотографа, волонтера и гуманиста' ['The life and fate of Dmitry Markov, a photographer, volunteer and humanist'], 22 February 2024, YouTube, www.youtube.com/watch?v=Iwjr9caAn_s.

185 **with outraged blog posts:** 'Псковская кондитерская посчитала извращением заказ торта с сексом оленей' ['Pskov baker decided an order of a cake with reindeer sex was perversion'], *Bumaga*, 23 December 2015, https://paperpaper.io/papernews/2015/12/23/cake

186 **'I think they're all dead'**: Shura Burtin, 'Душа за стеклом. К 40 дням со дня смерти гениального фотографа Дмитрия Маркова' ['The person behind the lens. Forty days since the death of the genius photographer Dmitry Markov'], Cherta, 26 March 2024, www.cherta.media/story/dusha-za-steklom

187 **against the door frame without waking him:** Markov, *Draft*, p. 8.

187 **climb an apple tree in the vicinity to read:** Stanislav Kuptsov, 'Фотографии Дмитрия Маркова – рассказ о тоске и жизни в регионах России' ['The photos of Dmitry Markov are a story of ennui and life in the Russian regions'], *Meduza*, 3 April 2021, www.meduza.io/feature/2021/04/03/fotografii-dmitriya-markova-rasskaz-o-toske-i-zhizni-v-regionah-rossii-a-ego-snimok-omonovtsa-pod-portretom-putina-stal-simvolom-presledovaniya-navalnogo

187 **collected by the police:** Markov, *Draft*, p. 7.

187 **'get your hands on everything':** Markov, *Draft*, p. 40.

188 **'You won't get very far on one leg':** 'Интервью с Александром Лапиным' ['Interview with Alexander Lapin'], 30-day-photo, 2012, https://30-day-photo.livejournal.com/1480944.html

188 **happiest periods of his life:** Markov, *Draft*, p. 103.

189 **beauty, glamour and even eroticism:** Author interview with Kirill Serebrennikov (23 February 2023).

190 **he would have been dead long ago:** For example, вДудь (vDud), 'Марков – как живет русская провинция' ['Markov – life in the

Russian provinces'], 18 November 2020, YouTube, www.youtube.com/watch?v=QDHYQ9Nd-GU.

190 **an expression of divine grace:** Polina Ivanushkina, '"Сиди хорошо"' ['"Sit tight"'], *Takie Dela*, 8 April 2021, www.takiedela.ru/2021/04/sidi-khorosho.

190 **'a little less inside me':** Markov, *Draft*, p. 41

191 **'an intellectual in adidas':** Vladimir Sevrinovsky, 'Интеллигентный человек в адидасе' ['An intellectual in Adidas'], *Takie Dela*, 23 April 2024, www.takiedela.ru/2024/04/intelligentnyy-chelovek-v-adidase

192 **'Justice is the realm of the devil; the realm of God is charity and forgiveness':** *vDud*, 'Markov – life in the Russian provinces'.

192 **Moscow's fancy bars, restaurants and cultural centres:** This idea was expressed by the Pskov journalist Svetlana Prokopyeva in *vDud*, 'Markov – life in the Russian provinces'.

193 **lived for a time with a paratrooper:** Vitaly Mikhailyuk, 'Как волонтер, снимающий социалку в инстаграм, попал в рекламу Apple' ['How a volunteer photographing social issues on Instagram was used in an Apple advert'], Afisha, 30 January 2017, www.daily.afisha.ru/culture/4376-kak-volonter-snimayuschiy-socialku-v-instagram-popal-v-reklamu-apple

194 **covering his eyes as he sobbed:** www.instagram.com/p/C3Ajscso88P/?hl=en&img_index=1

195 **'whether, indeed, that is even possible':** Дмитрий Марков (Dmitry Markov), 'Думаю, стоит прояснить на будущее, чтобы люди не тратились зря' ['I think I need to explain for the future, so people don't waste their time'], 7 February 2024, www.t.me/idcim/213

195 **raised the alarm:** 'Проект "ВЫЖИВШИЕ" [Project "Survivor"'], 'ДМИТРИЙ МАРКОВ | ЖИЗНЬ И СМЕРТЬ' ['DMITRY MARKOV | LIFE AND DEATH'], 22 February 2024, YouTube, www.youtube.com/watch?v=cnmNqVmC_Gs

196 **compared Dima to Henri Cartier-Bresson:** Author interview with Kirill Serebrennikov (23 February 2023).

196 **'invisible' people of Russian society 'visible':** Anton Khitrov, 'Умер фотограф Дмитрий Марков. Он показывал нам настоящую Россию и помогал полюбить ее' ['The photographer Dmitry Markov is dead. He showed us the real Russia and helped us love her'], *Meduza*, 18 February 2024, www.meduza.io/feature/2024/02/18/umer-fotograf-dmitriy-markov-on-pokazyval-nam-nastoyaschuyu-rossiyu-i-pomogal-polyubit-ee

196 **just a few months before his death:** Дмитрий Марков [Dmitry Markov], 'Кстати, я тут недавно обрел смысл жизни' ['Incidentally, I recently discovered the meaning of life'], 3 November 2023, Telegram, www.t.me/idcim/147'

CHAPTER FOURTEEN

198 **Ka-52 'Alligator' attack helicopters:** The Veret airfield outside Ostrov first received Ka-52 attack helicopters in 2014 (Oleg Yelensky, 'Под Псковом появились "Аллигаторы"' ['Near Pskov "Alligators" have appeared'], *Nezavisimaya Gazeta*, 16 May 2014, nvo.ng.ru/armament /2014-05-16/4_alligatory.html). They have proved a formidable weapon in Ukraine, particularly against Ukrainian units advancing during Kyiv's 2023 counter-offensive (Andrew Kramer and Eric Schmitt, 'Minefields and menace: Why Ukraine's pushback is off to a halting start', *The New York Times*, 26 June 2023, www.nytimes.com/2023/06/26/world/europe/ ukraine-counteroffensive.html).

199 **groundbreaking reporting on Russian atrocities in Ukraine:** For example, Dmitry Velikovsky and Yekaterina Fomina, 'Восемь псковских десантников в Буче' ['Eight Pskov paratroopers in Bucha'], iStories, 17 June 2022, www.istories.media/investigations/2022/06/17/vosem -pskovskikh-desantnikov-v-buche

201 **Followed by: 'Be one!':** Минобороны России [Russian Defence Ministry], 'Кем ты мечтал стать? В чем твоя сила? Какой путь ты хотел выбрать?' ['What do you dream of becoming? Where does your strength lie? What path would you choose?'], 19 April 2023, Telegram, www.t.me/mod_russia/25792

202 **pre-invasion force of some 45,000:** This figure was first given in 2023 by the founder of the Russian military Telegram channel Rybar, who is considered to be well-informed. However, it's unclear how it maps onto the exact numbers of killed and injured. See, for example, Dara Massicott, 'I'm surprised this person is putting this number out there — 50% of Russian VDV (airborne) lost Feb-September 2022', 31 January 2023, X, www.x.com/MassDara/ status/1620482712036597760

202 **managed to damage the runway:** For authoritative accounts of the battle of Hostomel, see: Liam Collins, Michael Kofman and John Spencer, 'The battle of Hostomel airport: A key moment in Russia's defeat in Kyiv', *War on the Rocks*, 10 August 2023, www.warontherocks.com/2023/08/ the-battle-of-hostomel-airport-a-key-moment-in-russias-defeat-in-kyiv/?s =03, Oksana Torop and Svyatoslav Khomenko, 'The fight for Hostomel airfield. How the gates to Kyiv stayed locked', BBC Russian Service, 29 February 2024, www.bbcrussian.substack.com/p/ukraine-war-the-fight -for-hostomel-airfield, and Holger Roonemaa and Eero Epner, 'How Estonia's military intelligence secretly helped Ukraine', *VSquare*, 15 September 2023, www.vsquare.org/how-estonias-military-intelligence -secretly-helped-ukraine

202 **Maps from 1989:** Simon Shuster, *The Showman: The Inside Story of the Invasion that Shook the World and Made a Leader of Volodymyr Zelensky*, London, UK: William Collins, 2024, p. 229

202 **lawlessness and looting:** 'Mapping the looting. 58 tonnes worth of packages shipped to Russian cities from the border with Ukraine (plus a military drone)', *Mediazona*, 27 May 2022, www.zona.media/article/2022/05/26/marauders

202 **month-long Russian occupation:** It may never be clear exactly how many people died in Bucha during the Russian occupation, but there were 501 names on a memorial opened in the summer of 2023 (Megan Specia and Oleksandr Chubko, 'Bucha gets a remake, but pain lingers behind the façade', *The New York Times*, 8 July 2023, www.nytimes.com/2023/07/08/world/europe/ukraine-bucha.html)

203 **investigations undertaken by media outlets:** These included: Yousur Al-Hlou, Masha Froliak, Dmitriy Khavin, Christoph Koettl, Haley Willis, Alexander Cardia, Natalie Reneau and Malachy Browne, 'Caught on camera, traced by phone: The Russian military unit that killed dozens in Bucha', *The New York Times*, 22 December 2022, www.nytimes.com/2022/12/22/video/russia-ukraine-bucha-massacre-takeaways.html, and Erika Kinetz, Oleksandr Stashevskyi and Vasilisa Stepanenko, 'How Russian soldiers ran a "cleansing" operation in Bucha', Associated Press, 3 November 2022, www.apnews.com/article/bucha-ukraine-war-cleansing-investigation-43e5a9538e9ba68a035756b05028b8b4

204 **Vuhledar, Marinka, Avdiivka and Bakhmut:** Josh Holder and Marco Hernandez, 'How Russia's offensive ran aground', *The New York Times*, 6 April 2023, www.nytimes.com/interactive/2023/04/06/world/europe/russia-offensive-maps.html

204 **week of the war up to that point:** Laura Gozzi, 'Russian soldier death rate highest since first week of war – Ukraine', BBC, 12 February 2023, www.bbc.com/news/world-europe-64616099.

208 **since the beginning of the war:** Other attacks include one on a helicopter base targeting Ka-52s ('Ukrainian defense intelligence reports destruction of two Ka-52 attack helicopters on Pskov airfield – 370 miles from Ukraine's border', *Meduza*, 31 October 2022, www.meduza.io/en/news/2022/10/31/ukrainian-defense-intelligence-reports-destruction-of-two-ka-52-attack-helicopters-on-pskov-airfield-370-miles-from-ukraine-s-border), and an attack on oil pipeline infrastructure (Natalya Anisimova, 'В Псковской области взрыв повредил здание нефтепровода' ['In Pskov Region an explosion damages the building of an oil pipeline'], *RBC*, 27 May 2023, www.rbc.ru/politics/27/05/2023/6471aa929a7947b35ab00e83)

208 **Ilyushin-76 transport aircraft used by the 76th:** 'Russian military repelling drone attack in Pskov, four planes damaged – officials', Reuters,

30 August 2023, www.reuters.com/world/europe/russian-military-repelling-drone-attack-pskov-four-planes-damaged-officials-2023-08-29

210 **Russian casualties from Ukraine:** Aleksei Alexandrov, 'Вечная память героям!' ['Eternal glory to the heroes!'], *Znamya Truda*, 10 November 2023, www.z-truda.ru/articles/kultura/vechnaya_pamyat_geroyam

210 **criminals used for the most dangerous missions:** Polina Nikolskaya and Maria Tsvetkova, '"They're just meat": Russia deploys punishment battalions in echo of Stalin', Reuters, 3 October 2023, www.reuters.com/world/europe/theyre-just-meat-russia-deploys-punishment-battalions-echo-stalin-2023-10-03

211 **lies close to the ancient ford:** 'Спустя почти год после обращения вдов погибших на войне в Украине к губернатору на кладбище в Выбуты пустили автобус' ['After a year of pleas to the governor from widows of Ukraine war dead, a bus service to Vybuty is launched'], *Pskovskaya Guberniya*, 20 September 2023, www.gubernia.media/news/spustya-pochti-god-posle-obrascheniya-vdov-pogibshih-na-voyne-v-ukraine-k-gubernator

CHAPTER FIFTEEN

212 **tried to kiss her:** Tikhon, *Everyday Saints*, p. 484.

212 **tinker with the mechanism below:** Tikhon, *Everyday Saints*, p. 472.

213 **'chased by the cats':** Khomich, *Monks Are God's Beloved Children*, p. 575.

216 **seriously ill and would soon pass away:** Tikhon, *Everyday Saints*, p. 424.

217 **generation of clerics and influential religious thinkers:** Author interview with Barbara Martin (30 January 2024).

217 **new, democratic Christian community:** Nikolai Shuvalov, '"Наш путь – это жажда свободы и воцерковления"' ['"Our Path is One of a Thirst for Freedom and Life in the Church"'], *Ostrov Svobody*, www.spb.iofe.center/node/199

217 **over 400 days in solitary confinement:** De Wolf, *Dissident for Life*, pp. 153–4.

217 **'it was a kind of mission':** Jim and Nancy Forest, 'Searching for Kitezh: A conversation with Alexander Ogorodnikov', *On Pilgrimage*, 4 March 2010, jimandnancyonpilgrimage.blogspot.com/2010/03/searching-for-kitezh.html

217 **regularly drew attention to Alexander's plight:** Bill Keller, 'Sakharov's list', *The New York Times*, 15 February 1987, www.nytimes.com/1987/02/15/magazine/sakharov-s-list.html

218 **describing him as an 'elder brother':** Tikhon, *Everyday Saints*, p. 489.

219 **referring to Raphael as 'Angel Raphael':** Khomich, *Monks Are God's Beloved Children*, p. 528.

220 **or even talking much about God:** Khomich, *Monks Are God's Beloved Children*, p. 551.

220 **attacked him and a group of other monks:** Tikhon, *Everyday Saints*, p. 454.

220 **despite the freezing slush of early winter:** Tikhon, *Everyday Saints*, p. 454.

220 **it had to be taken off the heat:** Khomich, *Monks Are God's Beloved Children*, p. 534.

221 **'took place because of him; and him alone':** Khomich, *Monks Are God's Beloved Children*, p. 602.

221 **when she asked for forgiveness:** Khomich, *Monks Are God's Beloved Children*, p. 571.

221 **jokingly call her his 'whore':** Khomich, *Monks Are God's Beloved Children*, p. 581.

221 **with a towel to mop up spilt tea:** Khomich, *Monks Are God's Beloved Children*, p. 583.

221 **'mustn't say anything to justify yourself':** Khomich, *Monks Are God's Beloved Children*, p. 553.

222 **resented the authority of the abbot:** Author interview with Father Dionisiy Zuban (2 February 2024).

222 **evident when it came to cars:** Khomich, *Monks Are God's Beloved Children*, p. 600 (2 February 2024).

222 **for no reason:** Khomich, *Monks Are God's Beloved Children*, p. 585.

222 **turn collaborator in exchange for a promotion:** Khomich, *Monks Are God's Beloved Children*, p. 591.

222 **when talking on his tapped phone:** Tikhon, *Everyday Saints*, pp. 466–7.

223 **received in the crash:** Petrova, *Monks Are God's Beloved Children*, p. 595.

223 **single dove landed on the wooden cross:** Khomich, *Monks Are God's Beloved Children*, p. 668.

223 **more on people's souls:** Author interview with Barbara Martin (30 January 2024).

224 **job for which he hired a group of thugs:** 'ещёнепознер' [stillnotpozner], 'Георгий Кочетков: "Все молчали. Мы молчать не должны"' ['Georgiy Kochetkov: "Everyone was silent. We should have not been silent"'], 29 October 2020, YouTube, www.youtube.com/watch?v=q6J2FTrGdWk, https://www.youtube.com/watch?v=q6J2FTrGdWk

224 **'people have been led to faith by him':** 'Проповедь митрополита Псковского и Порховского Тихона в 30-ю годовщину кончины иеромонаха Рафаила (Огородникова)' ['The sermon of Pskov and Porkhov Metropolitan Tikhon on the 30th anniversary of the death of

Hieromonk Rafael (Ogorodnikov)'], 18 November 2018, www.pskov-eparhia.ru/archives/3372

224 **face stained by tears:** '18 ноября 2018 года митрополит Псковский и Порховский Тихон совершил заупокойную литию на могиле иеромонаха Рафаила (Огородникова)' ['On 18 November 2018 Pskov and Porkhov Metropolitan Tikhon led a service for the repose of the soul at the grave of Hieromonk Rafael (Ogorodnikov)'], www.pskov-eparhia.ru/archives/3351

CHAPTER SIXTEEN

225 **'refused point-blank to leave and relinquish the house':** Maksimovskaya, *The Earth Is Silent*, p. 121.

225 **identify Jewish households:** Maksimovskaya, *The Earth Is Silent*, p. 62.

226 **'realized they were about to be executed':** Maksimovskaya, *The Earth Is Silent*, p. 92.

226 **about 800 men, women and children:** This is the figure given by the Holocaust memorial centre Yad Vashem.

227 **taken many of Grandma Hana-Riva's belongings:** Maria Konyukova, 'Невель в воспоминаниях петербуржцев' ['St Petersburg resident remembers Nevel'], *Novosti Jeps*, 9 July 2015, www.news.jeps.ru/lichnaya-istoriya/evrejskoe-mestechko-peterburzhczyi-vspominayut-nevel.html

227 **'that's why she never went to Nevel':** Maksimovskaya, *The Earth Is Silent*, p. 122.

227 **in the market, and at the well:** Maksimovskaya, *Keys to the Old House*, p. 10.

228 **'part of a life about which we knew nothing':** Maksimovskaya, *Keys to the Old House*, p. 29.

228 **some members of their family were buried there:** Maksimovskaya, *Keys to the Old House*, p. 32.

229 **70 per cent of the town's population:** Maksimovskaya, European University lecture, p. 1.

229 **leather, sheepskins, bristle and flax:** Maksimovskaya, European University lecture, p. 2.

229 **religious holidays were celebrated:** Maksimovskaya, *The Earth is Silent*, p. 25.

229 **were occasional tensions:** Matvei Kagan's first memory of hearing Russian words spoken in Nevel was being told 'I'll kill you' by Russian kids (Maksimovskaya, *Keys to the Old House*, p. 40).

229 **stretching from Amur to America:** Yudina, 'My Nevel', p. 116.

230 **'a source of fish':** Maksimovskaya, *Keys to the Old House*, p. 51.

230 **appalled by the sacrilege:** Rose, 'Religious life of Nevel Jews', p. 125.

230 **burning the now desecrated building to the ground:** Rose, 'Religious life of Nevel Jews', p. 123.

230 **Jews used rivers for ritual cleaning:** Rose, 'Religious life of Nevel Jews', p. 122.

231 **'get under the table and be silent':** Maksimovskaya, European University lecture, p. 16.

231 **others as many as three:** Rose, 'Religious life of Nevel Jews', p. 130.

232 **'Have you been to Blue Dacha? You must go there':** Maksimovskaya, *The Earth is Silent*, p. 110.

232 **almost refused entry to an MA programme:** Maksimovskaya, *Keys to the Old House*, p. 105.

232 **'belonged in Israel':** Maksimovskaya, *Keys to the Old House*, p. 125.

233 **Jews were not mentioned once:** G. V. Peterov, Невель [*Nevel*] Leningrad: Lenizdat, 1980.

233 **'fewer and fewer with each passing year':** Quoted in Maksimovskaya, 'Nevel at the end of the 1910s–start of the 1920s', p. 209.

234 **'what comes after that?':** Maksimovskaya, *Keys to the Old House*, p. 234.

235 **part of it was turned into a football pitch:** Maria Konyukova, 'St Petersburg resident remembers Nevel'.

CHAPTER SEVENTEEN

237 **Tiina Süvaorg's eyes were a washed-out blue:** The Seto were obliged to choose surnames – which they had not had before – in the 1920s when the entirety of *Setomaa* was part of Estonia. Many chose surnames after natural objects like forests or lakes. 'Süvaorg' means 'ravine'.

238 **referred to the Seto as 'Pskov Estonians':** Raun, 'The Petseri Region of the Republic of Estonia', p. 516.

238 **'town of heaven':** Hagu and Suhonen, *The Setu Epic*, p. 64.

238 **Pechory:** This is the transliteration of the town's Russian-language name. In Estonian and Seto, it is 'Petseri' (when pronounced in Estonian, the first 'e' is an abrupt, hard sound – in the Seto language it is softer).

238 **enormous conical silver brooches:** These brooches are traditionally worn by women until the age of forty or fifty along with necklaces of silver coins, usually sourced from Tsarist Russia. The whole outfit can weigh several kilograms, making it difficult to move quickly, and leaving bruises or welts on the back of the neck.

239 **the 'Seto Wall':** Jääts, 'Ethnic identity of the Setus', p. 662.

239 **almost all were eligible for Estonian citizenship:** On its establishment in 1991, Estonia followed the principle of continuity with the Estonian state that existed prior to 1940 (when it was annexed by the Soviet Union). Those who had lived in the first Estonian republic, and their descendants,

therefore, automatically were eligible for citizenship (whether or not they lived inside modern Estonia's borders). Pre-1940 Estonia included not only all of *Setomaa*, but the current Pskov Region's Pechory District.

240 **elderly parents live out their days in Russia:** Ogareva, *Ethnographic Notes from the Peasant People Seto*, p. 5.

240 **one Seto baptism a year, and no weddings:** Father Yevgeny was filmed for a documentary about the Seto in the early 2000s, which Tiina also appeared in: Peeter Brambat (dir.), 'Vahtsõ Ilma Veere Pääl' ['On The Edge of the New World'] Ikoon, 2004.

241 **visit friends and enjoy picnics:** One such incident is described by M. Kirillov-Ugryumov in Rakhmanina, *Vsevolod Smirnov*, p. 127 (Smirnov illegally takes Kirillov-Ugryumov and a foreign friend across the border into Estonia to celebrate Victory Day in the late 1990s).

241 **freed the following year in a spy exchange:** 'Russia and Estonia "exchange spies" after Kohver row', BBC, 26 September 2015, www.bbc.com/news/world-europe-34369853

241 **vans with blacked-out windows waiting on either side:** 'Estonia, Russia swap convicted spies after presidential pardons', Radio Free Europe/Radio Liberty, 11 February 2018, www.rferl.org/a/29032931.html

241 **violating Estonian airspace for a few seconds:** Shkurta Januzi, 'Estonia sends note of protest to Russia for violating its airspace in Koidula Region', Schengen.News, 11 August 2022, www.schengenvisainfo.com/news/estonia-sends-note-of-protest-to-russia-for-violating-its-airspace-in-koidula-region

244 **'buried in the same land':** Kataeva-Valk, *There, Where I Was Born*, p. 18.

246 **close relations with their parents:** Ogareva, *Ethnographic Notes from the Peasant People Seto*, p. 7.

249 **closed a consulate office in Pskov:** ' Эстония закрыла генеральное консульство в Санкт-Петербурге и представительство в Пскове' ['Estonia closes a general consulate in St Petersburg and a representative office in Pskov'], Interfax, 5 May 2022, www.tourism.interfax.ru/ru/news/articles/87524

249 **halted the issuance of visas to most Russian citizens:** 'Estonian Embassy in Moscow has stopped accepting visa applications from Russian citizens', Embassy of Estonia in Moscow, 15 March 2023, www.moscow.mfa.ee/estonian-embassy-in-moscow-has-stopped-accepting-visa-applications-from-russian-and-belarusian-citizens

249 **EU ban on allowing entry to Russian cars:** Mariya Krylova, 'Эстония запретила въезд автомобилей с российскими номерами' ['Estonia bans entry to cars with Russian number plates'], *Rossiyskaya Gazeta*, 13 September 2023, www.rg.ru/2023/09/13/estoniia-zapretila-vezd-avtomobilej-s-rossijskimi-nomerami.html

EPILOGUE

253 **working their way around the southern shore:** Author interview with Irina Külmoja (18 August 2023).

254 **simultaneous sun and rain on earth:** Morozova and Novikov, *The Folklore of the Old Believers of Estonia*, p. 18.

254 **waters of Lake Peipus:** Külmoja, *History and Culture of Old Believers in Estonia I*, p. 165.

255 **improvised houses on the ice for days at a time:** Morozova and Novikov, *The Folklore of the Old Believers of Estonia*, p. 95.

255 **Black ice was the most unpredictable:** Külmoja, *Essays on the History and Culture of Old Believers in Estonia III*, p. 300.

255 **think about hares:** In lots of cultures, including Slavic cultures, it is considered a bad omen if a hare runs across your path (in a similar way to black cats). There is a legend that Pushkin's life was saved by a hare: when living in Mikhailovskoye, he heard about the Decembrist revolt underway in St Petersburg and set out to join the insurrection, but turned back when a hare ran in front of his carriage. The Decembrists were eventually crushed, and many of their leaders executed.

255 **to encounter people with dubious reputations prior to going out on the lake:** Morozova and Novikov, *The Folklore of the Old Believers of Estonia*, p. 11.

255 **return empty-handed:** Morozova and Novikov, *The Folklore of the Old Believers of Estonia*, p. 104.

257 **attended by Putin, and Father Tikhon:** 'Putin unveils monument to legendary Russia prince', Agence France-Presse, 11 September 2021, www.france24.com/en/live-news/20210911-putin-unveils-monument-to-legendary-russia-prince

Bibliography

CHAPTER ONE

Tatyana Nefedova, Десять Актуальных Вопросов о Сельской России [*Ten Pressing Questions About Rural Russia*]. Moscow: URSS, 2017.

Y. A. Senkin-Tolstoy, Фердинанд, или Новый Радищев [*Ferdinand, or the New Radishev*]. Moscow: Novoe Literaturnoe Obozrenie, 2014.

CHAPTER THREE

Из Опыта Передовых Льноводов [*From the Experience of Frontline Flax Workers*]. Pskov: Pskovskoe Gazetno-Knizhnoe Izdatelstvo, 1951.

Ivan Frolov, *Мой опыт выращивания льна* [*My Experience of Growing Flax*]. Pskov: Oblpoligrafizdat, 1947.

A. V. Gladko, *Историко-Этнографические Очерки Псковского Края* [*Historical–Ethnographic Sketches of Pskov Region*]. Pskov, 1999.

Ivan Ilin, *Лен* [*Flax*]. Moscow: Moskovskiy Rabochi, 1966.

Y. B. Ponomarenko, *Льноводы Псковского Края* [*Pskov Region Flax Workers*]. Pskov, 2016.

L. P. Shershneva and T. A. Tikhonova, (eds) *Маленькой Город Большой России* [*A Small Town in Big Russia*]. Ostrov, 2005.

Gennady Smirnov, *Цвет и Соль Земли Дедовической* [*The Colour and Salt of Dedovichi Lands*]. Dedovichi, 2003.

A. Y. Solovyov, *Льноводство* [*Flax Cultivation*]. Moscow: Kolos, 1978.

Viktor Stepanenko, *Сказ о голубом цветке* [*Tales of a Blue Flower*]. Moscow: Sovetskaya Rossiya, 1983.

M. M. Trusha (ed.), *Лен-Долгунец* [*Flax-Dolgunets*]. Moscow: Kolos, 1976.

I. Vinogradov, *Рассказы Бывалых Льноводов* [*The Stories of Former Flax Workers*]. Pskov: Pskovizdat, 1950.

P. E. Zhelnin, *Условия Псковского Льноводство* [*The Conditions of Pskov Flax Growing*]. Leningrad: Izdanie Leningradskoi Oblastnoi Selsko-khozyaistvennoi Opytnoi Stantsii, 1929.

CHAPTER FIVE

Denis Kamalyagin, Aleksei Semyonov and Lev Shlosberg (eds), *Россия и Украина. Дни Затмения: Сборник статей, 2014–2017* [*Russia and Ukraine. Days of Eclipse: A Collection of Articles, 2014–2017*]. Pskov: Pskovskaya Guberniya, 2018.

CHAPTER SIX

Larisa Ageeva and Vladimir Lavrov, *Хранитель* [*Custodian*]. St Petersburg: Sovetskaya Pisatel Leningradskoe Otedelenie, 1990.

Iosif Budylin, *Пушкинский Заповедник: Музей и Жизнь* [*Pushkin's Zapovednik: Museum and Life*]. Moscow: Profizdat, 2009.

Thomas De Waal, 'Taking Pushkin off his pedestal', *Engelsberg Ideas*, 12 April 2023, www.engelsbergideas .com /essays /taking -pushkin -off -his -pedestal/ ?mc _cid =0f19075c56 &mc eid =be67525c6a

Sergei Dovlatov, *Pushkin Hills*. London: Alma Classics, 2013.

Semyon Geichenko, *У Лукоморье: Рассказы Хранителя Пушкинского За поведника* [*In Lukomoriye: Tales of a Curator of the Pushkin Zapovednik*]. St Petersburg, 2013.

Semyon Geichenko, *Завет Внуку* [*Testament to a Grandson*]. Moscow: Detskaya Literatura, 1986.

Semyon Geichenko, *В Стране Где Сороть Голубая* [*In a Country Where the Sorot Flows Blue*]. Moscow: Sovetskaya Rossiya, 1986.

Anna Kern, *Вспоминания Дневники Переписка* [*Memories, Diaries, Correspondence*]. Moscow: Pravda, 1989.

Boris Kozmin, *Миражи Памяти* [*The Mirages of Memory*]. Velikie Luki: Velikolukskaya Tipografiya, 2020.

Vyacheslav Kozmin, 'Про лося, кованый гвоздь и дом с видом на горку' ['About a moose, a forged nail, and a house with a view of a hill'], *Pushkinskiy Ugolok*, No. 3 (14), August 2015, p. 9.

Vyacheslav Kozmin, 'Тридцать первого тридцать лет тому назад' ['The thirty-first thirty years ago'], *Pushkinskiy Ugolok*, No. 2 (17), June 2016, p. 8.

Vyacheslav Kozmin, 'Пушкинское "Михайловское": ноябрь 1917–февраль 1918 гг.' ['Pushkin's Mikhalovskoye: November 1917–February 1918'], *Nauchno-prakticheskiy, istoriko-kraevedcheskiy zhurnal*, Pskov, No. 50, 2019, pp. 202–13.

Alexander Pushkin, *Eugene Onegin: A Novel in Verse*. London: Penguin, 2008.
Andrei Sinyavsky, *Strolls With Pushkin*. New York: Columbia University Press, 2017.
Dariya Timoshenko, *'Сделано: сожжен домик Пушкина'* ['It's done: Pushkin's house has been burnt down']. Velikie Luki Rubezh, 2016.
Dariya Timoshenko, *'. . . От Судеб Защиты Нет'* ['. . . There's no protection from fate']. Pskov: Pskovskaya Istoricheskaya Biblioteka, 2016.
Dariya Timoshenko and M. A. Timoshenko (eds), *Михайловский Рощи Кузьмы Афанасьева: Записки хранителя, 1935–1943* [*The Mikhailovskoye Groves of Kuzma Afanasiev: Notes of a Custodian, 1935–1943*]. Yaroslavl: Akademiya 76, 2018.
Vasily Zvontsov and Semyon Geichenko, *Как у Вас в Михайловским?* [*How's It Going in Mikhailovsoye?*]. Pskov, 2003.

CHAPTER SEVEN

'Мир нужен по воле Божией, уверен митрополит Тихон' ['Peace is needed by God's will, says Metropolit Tikhon'], 12 November 2022, Channel One https://smotrim .ru /video /2511850
'Осторожно: Собчак, Тихон Шевкунов: о России, церкви и войне' [Tikhon Shevkunov: 'On Russia, the Church and war'], 15 May 2023, www .youtube .com /watch ?v =zgxYomCL4d8
Charles Clover, 'Putin and the monk', *The Financial Times*, 25 January 2013, www .ft .com /content /f2fcba3e -65be -11e2 -a3db -00144feab49a
Anastasia Kashevarova, 'Митрополит Тихон: Переставая быть государственником, русский человек становится разрушителем' ['Metropolit Tikhon: If a Russian stops being a statist, they become a destroyer'], *Daily Storm*, 24 October 2021, dailystorm .ru /vlast /mitropolit -tihon -perestavaya -byt -gosudarstvennikom -russkiy -chelovek -stanovitsya -razrushitelem
Barbara Martin, 'Startsy, Samizdat and underground seminars: The "parallel polis" of young Russian Orthodox converts in the 1970s–1980s', *Religious Life in the Late Soviet Union*. London: Routledge, 2023.
Andrei Pertsev and Svetlana Reiter, 'Просвещенный русский национали ст' ['An enlightened Russian nationalist'], *Meduza*, 4 February 2021, www. meduza .io /feature /2021 /02 /04 /prosveschennyy -russkiy -natsionalist
Zoya Svetova, 'Тихон Шевкунов: "Я лишь немного знаю Путина"' ['Tikhon Shevkunov: "I only know Putin a little bit"'], Radio Liberty/Radio Free Europe, 14 November 2017, www .svoboda .org /a /28851429 .html
Zoya Svetova, '"Сечин в рясе". Как Тихон Шевкунов стал главным идеологом российской реакции' ['"Sechin in a cassock." How Tikhon Shevkunov became the main ideologue of Russian reaction'], MBK Media, 2 April 2019.

Tikhon (Shevkunov) (dir.) 'Псково-Печерская обитель' [Pskov-Pechersky Monastery], 1986
Tikhon Shevkunov (dir.) 'Гибель Империи. Византийский урок' ['Death of an empire. The lesson of Byzantium'], 2008.
Tikhon (Shevkunov), *Everyday Saints and Other Stories*. Dallas, TX: Pokrov Publications, 2012.
Tikhon (Shevkunov) (dir.) 'Гибель империи. Российский урок' ['Death of an empire. The lesson of Russia'], 2021
Sergei Ustinov, '"Всю свою жизнь я искал друга . . ."' ['"All my life I looked for a friend . . ."'], unpublished interview with Father Zenon (Teodor) supplied by interviewer.
Savva Yamshchikov, Архимандрит Алипий: Человек, Художник, Воин, Игумен [*Archimandrite Alipiy: Human, Artist, Warrior, Abbot*]. Moscow, 2004.
Кто он – "духовник Путина", что его на самом деле связывает с през идентом, и как с его подачи могло начаться дело Серебренникова [Who is "Putin's Confessor?", what links him to the president, and could he have initiated the case against Serebrennikov], Sergei Yerzhenkov and Vladislav Pushkarev, 15 November 2017, TV Rain, www.tvrain.tv/teleshow/reportazh/duhovnikfilm-450311/
Maria Zholobova, 'Пропагандист от бога' ['A propagandist from God'], iStories, 1 August 2022, www.storage.googleapis.com/istories/investigations/2022/08/01/propagandist-ot-boga/index.html
Dionisiy Zuban, *Псковская епархия Русской Православной Церкви в 1964–1991 гг.* [*The Pskov Eparchy of Russian Orthodox Church, 1964–1991*]. Moscow: Saint Tikhon's Orthodox University of Humanities, 2011.

CHAPTER EIGHT

Maria Berkovich, *Нестрашный Мир* [*Not A Scary World*]. St Petersburg: Seans, 2009.
Erving Goffman, *Asylums: Essays on the Social Situation of Mental Patients and Other Inmates*. London: Penguin, 1991.
Anna Klepnikov, *Наверно Я Дурак* [*I'm Probably an Idiot*]. St Petersburg: European University of St Petersburg, 2023.

CHAPTER NINE

Anton Chekhov, *Ward No. 6 and Other Stories, 1892–1895*. London: Penguin Books, 2002.

CHAPTER TEN

Antonina Antonova, 'Трагедия Волышова' ['The Tragedy of Volyshovo'], Pskov Manuscript: Kraevedicheskiy Album No. 3 (4), 2010, pp 170–90.
Galina Proskoryakova, *Волышовская Старина* [*The Good Old Days in Volyshovo*]. St Petersburg, 2008, https://text .pskovbook .ru /ProtectedView / App /Viewer
A. G. Sherbatov and S. A. Stroganov, *The Arabian Horse: A Survey*. London: J. A. Allen & Co., 1989.
Tatyana Veresova, 'На графских развалинах' ['On the count's ruins'], Pskov Manuscript: Kraevedicheskiy Album No. 1 (10), Pskov, 2019, pp. 160–75.

CHAPTER ELEVEN

Mikhail Minin, *Трудные Дороги к Победе* [*Difficult Roads to Victory*]. Pskov: Committee for Media of Administration of Pskov Region, 2001.
Mikhail Minin, 'Легенды и факты о штурме Рейхстага' ['Legends and facts about the storming of the Reichstag'], Archive of the Pskovo–Izborskiy United Museum-Zapovednik, I-32923, 2003.
Nikolai Yamskoi, *Кто Брал Рейхстаг: Герои по Умолчанию . . .* [*Who Took the Reichstag? Silent Heroes . . .*]. Moscow: OLMA-PRESS, 2006.

CHAPTER TWELVE

ПолитПсковЪ: Факты, расследование, комментарии [*PolitPskov: Facts, Investigation, Commentary*]. Pskov: Pskovskaya Istroicheskaya Biblioteka, 2013.
Yevgeny Mikhailov, *Бремя Имперской Наций* [*Burden of an Imperial Nation*], 1995, pamphlet supplied by the author.

CHAPTER THIRTEEN

Anton Makarenko, *Педагогическая Поэма* [*A Pedagogical Poem*]. Moscow: AST, 2022.
Dmitry Markov, *Черновик* [*Draft*]. Moscow: Treemedia, 2018.
Dmitry Markov, *Россия в квадрате* [Russia in squares]. Moscow: Treemedia, 2021.

CHAPTER FIFTEEN

Nikolai Bulchuk, '"У МЕНЯ БЫЛА ИДЕАЛЬНАЯ СОВЕТСКАЯ БИОГРАФИЯ" Беседа с христианским правозащитником Александ ром Огородниковым' ['"I HAD A PERFECT SOVIET BIOGRAPHY". An interview with Christian human rights activist Alexander Ogorodnikov'], Pravoslavie .r u, 10 June 2019, www.pravoslavie.ru/121693.html

Konraad De Wolf, *Dissident for Life. Alexander Ogorodnikov and the Struggle for Religious Freedom in Russia*. Cambridge: William B. Eeerdmans Publishing Company, 2013

Ksenia Kirillova, 'Александр Огородников о иеромонахе Рафаиле инеслучайных случайностях' ['Alexander Ogorodnikov on Hieromonk Rafael and coincidences for a reason'], *Pravmir*, 17 June 2013, www .pravmir .ru /aleksandr -ogorodnikov -o -brate -i -nesluchajnyx -sluchajnostyax

A. G. Khomich (ed.), *Монахи – Возлюбленные Дети Господни* [*Monks Are God's Beloved Children*]. Moscow, 2015.

CHAPTER SIXTEEN

S. Ansky, *The Enemy at his Pleasure: A Journey Through the Jewish Pale of Settlement During World War I*. New York: Metropolitan Books, 2002.

Katerin Clark and Michael Holquist, *Mikhail Bakhtin*. Cambridge, MA and London, UK: Belknap Press of Harvard University Press, 1984.

Caryl Emerson, *The First Hundred Years of Mikhail Bakhtin*. Princeton, NJ: Princeton University Press, 1997.

Nakhim Levit, 'Мама' ['Mum'], *Невелский Сборник 12* [*Nevel Collection 12*]. St Petersburg: Akropol, 2007, pp. 170–8.

Lyudmila Maksimovskaya, *Ключ от Старого Дома* [*Keys to the Old House*]. St Petersburg: Lema, 2012.

Lyudmila Maksimovskaya, *The Earth Is Silent . . . In Memory of the Nevel Ghetto*. St Petersburg: Lema, 2023.

Lyudmila Maksimovskaya, 'Невель в конце 10-х – начале 20-х гг. XX века' ['Nevel at the end of the 1910s–start of the 1920s'], *Невелский Сборник 12* [*Nevel Collection 12*]. St Petersburg: Akropol, 2007, pp. 207–40.

Lyudmila Maksimovskaya, Lecture given to the European University in St Petersburg (supplied by author), 30 October 2020.

Lyudmila Maksimovskaya and Lyubov Kuzmenko, *Путешествие в Невель* [*Journey to Nevel*]. St Petersburg: Lema, 2010.

Michael Rose, 'Религиозная жизнь невельских евреев в послереволюционную эпоху' ['Religious life of Nevel Jews in the post-revolution period'], *Невелский Сборник 10* [*Nevel Collection 10*]. St Petersburg: Akropol, 2005, pp. 120–35.

Elizabeth Wilson, *Playing with Fire: The Story of Maria Yudina, Pianist in Stalin's Russia*. New Haven, CT, and London: Yale University Press, 2022.

Vera Yudina, 'Мой Невель' ['My Nevel'], *Невелский Сборник 5* [*Nevel Collection 5*]. St Petersburg: Akropol, 2000, pp. 115–28.

CHAPTER SEVENTEEN

Oleg Artyushenko, 'Лет десять пройдёт, и никого не останется' ['In ten years' time, they'll be no one left'], *Pskovskaya Guberniya*, 1 June 2023, https://gubernia-media-2.tilda.ws/seto?fbclid=PAAaYH97fsK6Hkm7bm2Mg17Ne78UyAvJBsxHo1Rik2EDGn6pHT8HXofJ6vfRQ

Paul Hagu and Seppo Suhonen (eds), *Peko. Setu rahvuseepos – Setukaiseepos – The Setu Epic*. Kuopio (Finland): Snellman-instituutin, 1995.

Indrek Jääts, 'Ethnic identity of the Setus and the Estonian–Russian border dispute', *Nationalities Papers*, Vol. 28, No. 4, 2000, pp. 651–70.

Nadezhda Kataeva, *Там, где я родилась* [*There, Where I Was Born*]. Tartu: DIALOG, 2015.

Helen Külvik (ed.), *Setomaa*. Seto Institute, 2015.

Helen Külvik, *Setomaa: A Travel Guide*. Seto Institute, 2019.

Martha Merritt, 'A geopolitics of identity: Drawing the line between Russia and Estonia', *Nationalities Papers*, Vol. 28, No. 2, 2000, pp. 243–62.

Tatyana Ogareva, *Этнографические заметки из жизни крестьян Сето* [*Ethnographic Notes from the Peasant People Seto*]. St Petersburg: Giol, 2014.

Toivo Raun, 'The Petseri Region of the Republic of Estonia', *Jahrbücher für Geschichte Osteuropas*, 1991, Neue Folge, Bd. 39, H. 4 (1991), pp. 514–32.

Heiki Valk, Anti Selart and Anti Lillak, *Setomaa 2: Vanem ajalugu muinasajast kuni 1920* [*Setomaa 2: History from Ancient Times to 1920*]. Värska: Setomaa Museums, 2009.

EPILOGUE

Irina Külmoja (ed.), *Очерки по историй и культуре староверов Эстонии* I [Essays on the History and Culture of Old Believers in Estonia I]. Tartu: University of Tartu Press, 2004.

Irina Külmoja (ed.), *Очерки по историй и культуре староверов Эстонии II* [Essays on the History and Culture of Old Believers in Estonia II]. Tartu: University of Tartu Press, 2007.

Irina Külmoja (ed.), *Очерки по историй и культуре староверов Эстонии III* [Essays on the History and Culture of Old Believers in Estonia III]. Tartu: University of Tartu Press, 2012.

Leonid Mikhailov, *Поселения Причудья* [The Settlements of the Shore of Chudskoye Lake]. Tallinn: Absurdum Art, 2008.

Nadezhda Morozova and Yuri Novikov, *Фольклор староверов Эстонии* [The Folklore of the Old Believers of Estonia]. Tartu: HUMA, 2007.

Pavel Varunin, *Луководье: Взабылишные байки* [Forgotten Tales of Lukovodye]. Tartu: TAOS, 2016.

Select Bibliography

Olga Arakshuni, Народное Зодчество Пскова [*The Folk Architecture of Pskov*]. Moscow: Stroyizdat, 1987.

Catherine Belton, *Putin's People: How the KGB Took Back Russia and Then Took On the West*. London: William Collins, 2020.

Timothy Binyon, *Pushkin: A Biography*. London: HarperCollins, 2002.

Oliver Bullough, *The Last Man in Russia and the Struggle to Save a Dying Nation*. London: Allen Lane, 2013.

Ivan Bunin, *The Village*. London: Alma Classics, 2017.

Charles Clover, *Black Wind, White Snow: The Rise of Russia's New Nationalism*. New Haven, CT and London: Yale University Press, 2016.

Larry Cothren, *Outcast Visionary: Yurii Pavlovich Spegal'skii and the Reconstruction of Pskov*. Adelaide: Interweave Australia, 2016.

Victoria Donovan, *Chronicles in Stone: Preservation, Patriotism, and Identity in Northwest Russia*. DeKalb, IL: Northern Illinois University Press, 2019.

Alexander Etkind, *Warped Mourning: Stories of the Undead in the Land of the Unburied*. Stanford, CA: Stanford University Press, 2013.

Fiona Hill and Clifford G. Gaddy, *Mr Putin: Operative in the Kremlin*. Washington D.C.: Brookings Institute Press, 2013.

David E. Hoffman, *The Oligarchs: Wealth and Power in the New Russia*. New York: Public Affairs, 2002.

Paul Klebnikov, *Godfather of the Kremlin: Boris Berezovsky and the Looting of Russia*. New York: Harcourt, 2000.

Elena Kostyuchenko, *I Love Russia: Reporting from a Lost Country*. London: Penguin, 2023.

Lev Malyakov, Достопримечателности Псковской области [*The Sites of Pskov Region*]. Leningrad: Lenizdat, 1981.

Yelena Morozkina, *Pskov: A Guide*. Moscow: Raduga, 1984.

Yelena Morozkina, Псковская Земля [*Pskov Lands*]. Moscow: Iskusstvo, 1975.

Joy Neumeyer, 'Burying Homo Soveticus', *New Left Review* 129, May–June 2021, p. 153.

Arkady Ostrovsky, *The Invention of Russia: The Journey from Gorbachev's Freedom to Putin's War*. London: Atlantic Books, 2015.

Sergei Oushakine, *The Patriotism of Despair: Nation, War, and Loss in Russia*. Ithaca, NY: Cornell University Press, 2009.

Peter Pomerantsez, *Nothing is True and Everything is Possible: The Surreal Heart of the New Russia*. New York: Public Affairs, 2014.

Natalya Rakhmanina, Всеволод Смирнов: Архитектор, Художник, Кузнец [*Vsevolod Smirnov: Architect, Artist, Blacksmith*]. St Petersburg: Petropolis, 2010.

Sigrid Rausing, *Everything is Wonderful: Memories of a Collective Farm in Estonia*. New York: Grove Press, 2014.

Vladimir Sanin, Мы – Псковские*!* [*We Are From Pskov!*]. Moscow: Soviet Russia, 1970.

Serge Schmemann, *Echoes of a Native Land: Two Centuries of a Russian Village*. London: Abacus, 1998.

Gulnaz Sharafutdinova, *The Red Mirror: Putin's Leadership and Russia's Insecure Identity*. New York: Oxford University Press, 2020.

Boris Skobeltsyn, Псков Зимной и Псков Небесный [*Earthly Pskov and Heavenly Pskov*]. Pskov: My Pskopskie, 2003.

Boris Skobeltsyn, Земля Псковская [*Pskov Lands*]. Leningrad: Iskusstvo, 1972.

Mark B. Smith, *The Russia Anxiety and How History Can Resolve It*. London: Penguin, 2020.

Yuri Spegalsky, Псков [*Pskov*]. Leningrad: Lenizdat, 1972.

Yuri Spegalsky, По Пскову *XVII* Века [*In Pskov of the 17th Century*]. Leningrad: Lenizdat, 1974.

Shaun Walker, *The Long Hangover: Putin's New Russia and the Ghosts of the Past*. Oxford and New York: Oxford University Press, 2018.

Laura Lynne Williams, *The Storks' Nest: Life and Love in the Russian Countryside*. Arvada, CO: Fulcrum Publishing, 2008.

Joshua Yaffa, *Between Two Fires: Truth, Ambition, and Compromise in Putin's Russia*. London: Granta, 2020.

Savva Yamshchikov, Савва Ямщиков [*Savva Yamshchikov*]. Pskov: Vozrozhdenie, 2010.

Lea Ypi, *Free: Coming of Age at the End of History*. London: Penguin, 2022.

Mikhail Zygar, *All the Kremlin's Men: Inside the Court of Vladimir Putin*. New York: Public Affairs, 2016.

Acknowledgements

This book is based on hundreds of face-to-face interviews and encounters over the course of more than fifteen years (including almost two years living in Pskov Region). As a result, my first – and biggest – debt of gratitude is to those who patiently answered my questions. There are too many of them to name individually, but they all shaped the contents of *Russia Starts Here*.

When I first went to Pskov Region in the summer of 2007, my Russian was limited and my understanding of Russia even more so. For their friendship and understanding over many subsequent years, I would like to thank Artyom Sorokin, Alina Lobzina, Dasha, Olga V., Natasha, Alexandra Odynova and Aleksei Eremenko. I was privileged to experience the kindness and hospitality of Nina and Nikolai in Baranovo; Irina and Mikhail in Novopetrosvkoe (and Moscow); Valery and Natalia, Galina and Slava, and Sergei Nikolaevich in Porkhov; and Vyacheslav Kozmin in Pushkin Hills. Visiting Estonia in 2023, I was made to feel extremely welcome by Mike Cole, Lindsay Heather and Logan Carmichael.

Since embarking on the research and writing of *Russia Starts Here* in 2019, I have amassed a long list of people who have been generous with their thoughts, expertise, help and advice. Above all, I'd like to mention Nadezhda Belyakova, Larry Cothren, Sergei Grachev, Denis Kamalyagin, Natalia Kigai, Helen Külvik, Herman Krause, Aleksei Malov, Tatyana M., Barbara Martin, Sofiya Pugachyova, Svetlana Reiter, Sofia Simoes Coelho, Alina Slavinsky,

Zoya Svetova, Pavel Umbleja and Oleg Ustinov. Katya Fomina's assistance was crucial.

In the UK, I am thankful in the first instance to all those who helped coax *Russia Starts Here* into being. My agent Emma Finn was a reliable source of optimism, encouragement and inspiration and I am grateful to her and the rest of the team at C&W. I was fortunate to have had as many as three editors: Jamie Birkett, who commissioned *Russia Starts Here* and whose support was invaluable; Octavia Stocker, whose patience and creativity are apparently boundless; and Tomasz Hoskins, who deftly steered the manuscript into book form. My thanks to them, as well as to my copyeditor, Richard Mason, and everyone at Bloomsbury – particularly Fahmida Ahmed, Sarah Head and Jessica Gray.

In many ways, *Russia Starts Here* is the culmination of fifteen years thinking and writing about Russia. I learnt how to be a journalist at *The Moscow Times* in the early 2010s, and I will always be indebted to Justin Lifflander, Scott Rose and Nabi Abdullaev. This book has been influenced by the writing of many other colleagues, but I would like to single out the journalists at independent outlet *Pskovskaya Guberniya*. Reporting honestly on what is happening in Russia's regions has long been one of the most dangerous and badly-paid jobs in Russian journalism, and *Pskovskaya Guberniya* has been – and continues to be – an invaluable source of information.

As a first-time author, I've found that a few brief words of encouragement at the right moment can be of oversized importance. Thank you for such words at various points along the way to Andrew Monaghan, Tom Parfitt, Oliver Bullough, Ara Tadevosyan and Yulia Kushnarenko.

In different ways, the following all offered support, friendship and advice during the writing process: Dan Chandler, Shura Collinson, Max Colson, Emily Craig, Ilya Devedzhian, Caroline Eden, Andrei Gorianov, Edward Henderson, Mirela Ivanova, Oliver Kindeberg, Alec Luhn, Miles Mantle, Pyotr Mironenko, Philippa Mullins, Jesse Nicholls, Kevin O'Flynn, Marika Semenenko, David Sims, Michael Slavinsky, Florence Sutcliffe-Braithwaite, Dominik Tomenendal, Justin Varilek, Alex Winning and Edward Zychowicz-Coghill.

In particular, I would like to mention two people. Firstly, the immensely talented Dima Markov, who I describe in *Russia Starts Here* and whose powerful photos accompany the text. Dima died in early 2024 but his enthusiasm for this book, and foul-mouthed thoughts about Pskov and its people, were formative. Secondly, Peter Allwright, who taught me Russian with passion and discipline when I was a teenager, sparking an interest that continues to this day. Without him, my life would have taken a very different direction.

Of course, my most profound debts are to my family. To my inspirational grandmothers, Hazel and Kathleen; my impressive sisters, Josephine and Rachel; their partners Thomas and Richard; my niece Edith; and my nephews Otis and Leon. My wife, Anna, drove me around western Russia, read drafts and engaged in innumerable conversations about Pskov Region – I am immensely fortunate to have such a resilient and caring person by my side.

Finally, to my parents: my father, Roger, who spent many hours producing the book's wonderful illustrations, and my mother, Anne. Their empathy, example and love are foundational, and *Russia Starts Here* is dedicated to them.